MCSE Test Success™:
Networking Essentials

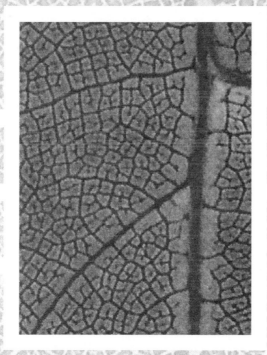

Todd Lammle

San Francisco • Paris • Düsseldorf • Soest

Associate Publisher: Guy Hart-Davis
Contracts and Licensing Manager: Kristine Plachy
Acquisitions & Developmental Editor: Bonnie Bills
Editor: Marilyn Smith
Project Editors: Jonathan Loucks, Lori Ash, Davina Baum
Technical Editor: Jim Cooper
Book Designers: Patrick Dintino, Bill Gibson
Graphic Illustrator: Andrew Benzie
Electronic Publishing Specialist: Bill Gibson
Production Coordinator: Katherine Cooley
Production Assistants: Beth Moynihan, Rebecca Rider
Indexer: Lynnzee Elze
Cover Designer: Archer Design
Cover Illustrator/Photographer: FPG International

Screen reproductions produced with Collage Complete.

Collage Complete is a trademark of Inner Media Inc.

SYBEX, Network Press, and the Network Press logo are registered trademarks of SYBEX Inc.

Test Success is a trademark of SYBEX Inc.

TRADEMARKS: SYBEX has attempted throughout this book to distinguish proprietary trademarks from descriptive terms by following the capitalization style used by the manufacturer.

Microsoft® Internet Explorer ©1996 Microsoft Corporation. All rights reserved. Microsoft, the Microsoft Internet Explorer logo, Windows, Windows NT, and the Windows logo are either registered trademarks or trademarks of Microsoft Corporation in the United States and/or other countries.

The author and publisher have made their best efforts to prepare this book, and the content is based upon final release software whenever possible. Portions of the manuscript may be based upon pre-release versions supplied by software manufacturer(s). The author and the publisher make no representation or warranties of any kind with regard to the completeness or accuracy of the contents herein and accept no liability of any kind including but not limited to performance, merchantability, fitness for any particular purpose, or any losses or damages of any kind caused or alleged to be caused directly or indirectly from this book.

SYBEX is an independent entity from Microsoft Corporation, and not affiliated with Microsoft Corporation in any manner. This publication may be used in assisting students to prepare for a Microsoft Certified Professional Exam. Neither Microsoft Corporation, its designated review company, nor SYBEX warrants that use of this publication will ensure passing the relevant exam. Microsoft is either a registered trademark or trademark of Microsoft Corporation in the United States and/or other countries.

Library of Congress Card Number: 98-84010
ISBN: 0-7821-2146-2

Manufactured in the United States of America

10 9 8 7 6 5 4 3 2 1

November 1, 1997

Dear SYBEX Customer:

Microsoft is pleased to inform you that SYBEX is a participant in the Microsoft® Independent Courseware Vendor (ICV) program. Microsoft ICVs design, develop, and market self-paced courseware, books, and other products that support Microsoft software and the Microsoft Certified Professional (MCP) program.

To be accepted into the Microsoft ICV program, an ICV must meet set criteria. In addition, Microsoft reviews and approves each ICV training product before permission is granted to use the Microsoft Certified Professional Approved Study Guide logo on that product. This logo assures the consumer that the product has passed the following Microsoft standards:

- The course contains accurate product information.
- The course includes labs and activities during which the student can apply knowledge and skills learned from the course.
- The course teaches skills that help prepare the student to take corresponding MCP exams.

Microsoft ICVs continually develop and release new MCP Approved Study Guides. To prepare for a particular Microsoft certification exam, a student may choose one or more single, self-paced training courses or a series of training courses.

You will be pleased with the quality and effectiveness of the MCP Approved Study Guides available from SYBEX.

Sincerely,

Holly Heath
ICV Account Manager
Microsoft Training & Certification

MICROSOFT INDEPENDENT COURSEWARE VENDOR PROGRAM

I would like to dedicate this book to Marilyn Smith, for without her brilliant editing, I can't imagine ever finishing this book! All my thanks to you, Marilyn!!!!

Acknowledgments

I would like to acknowledge my wife Monica for keeping me sane during the writing of this book.

I would also like to acknowledge James Chellis and Neil Edde. Their insight and friendship keep me going when I don't feel like going anymore.

Thanks also go to Jim Cooper, the technical editor, for his careful review and helpful suggestions.

Finally, I would like to acknowledge all the people at Sybex who helped produce this book: Bonnie Bills, developmental editor; project editors Jonathan Loucks, Lori Ash, and Davina Baum; Katherine Cooley, production coordinator; Beth Moynihan and Rebecca Rider, production assistants; Bill Gibson, electronic publishing specialist; and Andrew Benzie, illustrator.

Contents at a Glance

Introduction   *xiii*

Unit   1   Standards and Terminology   1

Unit   2   Planning   49

Unit   3   Implementation   123

Unit   4   Troubleshooting   183

Unit   5   Final Review   225

Appendix   Study Question and Sample Test Answers   243

Glossary   313

Index   *351*

Table of Contents

Introduction   *xiii*

Unit   1   **Standards and Terminology**   **1**

                      Defining Networking Terms   3
                            Network Description Terms   3
                            Network Topology Terms   5
                            Network Protocol Terms   6
                            Networking Service Terms   6
                      Comparing File, Print, and Application Servers   7
                      Comparing Client-Server and Peer-to-Peer Networks   8
                      Comparing User-Level Security with Access Permissions   10
                            Share-Level Security   10
                            Access Permissions   10
                      Comparing Connection-Oriented with Connectionless
                            Communications   11
                            Connectionless Communications   11
                            Connection-Oriented Communications   11
                      Distinguishing between SLIP and PPP   11
                      Defining Communications at the OSI Model Levels   12
                            The Application, Presentation, and Session Layers   13
                            The Transport and Network Layers   14
                            The Data Link and Physical Layers   14
                      Defining the Media Used in IEEE 802.3 and IEEE 802.5 Standards   15
                            802.3: Ethernet   16
                            802.5: Token Ring   17
                      Understanding NDIS and Novell ODI Standards   19
                            NDIS   19
                            ODI   19

Unit 2	**Planning**	**49**
	Selecting the Appropriate Media	52
	Communication Technologies	52
	Transmission Degradation	54
	Types of Cable Media	55
	Wireless Media	60
	Selecting the Appropriate Topology	63
	Bus Topology	64
	Ring Topology	64
	Star Topology	64
	Mesh Topology	66
	Selecting the Appropriate Protocols	66
	Protocols and the Windows NT Networking Structure	68
	The NetBEUI Protocol	69
	The Internet Protocol Suite	70
	The IPX/SPX Protocol Suite	71
	The AppleTalk Protocol Suite	72
	Selecting the Appropriate Connectivity Devices	74
	Repeaters	74
	Bridges	75
	Routers	76
	Brouters	77
	Gateways	77
	Selecting WAN Connection Services	78
	Analog versus Digital Signaling	78
	Dial-up versus Leased Lines	79
	Types of WAN Connection Services	79
Unit 3	**Implementation**	**123**
	Choosing an Administrative Plan	125
	Network Configuration	126
	Account Management	131
	File and Printer Shares	135

Security Management   137
Performance Management   140
Choosing a Disaster Recovery Plan   141
Backup Systems   142
UPS Systems   143
Fault-Tolerant Disk Schemes   144
Redundant WAN Links   144
Installing and Configuring Multiple Network Adapters   146
Multi-homing Techniques   146
Data Bus Architecture   148
Network Cabling and Connectors   148
Network Adapter Installation   149
Hardware Conflicts   149
Implementing a NetBIOS Naming Scheme   151
NetBIOS Names   151
Universal Naming Convention   151
Selecting the Appropriate Tools to Monitor Your Network 152
Protocol Analyzers   152
Performance Monitor   153

Unit 4   **Troubleshooting**   **183**

Identifying Common Communication Errors   185
Tools for Finding Errors   185
Common Sources of Communication Errors   188
Diagnosing and Resolving Common Connectivity Problems   191
Cable Problems   191
Connectivity Device Problems   193
NIC Problems   194
Ethernet and Token Ring Connectivity Problems   194
Resolving Broadcast Storms   195
Common Causes of Broadcast Storms   196
Tools for Resolving Broadcast Storms   197
Recognizing a Broadcast Storm   198

Identifying and Resolving Network Performance Problems 202

Common Sources of Network Performance Problems 202

Network Performance Troubleshooting Tools 203

Sources for Troubleshooting Information 206

Unit 5 **Final Review** **225**

Appendix **Study Question and Sample Test Answers** **243**

Glossary **313**

Index *351*

Introduction

One of the greatest challenges facing corporate America today is finding people who are qualified to manage corporate computer networks. Many companies have Microsoft networks, which run Windows 95, Windows NT, and other Microsoft BackOffice products (such as Microsoft SQL Server and Systems Management Server).

Microsoft developed its Microsoft certification program to certify those people who have the skills to work with Microsoft products and networks. The most coveted certification is MCSE, or Microsoft Certified Systems Engineer.

Why become an MCSE? The main benefits are that you will have much greater earning potential and that an MSCE carries high industry recognition. Certification can be your key to a new job or a higher salary—or both.

So what's stopping you? If it's because you don't know what to expect from the tests or you are worried that you might not pass, then this book is for you.

Is This Book for You?

This book is intended for those who already have some experience with Microsoft networks. It is especially well suited for:

- Students using courseware or taking a course to prepare for the exam, who would like to supplement their study material with test-based practice questions.

- Network engineers who have worked with Microsoft networks but want to make sure there are no gaps in their knowledge.

- Anyone who has studied for the exams—by using self-study guides, by participating in computer-based training, by taking classes, or by getting on-the-job experience—and wants to make sure that they're adequately prepared.

What Does This Book Cover?

This book provides you with the key to passing Exam 70-058, Networking Essentials. It covers exactly what you need to know, without wasting time on background material or detailed explanations. This book prepares you for the exam in the shortest amount of time possible.

In order to help you prepare for certification exams, Microsoft provides a list of exam objectives for each test. This book is based on the objectives specified for Exam 70-058.

For the Networking Essentials exam, the objectives are designed to measure your ability to design, administer, and troubleshoot Microsoft networks. The first four units in this book correspond to the Microsoft objectives groupings: Standards and Terminology, Planning, Implementation, and Troubleshooting. The fifth unit is a final review, which contains test questions pertaining to all the previous units.

In this book, you will find at-a-glance review sections, more than 400 study questions, and over 200 sample test questions to bolster your knowledge of the information relevant to each exam objective.

The review sections present the information concisely in easy-to-skim formats. The study questions are in various formats: fill-in-the-blank, true/false, list, and so on. The sample test questions are multiple-choice—just like the actual exam questions. In fact, some are even more difficult than what you'll find on the exam. If you can pass the sample tests at the end of each unit and the final review at the end of the book, you'll know that you're ready to take the test.

Understanding Microsoft Certification

Microsoft offers several levels of certification for network professionals working with Microsoft products:

- Microsoft Certified Professional (MCP)

- Microsoft Certified Systems Engineer (MCSE)

- Microsoft Certified Professional + Internet

- Microsoft Certified Systems Engineer + Internet

- Microsoft Certified Trainer (MCT)

The one you choose depends on your area of expertise and your career goals.

For the most up-to-date certification information, visit Microsoft's Web site at www.microsoft.com/train_cert.

Microsoft Certified Professional (MCP)

MCP certification is for individuals with expertise in one specific area. MCP certification is often a stepping stone to MCSE certification and allows you some of the benefits of Microsoft certification after just one exam.

By passing one core exam (an operating system exam), you become an MCP.

Microsoft Certified Systems Engineer (MCSE)

Becoming an MCSE requires commitment. You need to complete all of the steps required for certification. Passing the exams shows that you meet the high standards that Microsoft has set for MSCEs.

The following list applies to the Windows NT 4.0 track. Microsoft still supports a track for 3.51, but 4.0 certification is more desirable because it applies to the current operating system.

To become an MCSE, you must pass a series of six exams: four core requirements and two electives. The core exams are:

- Networking Essentials (waived for Certified Novell Engineers, or CNEs)
- Implementing and Supporting Microsoft Windows NT Workstation 4.0, or Installing and Supporting Windows 95
- Implementing and Supporting Microsoft Windows NT Server 4.0
- Implementing and Supporting Microsoft Windows NT Server 4.0 in the Enterprise

Some of the electives include:

- Internetworking with Microsoft TCP/IP on Microsoft Windows NT 4.0
- Implementing and Supporting Microsoft Internet Information Server 4.0
- Implementing and Supporting Microsoft Exchange Server 5.5
- Implementing and Supporting Microsoft SNA Server 4.0
- Implementing and Supporting Microsoft Systems Management Server 1.2
- Implementing a Database Design on Microsoft SQL Server 6.5
- System Administration for Microsoft SQL Server 6.5

Microsoft Certified Trainer (MCT)

As an MCT, you can deliver Microsoft certified courseware through official Microsoft channels.

The MCT certification is more costly than the other types of certification because in addition to passing the exams, you must sit through the official Microsoft courses. You also need to submit an application that must be approved by Microsoft. The number of exams you are required to pass depends on the number of courses that you want to teach.

Preparing for the MCSE Exams

To prepare for the MCSE certification exams, you should try to work with the product as much as possible. In addition, there are a variety of resources from which you can learn about the products and exams:

- You can take instructor-led courses.

- Online training is an alternative to instructor-led courses. This is a useful option for people who cannot find any courses in their area or who do not have the time to attend classes.

- If you prefer to use a book to help you prepare for the MCSE tests, you can choose from a wide variety of publications. These range from complete study guides (such as the Network Press *MCSE Study Guide* series, which cover the core MCSE exams and key electives) through test-preparedness books similar to this one.

After you have completed your courses, training, or study guides, you'll find the *MSCE Test Success* books an excellent resource for making sure that you are prepared for the test. You will discover if you've got it covered or if you still need to fill in some holes.

Scheduling and Taking an Exam

When you've decided that you're ready to take an exam, call Prometric Testing Centers at (800)755-EXAM (800-755-3926) to find the closest testing center. Before you call, get out your credit card because each exam costs $100. (If you've used this book to prepare yourself thoroughly, chances are you'll have to shell out that $100 only once!)

You can schedule the exam for a time that is convenient for you. The exams are downloaded from Prometric to the testing center, and you show up at your scheduled time and take the exam on a computer.

Once you complete the exam, you will know right away whether you have passed or not. At the end of the exam, you will receive a score report. The report will list the areas that you were tested on and how you performed. If you pass the exam, you don't need to do anything else—Prometric uploads the test results to Microsoft. If you don't pass, you'll need to try again. But at least you will know from the score report where you did poorly, so you can study that particular information more carefully.

Test-Taking Hints

If you know what to expect, your chances of passing the exam will be much greater. The following are some tips that can help you achieve success.

Get There Early and Be Prepared   This is your last chance to review. Bring your *MSCE Test Success* book and scan any material areas you feel unsure of. If you need a quick drink of water or a visit to the restroom, take the time before the exam. Once your exam starts, it will not be paused for these needs.

When you arrive for your exam, you will be asked to present two forms of ID. You will also be asked to sign a piece of paper verifying that you understand the testing rules (for example, the rule that says that you will not cheat on the exam).

Before you start the exam, you will have an opportunity to take a practice exam. It is not related to Windows NT and is simply offered so that you will have a feel for the exam-taking process.

What You Can and Can't Take with You   These are closed-book exams. The only thing that you can take in is scratch paper provided by the testing center. Use this paper as much as possible to diagram the questions. Many times, diagramming questions will help make the answers clear. You will need to give this paper back to the test administrator at the end of the exam.

Many testing centers are very strict about what you can take into the testing room. Some testing centers will not even allow you to bring in items like zipped-up purses. If you feel tempted to take in any outside materials, be aware that many testing centers use monitoring devices, such as video and audio equipment (so don't swear, even if you're alone in the room!).

Your Approach to the Test As you take the test, if you know the answer to a question, fill it in and move on. If you're not sure of the answer, mark your best guess, then "mark" the question.

At the end of the exam, you can review the questions. Depending on the amount of time remaining, you can then view all of the questions again, or you can view only the questions that you were unsure of. I always like to double-check all of my answers, just in case I misread any of the questions on the first pass. (Sometimes half of the battle is in trying to figure out exactly what the question is asking you.) Also, sometimes I find that a related question provides a clue for a question that I was unsure of.

Be sure to answer all questions. Unanswered questions are scored as incorrect and will count against you. Also, make sure that you keep an eye on the remaining time so that you can pace yourself accordingly.

If you do not pass the exam, note everything that you can remember while the exam is still fresh in your mind. This will help you prepare for your next try. Although the next exam will not be exactly the same, the questions will be similar, and you don't want to make the same mistakes.

After You Become Certified

Once you become an MCSE, Microsoft kicks in some goodies, including:

- A one-year subscription to Microsoft TechNet, a valuable CD collection that contains Microsoft support information.

- A one-year subscription to the Microsoft Beta Evaluation program, which is a great way to get your hands on new software. Be the first kid on the block to play with new and upcoming software.

- Access to a secured area of the Microsoft Web site that provides technical support and product information. (This benefit is also available with MCP certification.)

- Permission to use the Microsoft Certified Professional logos (each certification has its own logo), which look great on letterhead and business cards.

- An MCP certificate (you will get a certificate for each level of certification you reach), suitable for framing and sending copies to Mom.

- A one-year subscription to *Microsoft Certified Professional Magazine*, which provides information on professional and career development.

How to Use This Book

This book is designed to help you prepare for the MCSE exam. It reviews each objective and relevant test-taking information, and offers you a chance to test your knowledge through study questions and sample tests.

For each unit:

1. Review the exam objectives list at the beginning of the unit. (You may want to check the Microsoft Train_Cert Web site to make sure that the objectives haven't changed.)

2. Read through or scan the reference material that follows the objectives list. This material is organized according to the objectives and is designed to help you brush up on the information that you need to know for the exam.

3. Review your knowledge by answering the study questions. These are straightforward questions designed to test your knowledge of the specific topic. You'll find the answers to the study questions in the Study Question and Sample Test Answers appendix at the back of the book.

4. Once you feel sure of your knowledge of the area, take the sample test. The sample test's content and style matches that of the real exam. Set yourself a time limit based on the number of questions: A general rule is that you should be able to answer 20 questions in 30 minutes. When you've finished, check your answers against those in the Study Question and Sample Test Answers appendix in the back of the book. If you answer at least 85 percent of the questions correctly within the time limit (the first time you take the sample test), you're in good shape. To really prepare, you should note the questions you missed and be able to answer 95 to 100 percent correctly on subsequent tries.

5. After you successfully complete Units 1 through 4, you're ready for the Final Review in Unit 5. Allow yourself 90 minutes to complete the test of 58 questions. If you answer 85 percent of the questions correctly on the first try, you're well prepared. If not, go back and review the areas you struggled with. Then take the test again.

6. Immediately before you take the Networking Essentials exam, scan the reference material at the beginning of each unit to refresh your memory.

At this point, you are well on your way to becoming certified!
Good luck!

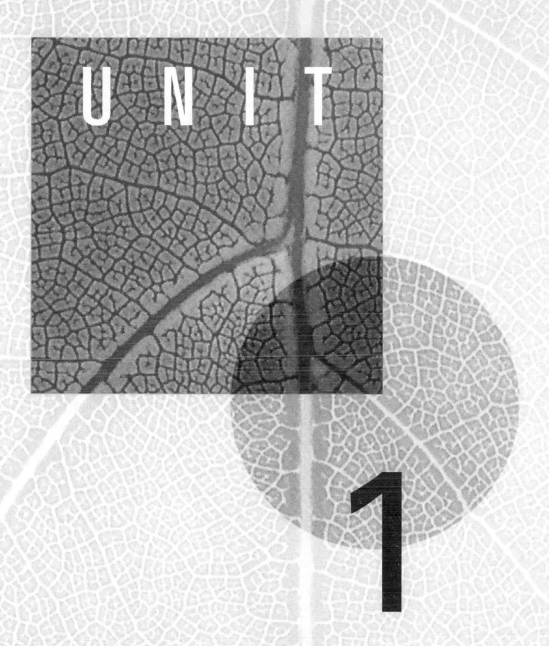

UNIT 1

Standards and Terminology

Test Objectives: Standards and Terminology

- Define common networking terms for LANs and WANs.

- Compare a file-and-print server with an application server.

- Compare a client-server network with a peer-to-peer network.

- Compare user-level security with access permission assigned to a shared directory on a server.

- Compare the implications of using connection-oriented communications with connectionless communications.

- Distinguish whether SLIP or PPP is used as the communications protocol for various situations.

- Define the communication devices that communicate at each level of the OSI model.

- Describe the characteristics and purpose of the media used in IEEE 802.3 and IEEE 802.5 standards.

- Explain the purpose of NDIS and Novell ODI network standards.

Exam objectives are subject to change at any time without prior notice and at Microsoft's sole discretion. Please visit Microsoft's Training & Certification website (www.microsoft.com/Train_Cert) for the most current exam objectives listing.

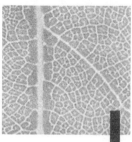

In this unit, we'll review the standards and terminology used in today's networking environment. We'll begin with some definitions of common networking terms, and then describe types of network servers and networks. Next, we'll review types of communications methods and the OSI reference model. Then we'll go over the IEEE standards for Ethernet and Token Ring networks. Finally, we'll discuss the NDIS and ODI network standards.

Defining Networking Terms

We'll define common terms in four categories: network description, network topology, network protocol, and networking service.

Network Description Terms

The following are the terms commonly used when describing a network, beginning with the most basic one:

Network   A group of interconnected computers that share resources and information. For example, some hardware resources typically shared on a network are printers, fax-modems, and hard disks.

Transmission media   The physical pathway on which the computers are connected. Cable and wireless media can connect the computers in a network.

Stand-alone computer   A computer that is not connected to a network.

Local area network (LAN)   A group of computers interconnected within a building or campus (see Figure 1.1). For example, a LAN may consist of computers located on a single floor of a building or it might link all the computers in a small company.

Metropolitan area network (MAN)   A network of LANs that covers a city or large campus environment (see Figure 1.2).

Wide area network (WAN)   A network consisting of computers or LANs connected across a distance (see Figure 1.3). WANs can cover small to large distances using different physical topologies, such as telephone lines, fiber-optic cabling, satellite transmissions, and microwave transmissions.

FIGURE 1.1

An example of a local area network (LAN)

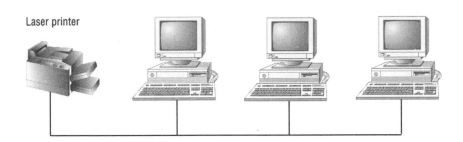

FIGURE 1.2

An example of a metropolitan area network (MAN)

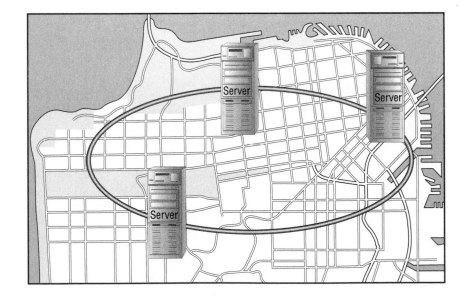

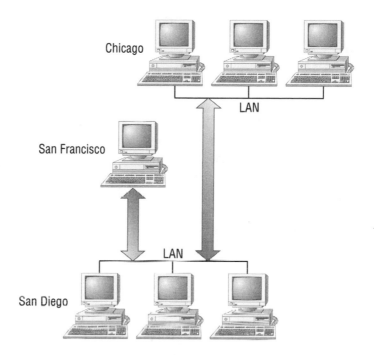

Network Topology Terms

Network *topologies* are the physical cable or transmitters on the network. The
following are the different types of physical topologies:

Bus   All computers are connected with a single cable with a terminator on
each end. An example is an Ethernet network connected with Thinnet
coaxial (10Base2) cable.

Star   All computers are connect to a central device, typically a hub or
switch. An example is an Ethernet network connected with twisted-pair
(10BaseT) cable.

Ring   All computers or network devices are attached directly to each other
in a ring fashion. An example is an FDDI (Fiber Distributed Data Interface)
network, where all the hubs connect to each other in a ring.

See Unit 2 for more details about network topologies and their uses.

Network Protocol Terms

Computers use *protocols* to communicate with each other. A protocol is a language, or a set of rules the computers in a network need to follow in order to understand each other.

A *protocol suite* is a group of protocols that are loaded together. An example of a protocol suite is TCP/IP.

The following are some common network protocols:

- **TCP (Transmission Control Protocol)** The Internet protocol suite's transport service protocol.

- **IP (Internet Protocol)** The Internet protocol suite's protocol for defining and routing datagrams.

- **IPX/SPX ((Internetwork Packet Exchange/Sequenced Packet Exchange)** Routable protocols created by Novell for NetWare networks.

- **NetBEUI (NetBIOS Extended User Interface)** A protocol created by IBM for small workgroups.

- **HTTP (Hypertext Transfer Protocol)** The WWW (World Wide Web) protocol used to transfer Web pages across the Internet.

See Unit 2 for more details about network protocols and their uses.

Networking Service Terms

The following are three terms related to TCP/IP networking services:

WINS (Windows Internet Name Service) A TCP/IP network service for Microsoft networks that resolves NetBIOS names and facilitates browsing across subnetworks.

DNS (Domain Name Service)   A TCP/IP network service that translates host names to Internet Protocol (IP) addresses.

DHCP (Dynamic Host Configuration Protocol)   A method for automatically assigning IP addresses to client computers on a network.

See Unit 3 for more details about networking services and their uses.

Comparing File, Print, and Application Servers

A *server* in a network is dedicated to performing specific tasks in support of other computers on the network. In a server-based network, not all servers are alike:

- *File servers* offer services that allow network users to share files. File services include storing, retrieving, and moving data. File and print servers do not do processing for the client computers.

- *Print servers* manage and control a single printer or a group of printers on a network. The print server controls the queue or spooler. Clients send print jobs to the print server, and the print server uses the spooler to hold the jobs until the printer is ready.

- *Application servers* allow client PCs to access and use extra computing power and expensive software applications that reside on a shared computer. Application servers offload work from the client by running programs for the client and sending the results back to the client. For example, when a client asks a Microsoft SQL Server server to find a record, SQL Server does all the processing to find the answer, and then sends the results back to the client.

Running applications from an application server rather than from separate client machines can reduce your licensing costs. With this setup, you can purchase licenses for every connection to the application. For example, if you have 100 users but only 50 users use the application at a time, you would buy a 50-user license.

File, print, and application services are the main services that servers provide. Although you can dedicate a server to a particular service, such as having a computer that serves only as a print server, you do not need a different server for each type of service. One server can function as a file, print, and application server.

Comparing Client-Server and Peer-to-Peer Networks

There are three roles for computers in a network:

- A *client* is a workstation used only to request services from a network service provider, such as a dedicated server or another workstation (see Figure 1.4).

FIGURE 1.4

A client computer requests services.

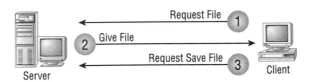

- A *server* provides services to service requestors (see Figure 1.5). A *dedicated* server functions only as a server; it is not used as a client or workstation. The use of a dedicated server is recommended for networks with more than ten clients.

- A *peer* both requests and provides network services.

In a server-based *(client-server)* network, a dedicated server is used to provide services to clients. For example, the server might provide file, print, message, database, and application services to the clients in the network.

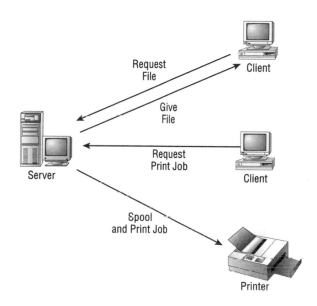

Request
File

Client

Give
File

Server

Request
Print Job

Client

Spool
and Print Job

Printer

In a peer-to-peer network, each computer is equal (peer) in the sharing of
resources (see Figure 1.6). A peer-to-peer network does not have a dedicated
server, and there is no hierarchy among the computers. Each peer is responsible
for its own security. Usually, the computer users determine what data on their
computer will be shared on the network.

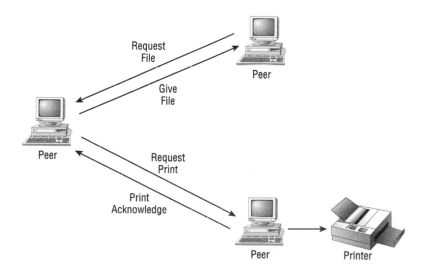

Request
File

Peer

Give
File

Peer

Request
Print

Print
Acknowledge

Peer   Printer

A *hybrid* network is a combination client-server/peer-to-peer network. Typically, hybrid networks are client-server networks that also include some peers.

Comparing User-Level Security with Access Permissions

One large difference in the way peer-to-peer and server-based networks operate is in how they implement security.

Share-Level Security

Peer-to-peer networks are usually less secure than server-based networks because peer-to-peer networks commonly use *share-level security*, also known as *password-protected security*.

With share-level security, each network resource can be assigned a password. For example, on a Windows 95 system, you can assign a password to a certain directory. Then, before a user can gain access to that directory, he or she must enter the correct password.

Share-level security can be used with both FAT and NTFS partitions. This type of security works at the directory (folder) level, which means that it applies to all the files within the specified directory.

Access Permissions

Server-based networks commonly use access permission security, also known as *file-level* or *user-level* security. With this type of security, an administrator assigns rights to a user or group so that the user or group can access a certain network resource.

Rather than entering a password for access to each shared resource, the user first enters a user name and password to gain access to the network itself. Then the user's access is controlled by the permissions he or she has been granted or denied. In a system using access permissions. all share access is evaluated on the basis of account information. For example, a user must log on to a Windows NT domain before being able to request to use a network printer, and that user will have access to that printer if that user's account has permissions for that network resource.

Access permission security works only with NTFS partitions and can apply to indivdual files.

Comparing Connection-Oriented with Connectionless Communications

There are two ways that communication between computers can be arranged: connectionless methods and connection-oriented methods.

Connectionless Communications

Connectionless methods do not guarantee delivery, and thus are faster than connection-oriented methods. An analogy is using the postal service to send a postcard or letter—it will probably get to its destination but there is no guarantee.

Examples of protocols that use connectionless communications are IP (Internet Protocol), UDP (User Datagram Protocol), and IPX (Internetwork Packet eXchange).

Connection-Oriented Communications

Connection-oriented methods guarantee delivery, but they are slower than connectionless methods. An analogy is sending a registered letter, where extra steps are taken to ensure that it arrives at its destination.

Examples of protocols that use connection-oriented communications include TCP (Transmission Control Protocol), SPX (Sequence Packet eXchange), and X.25 (a WAN protocol).

Distinguishing between SLIP and PPP

SLIP (Serial Line Internet Protocol) and PPP (Point-to-Point Protocol) are two common protocols used to transmit IP packets over serial line and telephone connections, most often as part of a dial-up Internet connection.

SLIP, the original serial framing transport for TCP/IP, and PPP, the newer serial protocol, are similar. There are, however, some key differences that make PPP a more efficient and secure transport option. Table 1.1 shows these differences.

TABLE 1.1 SLIP versus PPP	SLIP	PPP
	Supports TCP/IP only	Supports multiple protocols
	Does not provide error checking for bad frames (very little overhead)	Provides error checking for each frame (more overhead)
	Requires manual IP addressing	Provides dynamic addressing
	Does not support encrypted authentication	Supports encrypted authentication, both login and password

Defining Communications at the OSI Model Levels

There are seven layers that define the OSI reference model (see Figure 1.7). Table 1.2 lists the layers, from bottom to top.

FIGURE 1.7

The OSI reference model and its functions

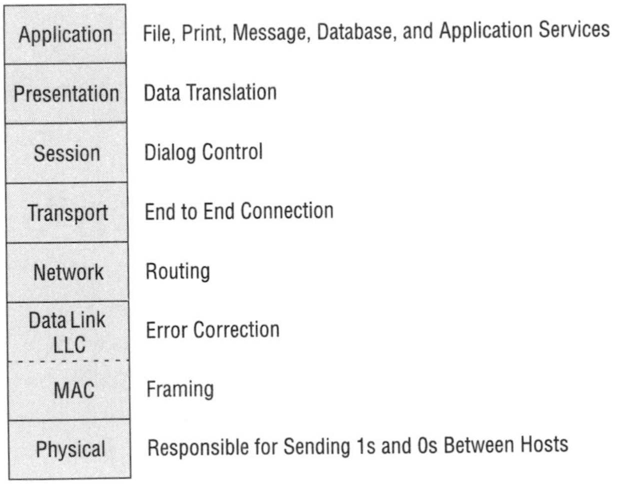

Application	File, Print, Message, Database, and Application Services
Presentation	Data Translation
Session	Dialog Control
Transport	End to End Connection
Network	Routing
Data Link LLC	Error Correction
MAC	Framing
Physical	Responsible for Sending 1s and 0s Between Hosts

	Layer	Function	Communication Devices
TABLE 1.2 OSI Reference Model Layers	Physical	Handles sending bits (ones and zeros) from one computer to another.	Hubs, switches, repeaters, cables, connectors, transmitters, receivers, multiplexers

	Data Link
	  LLC sublayer
	  MAC sublayer
		Provides for the flow of data over a single link from one device to another	Switches, bridges, intelligent hubs

	Network	Makes routing decisions and forwards packets (also known as *datagrams*) for devices that could be farther away than a single link	Routers, brouters, gateway services
	Transport	Ensures that packets are delivered error-free, in sequence, and without losses or duplication	Routers, brouters, gateway services
	Session	Allows applications on separate computers to share a connection (called a *session*)	Application interfaces, gateways
	Presentation	Translates data between the formats the network requires and the formats the computer expects	Application interfaces, gateways
	Application	Provides services that directly support user applications, such as database access, e-mail, and file transfer	Application interfaces, gateways

The Application, Presentation, and Session Layers

The top three layers in the OSI reference model—Application, Presentation, and Session—deal mostly with functions that aid applications in communicating with other applications. They specifically deal with tasks like filename formats, code sets, user interfaces, compression, encryption, and other functions that relate to the exchange occurring between applications.

Application interfaces like Microsoft's NetBIOS and Novell's NCP (Net-Ware Core Protocol) run at these levels. Another connectivity device that operates at the upper layers of the OSI reference model is a gateway. A *gateway* rebuilds a protocol stack from one type of application so that it can be understood by another type of application.

The Transport and Network Layers

The middle layers in the OSI reference model—Transport and Network—deal with the logical transmission of data. They take care of the sizing of packets, also called *datagrams*, sent and received from each application, and then handle the routing of those packets. These layers also set the degree of reliability for packets reaching their destination and the logical addressing of each machine. Several connectivity devices work at these levels:

- *Gateways* can rebuild a complete protocol stack, as explained in the description of the upper layers. If you are running a TCP/IP network and want to communicate with an IPX network, you need a gateway to be able to communicate between the two networks.

- *Routers* route packets through an intranetwork and the Internet. A router is a lot like a postman; he needs to know all the streets to be able to deliver mail. A router keeps track of all the network segments and communicates this information with other routers.

- *Brouters* are used when you have more then one type of protocol on your network, but one of the protocols is not routable. For example, the Net-BEUI protocol cannot be routed, so it would be bridged instead. Brouters are typically run with software in a router.

 See Unit 2 for more details about network connectivity devices and their uses.

The Data Link and Physical Layers

The bottom layers in the OSI reference model—Data Link and Physical—handle the physical transmission of data. They take what is passed down to them and put it into a format that can be sent over a variety of physical transmission media.

The Data Link layer, which packages the data units into *frames*, is divided into two sublayers:

LLC (Logical Link Control)   Top sublayer; establishes and maintains links between communicating devices. This sublayer is also responsible for frame error correction and hardware addresses.

MAC (Media Access Control)   Bottom sublayer; controls how devices share a media channel. There are two main methods:

- With *contention*, all devices attached to the network can transmit whenever they have something to communicate. Ethernet is an example of a contention network.

- With *token passing*, computers on the network cannot transmit onto the network cable until they are given a frame or token. Token Ring, ARCnet, and FDDI are examples of networks that use token-passing media access.

Some of the hardware devices that communicate at the Data Link and Physical layers are hubs, switches, repeaters, cables, connectors, transmitters, and receivers. Also, *bridges*, which are devices that connect network segments, operate at the Data Link layer. Bridges can selectively determine the appropriate segment that should receive a signal, and they are used with nonroutable protocols, such as NetBEUI.

Defining the Media Used in IEEE 802.3 and IEEE 802.5 Standards

In February 1980, the Institute for Electrical and Electronic Engineers, Inc. (IEEE) formed a project called project 802 (after the year and month) to help define certain standards. The 802 specifications fall into 12 categories that are identified by the 802 numbers:

802.1   Internetworking and Management

802.2   Logical Link Control

802.3   Carrier Sense with Multiple Access and Collision Detection (CSMA/CD or Ethernet)

802.4	Token Bus LAN
802.5	Token Ring LAN
802.6	Metropolitan Area Network (MAN)
802.7	Broadband Technical Advisory Group
802.8	Fiber-Optic Technical Advisory Group
802.9	Integrated Voice/Data Networks
802.10	Network Security
802.11	Wireless Network
802.12	Demand Priority Access LAN, 100BaseVG-AnyLAN

IEEE 802.3 (Ethernet) and 802.5 (Token Ring) are the most commonly used standards for physical and logical topologies.

802.3: Ethernet

The Ethernet protocol implements a logical bus network that can transmit at 10 or 100Mbps. Every computer receives the information, but only the intended destination acknowledges the transmission.

CSMA/CD

Ethernet uses the CSMA/CD access method to share network media. The CSMA/CD protocol can be broken down as follows:

CS (Carrier Sense)   Before transmitting, listen for a signal; if none is found, it is okay to transmit.

MA (Multiple Access)   All computers share the same cable and signaling techniques.

CD (Collision Detect)   Detect collisions, wait, and retransmit.

Ethernet Cabling Systems

There are four commonly used Ethernet cabling systems, which are listed in Table 1.3.

TABLE 1.3	Cable	Description
Ethernet Cabling	10Base5	Also known as RG-8 or Thicknet coaxial cable; carries signals up to 500 meters (1640 feet) at 50 ohms
	10Base2	Also known as RG-58 or Thinnet coaxial cable; carries signals 185 meters (607 feet) at 50 ohms
	10BaseT	Also known as twisted-pair; the most popular of all Ethernet topologies, categories include 3, 5, and 6 (UTP, or unshielded twisted pair) cable at up to 100Mbps speeds; carries signals up to 100 meters (330 feet)
	100BaseT	Also known at twisted-pair; uses category 5 for speeds up to 100Mbps and category 6 for speeds up to 155Mbps; carries signals up to 100 meters (330 feet)

See Unit 2 for more details about network cable types and their uses.

802.5: Token Ring

Token Ring is a logical ring network that looks like a star network (because the ring is actually formed inside a central hub). Token Ring devices can transmit at 4Mbps or 16Mbps.

Hubs in a Token Ring network are called MSAUs or MAUs (both for multistation access units).

Token Passing

Token Ring networks use token passing to determine who may transmit at any one moment. Unlike an Ethernet network, computers in a Token Ring network can transmit only when they receive a frame known as a *token*. The token goes around the logical ring, and only the computer that has the token can transmit. Since the computer must have a token before transmitting, no collisions occur.

Active monitors, sometimes referred to as *token masters*, are in charge of keeping track of where the token is and making sure that there is only one token on the network at a time.

Token Ring is a very resilient network. Network interface cards in Token Ring networks can run diagnostics on themselves and take themselves off and on the network.

Token Ring Cabling Types

Standard cable types for Token Ring include Types 1 through 6, 8, and 9, as listed in Table 1.4.

TABLE 1.4 Token Ring Cabling	Cable	Description
	Type 1	STP (shielded twisted-pair), used to connect terminals and distribution panels
	Type 2	STP, used to connect terminals located in the same physical area or room
	Type 3	UTP (unshielded twisted-pair), which has four pairs, each twisted two times for every 3.6 meters (12 feet) of length
	Type 5	Optical cable used only on the main ring path
	Type 6	STP that does not carry signals as far as Type 1 or 2, used as patch cable or extensions in wiring closets
	Type 8	Used for runs under carpets
	Type 9	Plenum-rated, used for runs in ceilings

Understanding NDIS and Novell ODI Standards

Computer users want to able to load multiple protocols on their workstation but install only one network interface card. The solution to this problem is driver interfaces, which allow multiple cards to be bound to multiple transport protocols. Two such driver interfaces exist: NDIS and ODI.

NDIS

In Windows NT, Windows 95, OS/2, and Windows for Workgroups, the network driver is implemented by NDIS (Network Driver Interface Standard) 3.0. NDIS is a small code wrapper that controls the interface between NDIS-compliant drivers and transport protocols. NDIS 3.0 allows multiple adapter drivers to be bound to an unlimited number of transport protocols.

ODI

ODI (Open Data Link Interface) was developed by Apple and Novell to simplify driver development and to provide support for multiple protocols in a single network adapter card. Similar to NDIS, ODI allows Novell NetWare drivers to be written without concern for the protocol that will be used on top of them.

```
STUDY QUESTIONS
```

Defining Networking Terms

1.   Define what a network is.

_____

2.   True/False. Transmission media is the analog signal used in wireless transmissions.

3.   If a computer is not connected to a network, it is known as a _____
_____ computer.

4.   A LAN is typically defined as a _____.

5.   Which type of network can typically span large geographic areas?

_____

6.   The most common LAN network topology is _____.

7.   What does WAN stand for?

_____

8.   Define network topology.

_____

9.   List two of the physical topologies used in WANs.

_____

_____

10.   In which type of physical topology would you use Thinnet cable?

_____

11.   Define a bus physical topology.

_____

12.   In which type of physical topology would you find an FDDI network?

_____

13.   In which type of physical topology would you find a 10BaseT network?

_____

14.   In which physical topology would you find connecting hubs all connected in a ring, passing a token through all the hubs until it reaches the originating hub?

_____

15.   What is a protocol?

_____

16. True/False. When loading TCP/IP on a workstation, you are actually loading the IP protocol suite.

17. True/False. TCP/IP is one protocol.

18. What is Novell's primary protocol?

_____

19. What does NetBEUI stand for?

_____

20. Which protocol does the World Wide Web use to transmit pages on the Internet?

_____

21. True/False. IBM originally created the NetBEUI protocol for large workgroups.

22. True/False. WINS is a network service that translates host names into Internet Protocol (IP) addresses.

Comparing File, Print, and Application Servers

23. Which service on the server provides storage, retrieval, and file transfer?

_____

24. Which service on the server manages and controls printing on a network?

_____

25. How many servers do you need if you want to run file, print, and application services?

_____

26. What does spooling a job mean?

_____

27. True/False. You need a print server for every five printers running on your network.

28. True/False. The printer spooler runs on the client requesting the print job.

29. True/False. Application servers allow all clients to access and use extra computing power and software applications that reside on a shared computer.

30. True/False. One advantage of storing applications on a network server instead of a client computer is lower licensing cost.

31. True/False. A SQL Server server will send data to the client computer for processing. The client will then send the information back to the SQL Server server for storage.

32. When would you install an application server?

_____

33. True/False. Application servers do not need more power or storage than clients do.

34. What is the main difference between a file server and an application server?

_____

Comparing Client-Server and Peer-to-Peer Networks

35. True/False. Clients request services from service requestors.

36. What type of networking does Windows 95 implement?

_____

37. How large should you make a peer-to-peer network?

_____

38. Which network is less expensive: peer-to-peer or server-based?

_____

39. A client workstation is used only as a service _____.

40. True/False. A dedicated server functions only as a server and is not used as a client or workstation.

41. What type of computer can be both a service provider and a service requestor?

_____

42. True/False. In a peer-to-peer network, some of the computers are equal and therefore are known as peers.

43. If you are using a hybrid network, what type of network(s) are you using?

_____

Comparing User-Level Security with Access Permissions

44. Peer-to-peer networks use _____ security; server-centric networks use _____ security.

45. True/False. Peer-to-peer networks are usually less secure than server-based networks.

46. In what type of network is file-level security typically used?

_____

47. Password-protected shares are also known as _____.

48. Access permissions are also known as _____.

49. True/False. When assigning access permissions, the administrator can assign rights to both users and groups.

50. True/False. In both share-level and file-level security, a user only needs to supply a password to get access to a network resource.

Comparing Connection-Oriented with Connectionless Communications

51. Which type of connection method is like sending a postcard?

52. True/False. Connectionless methods do not guarantee delivery, which makes them slower than connection-oriented methods.

53. For each protocol listed below, indicate whether it is connection-oriented or connectionless.

IP: _____

TCP: _____

SPX: _____

IPX: _____

54. When would you decide to run a connectionless program, and when would you decide to turn on connection-oriented protocols?

_____

Distinguishing between SLIP and PPP

55. SLIP stands for _____.

56. PPP stands for _____ .

57. True/False. SLIP has more overhead than PPP.

58. True/False. SLIP supports only TCP/IP; PPP supports multiple protocols.

59. True/False. When using PPP, the protocol information is typically assigned to the host dynamically.

60. When using SLIP, authentication is not supported; PPP supports both
_____ and _____ .

Defining Communications at the OSI Model Levels

61. How many layers are in the OSI reference model?

_____

62. The Logical Link Control is a sublayer of which layer of the OSI reference model?

_____

63. Which device resides at the Network layer of the OSI reference model and makes decisions on how to send packets through an intranetwork?

_____

64. Which device tears down a frame and rebuilds it to accommodate a different protocol stack?

_____

65. Which layer of the OSI reference model is responsible for framing?

_____

66. If you are using NetBEUI, which device and at which layer of the OSI reference model do you need to use to segment your network?

Device: _____

Layer: _____

67. At which layer of the OSI reference model is digital signaling defined?

_____

68. At which layer of the OSI reference model are hardware addresses defined?

_____

69. In the spaces below, write in the layers of the OSI reference model from top to bottom and their corresponding functions.

Layer   Function

_____   _____

_____   _____

_____   _____

_____   _____

_____   _____

_____   _____

_____   _____

70. Which layer of the OSI reference model is typically responsible for connection-oriented transmission of data?

_____

71. Which layer of the OSI reference model handles the actual transmission of 1s and 0s across the cable media?

_____

72. At which layer of the OSI reference model would a redirector reside?

_____

73. At which layer of the OSI reference model is the physical topology defined?

_____

74. At which layer of the OSI reference model is the logical topology defined?

_____

75. Which communication device actually uses all seven layers of the OSI reference model?

_____

76. At which layer of the OSI reference model are compression, expansion, encryption, and decryption performed?

_____

Defining the Media Used in IEEE 802.3 and IEEE 802.5 Standards

77. True/False. Project 802 was named because the IEEE is responsible for eight hundred and two projects.

78. True/False. The 802.1 group is responsible for Internetworking and Management.

79. 802.2 is defined as _____.

80. 802.3 is defined as _____, or Ethernet.

81. True/False. 802.4 is known as Token Ring LAN.

82. True/False. 802.5 is known as Token Bus LAN.

83. A metropolitan area network (MAN) is described in which IEEE specification?

_____

84. True/False. 802.7 is an advisory group for broadband technology.

85. The 802.9 group was put together to come up with which specifications?

_____

86. True/False. The 802.8 specifications are for hardware modems.

87. The Fiber-Optic Technical Advisory Group has which specification number?

_____

88. Network security is specified with which number?

_____

89. True/False. Wireless networks are defined with 802.11 specifications.

90. 802.12 specifies which protocol?

_____

91. True/False. The Ethernet protocol implements a physical bus network that can transmit at 10Mbps.

92. Define the following terms:

CS _____

MA _____

CD _____

93. Which type of cable can carry a signal 500 meters at 50 ohms?

_____

94. Which Ethernet cabling is specified to be able to carry a signal 185 meters at 50 ohms?

_____

95. Twisted-pair cable can run what distance and still be within its specifications?

_____

96. What are the categories that twisted-pair cable comes in?

_____

97. Why is Token Ring called Token Ring, even though it is a physical star network?

_____

98. True/False. Token Ring is faster than 10BaseT.

99. Token Ring devices can transmit at _____ or
_____ Mbps.

100. Token Ring is also know as 802._____.

101. What type of media-access method does Token Ring use so that no collisions will occur?

_____

102. True/False. Shielded twisted-pair (STP) is the most popular of all cables used for LANs.

103. How many wires are there in a 10BaseT category 3 cable?

_____

104. Which type of Token Ring cable is plenum-rated and used for runs in ceilings?

_____

Understanding NDIS and Novell ODI Standards

105.   Which companies developed NDIS?

_____

106.   Which companies developed ODI?

_____

107.   At which layer of the OSI reference model is the ODI defined?

_____

108.   What is the goal for NDIS and ODI?

_____

SAMPLE TEST

1-1 You must link together a small number of computers in an office building. Which kind of network should you install?

    A. LAN

    B. WAN

    C. MAN

    D. CAN

1-2 You manage eight computers for a small marketing firm. You are told that it is time to install a network. Cost is an issue, and you can trust the users to manage their own computers with a minimum of help from you. What kind of network best fits your situation?

    A. Server-based

    B. Peer-to-peer

    C. Hybrid

    D. Mainframe/terminal

1-3 You would like security on your network to be as tight as possible, but you would also like to be able to control access to resources on an account-by-account basis. What kind of security should you implement?

    A. Peer-based (password-protected shares)

    B. Server-based (file and directory security)

    C. Physical (guards and keys)

    D. Hybrid (both peer-based and server-based)

1-4 You need file, print, message, and database services on your 100-user network. How many servers do you need?

    A. One

    B. Two

    C. Three

    D. Four

1-5 Your 10Base2 Ethernet network is improperly terminated. At which layer of the OSI reference model does the problem reside?

    A. Physical

    B. Data Link

    C. Network

    D. Transport

1-6 You are installing a network to support 95 computers. Security is the most important issue. You must control how data is shared on the network so that the sensitive data is not compromised (users must not be able to establish their own shares). Your network must support DOS and Windows programs. What type of network should you implement?

    A. Server-based

    B. Peer-to-peer

    C. Hybrid

    D. Mainframe/terminal

SAMPLE TEST

1-7   You have an Ethernet network and a Token Ring network connected by a router. You are using TCP/IP on both networks, but from any computer on one network, you cannot access resources on the other network. You suspect that the router is configured improperly. At which layer of the OSI reference model does the problem reside?

    A. Physical

    B. Data Link

    C. Network

    D. Transport

1-8   You would like to get the IEEE specification for Ethernet over fiber-optic cable. Which specification are you looking for?

    A. 802.1

    B. 802.5

    C. 802.8

    D. 802.12

1-9   Which layer of the OSI reference model is responsible for bridging?

    A. Physical

    B. Data Link

    C. Network

    D. Transport

SAMPLE TEST

1-10   Which of the following specifications allows multiple protocols to run on one adapter? (Choose all that apply.)

    A. NDIS

    B. ODI

    C. OSI

    D. TCP/IP

1-11   Which is faster: TCP or UDP?

    A. TCP

    B. UDP

    C. Neither

    D. They cannot be compared

1-12   Which kind of network should you create when you need to link together the various branch offices around the state for your company?

    A. LAN

    B. WAN

    C. MAN

    D. CAN

1-13   Which media-access methods use tokens? (Choose all that apply.)

    A. Ethernet

    B. Token Ring

    C. FDDI

    D. ARCnet

1-14   At which layer of the OSI reference model is bit synchronization performed?

   A. Physical

   B. Data Link

   C. Network

   D. Transport

1-15   You have been hired as the administrator for a small network of around 10 computers. You do not need to worry about security, and the users are computer-literate. Which kind of network best fits your needs?

   A. Peer

   B. Single server

   C. Multi-server

   D. Multi-server with a high-speed backbone

1-16   You need to set up and perform central backups and account administration for a small network. The data transfer and storage requirements are relatively light. Which kind of network is best for your firm?

   A. Peer

   B. Single server

   C. Multi-server

   D. Enterprise

| S A M P L E   T E S T |

1-17 Which type of network should you install if you must link together the computers on eight floors in a office building?

    A. LAN

    B. WAN

    C. MAN

    D. CAN

1-18 You want to switch from share-level security to user-level security on your Windows 95 clients. You go to Control Panel, Network, Access Control, Option and enter the name of your Windows 95 workgroup. You then receive an error message. What could the problem be?

    A. You misspelled the workgroup name

    B. Windows 95 does not support user-level security

    C. The Windows 95 machine is not attached to the network

    D. It's normal. Click OK to continue

1-19 Another Ethernet adapter is set to the same MAC address as yours, causing network problems for these two machines. At which layer of the OSI reference model does the problem reside?

    A. Physical

    B. Data Link

    C. Network

    D. Transport

1-20 Which dial-in protocol provides error checking for frames?

    A. TCP/IP

    B. LLC

C. SLIP

D. PPP

1-21   When would you use the WINS service? (Choose all that apply.)

   A. When you need to give each host an IP address

   B. When you need to resolve host names to IP addresses

   C. When you need to resolve NetBIOS names to IP addresses dynamically

   D. When you need to resolve NetBIOS names to IP addresses statically

1-22   What does NetBEUI stand for?

   A. NetBIOS Extended User Interface

   B. NetBIOS Exchange User Interface

   C. NetBEUI Extended User Interface

   D. NetBEUI Exchange User Interface

1-23   When would you use DNS? (Choose all that apply.)

   A. When you need to resolve NetBIOS names to IP addresses dynamically

   B. When you need to resolve host names to IP addresses dynamically

   C. When you need to resolve host names to IP addresses statically

   D. When you need to resolve NetBIOS names to IP addresses statically

1-24   At which layer of the OSI reference model does network cabling specification take place?

   A. Physical

   B. Data Link

   C. Network

   D. Transport

1-25 You have just been hired to manage a small network of around 30 computers. Business requirements dictate that you use central administration and data backup of important files, but some power users would like to be able to share files and peripherals from their own computers. Which kind of network best fits your needs?

    A. Server-based

    B. Peer-to-peer

    C. Hybrid

    D. Mainframe/terminal

1-26 FDDI uses which type of physical topology?

    A. Bus

    B. Ring

    C. Star

    D. Mesh

1-27 At which layer of the OSI reference model are file and print services specified?

    A. Transport

    B. Session

    C. Presentation

    D. Application

1-28 Which devices function at the Data Link layer of the OSI reference model? (Choose all that apply.)

    A. Multiplexers

    B. Switches

    C. Intelligent hubs

    D. Bridges

SAMPLE TEST

1-29   At which layer of the OSI reference model does UDP reside?

  A. Physical

  B. Data Link

  C. Network

  D. Transport

1-30   Which media-access network tries to detect collisions instead of avoiding collisions?

  A. Token Ring

  B. ARCnet

  C. CSMA/CD

  D. CSMA/CA

1-31   When you install a 10Base2 network, what must you make sure to do?

  A. Terminate each end with a 93-ohm terminator

  B. Terminate each end with a 75-ohm terminator

  C. Terminate each end with a 50-ohm terminator

  D. Connect both ends together to make a loop

1-32   What is 10Base5 also called?

  A. Thicknet

  B. Thinnet

  C. Token Ring

  D. Routing

1-33   How many tokens can exist on a Token Ring network at the same time?

   A. As many as it takes

   B. One

   C. Two

   D. One for each workstation

1-34   Which protocol does a Web browser use to communicate?

   A. TCP/IP

   B. HDLC

   C. HTTP

   D. HTML

1-35   A physical star network uses which type of logical topology?

   A. Bus

   B. Ring

   C. Star

   D. Mesh

1-36   Which type of resource-sharing architecture does Windows for Workgroups use?

   A. NTFS permissions

   B. Access permissions

   C. File-level security

   D. Share-level security

1-37   In file-level access, how many passwords do the network resources have?

    A. One

    B. Two

    C. Unlimited

    D. None

1-38   You dial into your ISP but you do not receive an IP address. You must type it in manually. Which type of dial-up protocol are you using?

    A. TCP/IP

    B. PPP

    C. SLIP

    D. None

1-39   LLC is a sublayer of which OSI reference model layer?

    A. Physical

    B. Data Link

    C. Network

    D. Transport

1-40   Windows 95 implements which type of networking?

    A. File-level security

    B. Server-based

    C. Peer-to-peer

    D. None

SAMPLE TEST

1-41   Ethernet is a physical star, logical bus network. What is Token Ring?

   A. Physical star, logical bus

   B. Logical star, physical ring

   C. Physical bus, logical ring

   D. Physical star, logical ring

1-42   Datagrams are associated with which layer of the OSI reference model?

   A. Physical

   B. Data Link

   C. Network

   D. Transport

1-43   What is the name of a hub in a Token Ring network?

   A. Switch

   B. Hub

   C. Bridge

   D. MSAU

1-44   Which layer of the OSI reference model is concerned with framing?

   A. Physical

   B. Data Link

   C. Network

   D. Transport

1-45   What is the maximum distance of cable runs in a 10Base2 network?

    A. 100 meters

    B. 1000 meters

    C. 185 meters

    D. 1100 feet

UNIT

2

Planning

Test Objectives: Planning

■ Select the appropriate media for various situations. Media choices include:

- Twisted-pair cable
- Coaxial cable
- Fiber-optic cable
- Wireless

Situational elements include:

- Cost
- Distance limitations
- Number of nodes

■ Select the appropriate topology for various token-ring and Ethernet networks.

■ Select the appropriate network and transport protocol or protocols for various token-ring and Ethernet networks. Protocol choices include:

- DLC
- AppleTalk
- IPX
- TCP/IP
- NFS
- SMB

■ Select the appropriate connectivity devices for various token-ring and Ethernet networks. Connectivity devices include:

- Repeaters
- Bridges
- Routers
- Brouters
- Gateways

■ List the characteristics, requirements, and appropriate situations for WAN connection services. WAN connection services include:

- X.25
- ISDN
- Frame relay
- ATM

Exam objectives are subject to change at any time without prior notice and at Microsoft's sole discretion. Please visit Microsoft's Training & Certification website (www.microsoft.com/Train_Cert) for the most current exam objectives listing.

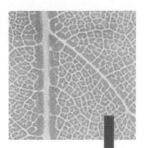

In this unit, we will study planning your network. Planning includes selecting the most suitable media type and topology for your network. You also need to know about connectivity devices, protocols, and WAN connection services.

Selecting the Appropriate Media

Computers must communicate through some form of transmission media. The most common types of media are twisted-pair and coaxial cable (copper media), followed by fiber-optic cable (glass media). Wireless media include radio wave, microwave, and infrared. These types are still much slower than copper of glass media, but they are the most suitable choice for certain situations.

First we will look at an overview of communication technologies and the problems that degrade transmissions through various types of media. Then we will review the specific characteristics of different media.

Communication Technologies

The following are some technologies that apply to communications:

- *Broadband transmission* enables two or more communication channels to share the bandwidth of the transmission media (see Figure 2.1). Broadband networks can simultaneously accommodate video, voice, and data. ISDN is an example of a WAN communication service that can provide broadband transmissions.

Bandwidth is basically the difference between the highest and lowest frequencies in a given range. This refers to the capacity of the media. The greater the bandwidth, the faster the data-transfer capabilities. For example, Ethernet has a bandwidth of 10 megabits per second (Mbps) and Token Ring has a bandwidth of either 4Mbps or 16Mbps.

- *Baseband transmission* uses digital signals over a single frequency (see Figure 2.1). With baseband transmission, the entire communication-channel capacity is used to transmit a single data signal. Most LANs use baseband technology.

FIGURE 2.1

Broadband and base-band technologies

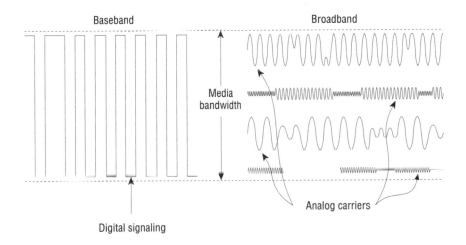

- *Multiplexing* divides a transmission facility into two or more channels (see Figure 2.2). The two main ways to share a channel are time-division multiplexing (TDM) and frequency-division multiplexing (FDM). *Demultiplexing* recovers the original separate channels from a multiplexed signal. A *multiplexer*, also called a *mux*, can perform both multiplexing and demultiplexing.

FIGURE 2.2

Multiplexing and
demultiplexing

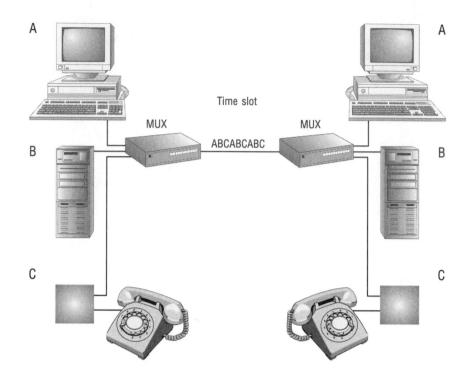

Transmission Degradation

Depending on the media type, the following problems can affect the quality of transmissions:

- *Attenuation* refers to loss of signal as it goes through the transmission medium, measured in decibels (dB).

- *Electromagnetic interference* (EMI) is electrical background noise that disturbs or distorts a signal as it travels down the transmission media. Fiber-optic cable is usually immune to EMI because it uses light rather than electronic signals to transfer data.

- *Crosstalk* is a form of EMI caused by wires next to each other interfering with signals as they travel through the transmission media.

- *Dispersion* applies to fiber-optic cables. Chromatic dispersion occurs when light enters the core at different angles and spreads apart slightly as it travels to the destination.

Types of Cable Media

The following types of cabling are used in networks:

- Twisted-pair—unshielded twisted pair (UTP) and shielded twisted-pair (STP)

- Coaxial—Thinnet and Thicknet

- Fiber-optic

These types are compared in Table 2.1 and described in the following sections.

TABLE 2.1: Characteristics of Cable Media

Cable Type	Cost	Max. Distance	Max. Number of Nodes	Common Usage
UTP	Very low	Commonly 100 meters (330 feet)	1024	Star networks; 2 to 155Mbps
STP	Fairly expensive—more than UTP or Thinnet	Commonly 100 meters (330 feet)	270	IBM Token Ring; 4 or 16Mbps
Thinnet	Relatively inexpensive—less than STP or UTP	185 meters (610 feet)	30 per segment	Thinnet Ethernet; 2 to 10Mbps
Thicknet	Fairly expensive—more than Thinnet, STP, or UTP; less than fiber-optic	500 meters (1650 feet)	100 per segment	Thicknet Ethernet; 2 to 10Mbps
Fiber-optic	Most expensive, but costs are dropping	20 kilometers (12.5 miles)	No limit for nodes; hubs limited to manufacturer's specifications	FDDI; commonly 100Mbps; also for connections between buildings or wiring closets

Twisted-Pair Cable

Twisted-pair cable uses one or more pairs of two twisted copper wires to transmit signals. The twists in twisted-pair cable decrease crosstalk because the radiated signals from the twisted wires tend to cancel each other out.

Twisted-pair cable is commonly used as telecommunications cable and has become the most popular type for LANs that use copper cables. It is very inexpensive and easy to install.

UTP   UTP cable consists of a number of twisted pairs with a simple plastic casing (see Figure 2.3). Transmissions across copper wire tend to attenuate rapidly. However, engineers have reduced UTP's problems of radiated noise and susceptibility to EMI, and some categories of UTP are capable of speeds up to 100 Mbps. UTP is available in six categories, which are listed in Table 2.2.

F I G U R E 2.3

Unshielded twisted-pair (UTP) cable

T A B L E 2.2	Category	Description
UTP Categories	1 and 2	Voice grade; very low data rates
	3	Four-twisted pairs with three twists per foot; data rates up to 10Mbps
	4	Four twisted pairs; data rates up to 16Mbps (not commonly used)
	5	Four twisted pairs; data rates up to 100Mbps (currently the most popular UTP)
	6	Four twisted pairs; data rates up to 155Mbps (soon to be the most popular UTP)

STP The only difference between STP and UTP is that STP cable has a shield between the outer jacket or casing and the wires (see Figure 2.4). The shield, which is usually made of aluminum/polyester, makes STP less vulnerable to EMI because the shield is electrically grounded; however, STP is not much less susceptible to attenuation than UTP.

A *ground* is a portion of the device that serves as an electrical reference point.

FIGURE 2.4

Shielded twisted-pair (STP) cable

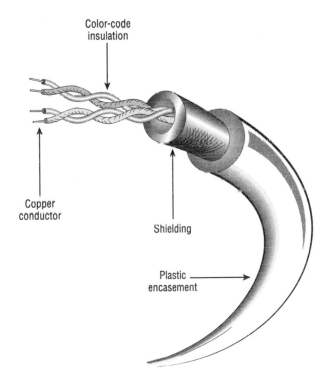

Color-code insulation

Copper conductor

Shielding

Plastic encasement

Coaxial Cable

Coaxial cable, commonly called *coax*, has two conductors that share the same axis. A solid or stranded copper wire runs down the center of the cable, and this wire is surrounded by plastic foam insulation (see Figure 2.5). Coax cable suffers less attenuation than either UTP or STP cable. Coaxial cable comes in different sizes, which are listed in Table 2.3.

	Size	Description
T A B L E 2.3	50-ohm, RG-8, and RG-11	Used for Thicknet Ethernet, also known as 10Base5
Coaxial Cable Sizes	50-ohm, RG-58	Used for Thinnet Ethernet, also known as 10Base2
	75-ohm, RG-59	Used for cable TV
	93-ohm, RG-62	Used for ARCnet

F I G U R E 2.5

Coaxial cable

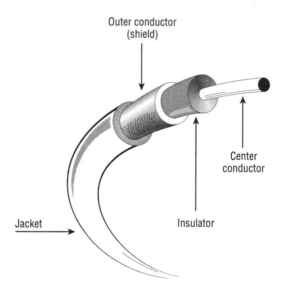

Outer conductor
(shield)

Center
conductor

Jacket

Insulator

Fiber-Optic Cable

Fiber-optic cable transmits light signals rather than electrical signals. Each fiber has an inner core of glass or plastic that conducts light. A layer of glass that reflects the light back into the core, called *cladding*, surrounds the inner core. A plastic sheath surrounds each fiber. The sheath can either be tight or loose (see Figure 2.6).

FIGURE 2.6

Fiber-optic cable: loose
and tight configurations

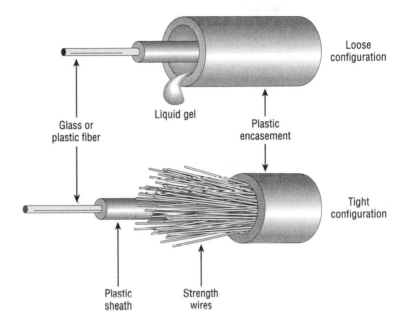

Fiber-optic cable is enormously more efficient than the other network cable media. It has much lower attenuation than copper wires, mainly because the light is not radiated out in the way that electricity is radiated from copper cables. Current fiber-optic technologies allow data rates from 100Mbps to 2Gbps. Two disadvantages of fiber-optic cable are that it is more expensive than the other types of cable media and that it is more difficult to install.

Connectors

Three types of connectors are commonly use to connect cables to network interface cards (NICs). These are listed in Table 2.4.

TABLE 2.4

Common Connector
Types

Connector	Description
RJ-45	Used to connect UTP cables; 8 conductors
RG-58	Coaxial BNC connector used to connect Thinnet or 10Base2 cables
AUI	15-pin connector used for to connect AUI (Attachment Unit Interface) drop cable

Wireless Media

Wireless media do not use an electrical or optical conductor. In most cases, the Earth's atmosphere is the physical path for the data. Wireless media is therefore useful when distance or obstructions make bounded media more difficult.

There are three main types of wireless media:

- Radio waves—low-power, single frequency; high-power, single frequency; and spread-spectrum
- Microwave
- Infrared

These types are compared in Table 2.5 and described in the following sections.

T A B L E 2.5: Characteristics of Wireless Media

Wireless Type	Cost	Max. Distance	Max. Number of Nodes	Common Usage
Low-power, single-frequency radio wave	Moderately priced compared with other wireless systems	20 to 30 meters (65 to 100 feet)	Depends on the application and manufacturer; typically about 30 stations per transmitter	For roving users and hard-to-wire locations; 2 to 10Mbps
High-power, single-frequency radio wave	Relatively inexpensive	Depends on power and manufacturer; can go hundreds of kilometers (or miles)	Depends on the application and manufacturer	For traveling users, communications between remote offices; 2 to 10Mbps
Spread-spectrum radio wave	Varies in price depending on the amount of channels and power	Depends on power; high power improves resistance to attenuation	Depends on the application and manufacturer	For redundancy and security; 2 to 6Mbps
Microwave	Varies in price depending on power	Depends on power; affected by weather and objects	Depends on the application; typically the same as an Ethernet LAN	In LANs between buildings or across large, flat, open areas (e.g., bodies of water or the desert); 2 to 10Mbps

T A B L E 2.5: Characteristics of Wireless Media *(continued)*

Wireless Type	Cost	Max. Distance	Max. Number of Nodes	Common Usage
Infrared	Varies in price depending on system; high-power lasers are very expensive	Depends on quality of emitted light and its purity, as well as general atmospheric conditions and signal obstructions	Depends on the application	For connections between buildings or wiring closets; 115Kbps to 2Mbps

Radio Waves

Radio waves have frequencies between 10 kilohertz (KHz) and 1 gigahertz (GHz). The range of the electromagnetic spectrum between 10KHz and 1GHz is called *radio frequency* (RF).

Radio waves fall into three categories:

- *Low-power, single frequency* transceivers operate at only one frequency.

- *High-power, single frequency* transmissions are similar to low power, but can cover larger distances and go through and around objects. High-power rates improve the signal's resistance to attenuation, and repeaters can be used to extend the signal range.

- *Spread-spectrum* broadcasts signals over a range of frequencies. The signal is coded with a technique called *chips*, which gives the technology both security and redundancy. The available frequencies are divided into *channels* or *hops*. The adapters tune into a specific frequency for a pre-determined length of time and then switch to a different frequency.

Microwave

Microwave is currently the most popular long-distance transmission method in the United States. It uses line-of-sight communication. Microwave systems consist of two radio transceivers: one to transmit and one to receive. These antennas are often installed on towers to give them more range and raise them above anything that might block their signals.

Microwave communications comes in two types:

- *Terrestrial microwave* uses Earth-based transmitters and receivers in the low gigahertz range of frequencies (see Figure 2.7). Communications are line-of-sight and cannot go around corners or through buildings.

FIGURE 2.7

Terrestrial microwave connecting two buildings

- *Satellite microwave* uses communication satellites that operate in geosynchronous orbit (rotate with the Earth) at 22,300 miles above the Earth (see Figure 2.8). Parabolic antennas are used to communicate with the satellite. You might consider satellite transmission for locations that wires cannot reach (such as far out at sea) or when you need to connect thousands of locations worldwide (making cable media very expensive).

Infrared

Infrared media use infrared light to transmit signals. LEDs (light-emitting diodes) or ILDs (interjection-laser diodes) transmit the signals, and photodiodes receive the signals. Because infrared signals are in the terahertz (higher frequency) range, they have good throughput. The disadvantages of infrared signals are that they cannot penetrate walls or other objects and they are diluted by strong light sources.

FIGURE 2.8

Satellite microwave
transmission

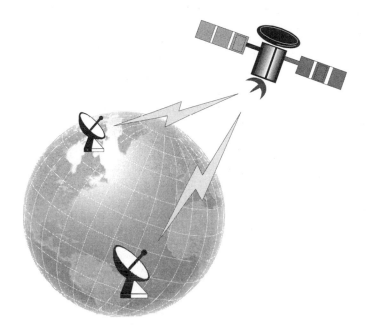

Selecting the Appropriate Topology

Four physical topologies are typically used for networks:

- Bus
- Ring
- Star
- Mesh

Physical topology refers to the actual layout of the physical cabling or transmission media. *Logical topology* refers to the logical path of the signal as it travels through the physical topology.

Bus Topology

A bus topology is commonly used for 10Base2 or 10Base5 networks. A typical bus network uses just one or more cables, with no active electronics to amplify the signal or pass it along from computer to computer (see Figure 2.9). When one computer sends a signal up and down the wire (sometimes referred to as a *backbone*), all the computers on the network receive the information but only one computer will accept the information; the rest disregard the information.

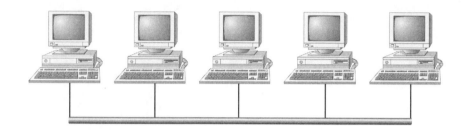

Ring Topology

In a ring topology, each computer is connected to the next computer, with the last one connected to the first (see Figure 2.10). Each device has a receiver and a transmitter that serves as a repeater, passing the signal to the next computer.

Token Ring is *not* a physical ring topology; it is a logical ring topology running on a physical star topology.

Star Topology

Star is the standard physical topology for both Ethernet (10BaseT) and Token Ring networks. In a star topology, all the cables run from the computers to a central location, where they are connected by a device called a *hub* or a *switch* (see Figure 2.11). The hub or switch receives the signals from other computers and routes the signals to the proper destination. If you connect more than one hub together, it is referred to as a *tree* or *hierarchical* topology.

A star physical topology is run as a logical bus topology, which means that all computers receive the signal but only the destination accepts the signal; the rest disregard the information.

FIGURE 2.10

A physical ring network

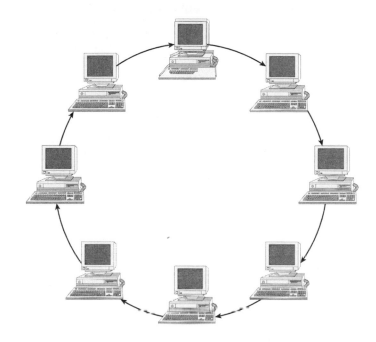

FIGURE 2.11

A physical star network

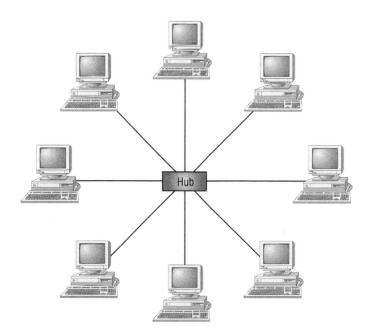

Four types of hubs are used with star physical topologies:

- *Passive hubs* receive the signal and pass it along without regenerating the signal.

- *Active hubs* receive the signal and pass it along, regenerating or amplifying the signal.

- *Intelligent hubs* are the same as active hubs, but they have a management card for administration.

- *Switches*, unlike the other types of hubs, receive a signal and send it only to the port(s) it is destined for. The other types of hubs receive the signal and pass it along to all other ports.

 The 5-4-3 rule of thumb applies to the topology of Ethernet networks. This rule states that in an Ethernet network, you can have up to five segments and four repeaters, with only three segments populated.

Mesh Topology

The mesh topology is distinguished by redundant links between devices. Most mesh topology networks are not true mesh networks. Instead, they are hybrid mesh networks, with some redundant links rather than all redundant links (see Figure 2.12).

Selecting the Appropriate Protocols

The main Token Ring and Ethernet protocols are listed in Table 2.6 and discussed in the following sections.

FIGURE 2.12

Physical true mesh and
hybrid mesh networks

True mesh

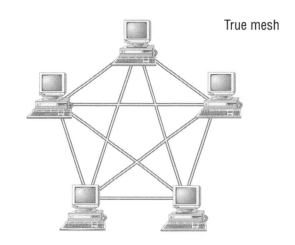

Hybrid mesh

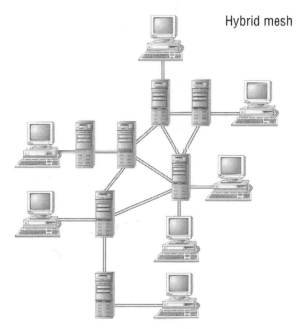

	Protocol	Description
TABLE 2.6 Token Ring and Ethernet Protocols	DLC (Data Link Control)	An IBM SNA (Systems Network Architecture) protocol, used to communicate with IBM mainframes and HP Jet Direct cards
	AppleTalk	A protocol suite designed for the Apple Macintosh
	IPX (Internetwork Packet eXchange)	Novell's main Network layer protocol, which deals with addressing, route selection, and connection services
	TCP/IP (Transmission Control Protocol/Internet Protocol)	The best-known protocols that make up the Internet protocol suite
	SMB (Server Message Blocks)	A protocol used by Windows systems for file and print sharing
	NetBEUI	A nonroutable protocol designed by IBM for small networks
	NFS (Network File System)	An Application layer protocol, created by Sun Microsystems, that provides file and remote-operation services

Protocols and the Windows NT Networking Structure

In the Windows NT networking structure (see Figure 2.13), the NDIS interface, NDIS wrapper, and NDIS-compatible drivers enable the TCP/IP, NWLink, NetBEUI, AppleTalk, and DLC protocols to interact simultaneously with the lower layers.

The TDI (Transport Driver Interface) is an interface that enables the server, redirector, and file system drivers to remain independent of the transport protocol.

Windows NT, Windows 95, Windows 3.1, and Windows for Workgroups use SMB for file and print sharing.

DLC is used in Windows NT environments that include HP Jet Direct cards with printers. This protocol is used as a connectivity protocol for IBM mainframes, but it cannot be used as a communication protocol between Microsoft hosts.

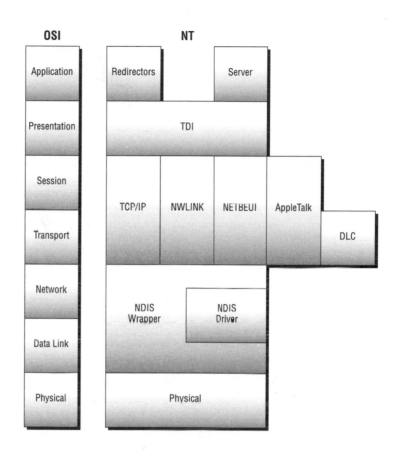

FIGURE 2.13

Windows NT
networking architecture

Windows NT uses its own compatible implementation of Novell's IPX/SPX, called NWLink. NWLink is faster than TCP/IP and is a good choice for small networks.

The NetBEUI Protocol

The NetBEUI protocol is an extension of Microsoft's NetBIOS (Network Basic Input/Output System). This protocol is supplied with all Microsoft network products.

NetBEUI has several advantages:

- It is speedy compared with other protocols.

- It has a small stack size.

- It is compatible with all Microsoft products.

It also has several disadvantages:

- It was designed for small networks.
- It is not routable (but it can be bridged).
- It is generally limited to Microsoft-based networks.

IBM OS/2 LAN Server also supports a compatible NetBEUI protocol.

Because of the NDIS standard, NetBEUI can coexist with other, routable protocols. For example, you can use NetBEUI on your LAN and use TCP/IP for your WAN segments. If you use NetBEUI, you must use a bridge or brouter to segment your network.

The Internet Protocol Suite

The Internet protocol suite was developed along with its namesake, and these protocols have become the de facto standard because of the success of the Internet. The entire protocol suite is sometimes referred to as TCP/IP. Table 2.7 lists the protocols in the Internet protocol suite (see Figure 2.14).

FIGURE 2.14

The Internet Protocol suite compared to the OSI reference model

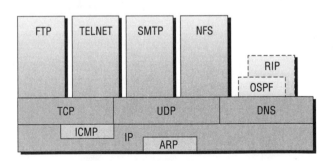

TABLE 2.7	Protocol	Description
Protocols in the Internet Protocol Suite	IP (Internet Protocol)	A connectionless protocol that runs at the Network layer and is responsible for datagram addressing
	ARP (Address Resolution Protocol)	A protocol that maps IP addresses (network-based) to data-link addresses (hardware-based)
	RIP (Routing Information Protocol)	A routing protocol that performs route discovery by using hop counts
	OSPF (Open Shortest Path First)	A routing protocol that performs route discovery by using calculations based on bandwidth (not hops)
	TCP (Transmission Control Protocol)	A connection-oriented protocol that runs at the Transport layer and provides reliable, end-to-end delivery of segments using sequencing and acknowledgments
	UDP (User Datagram Protocol)	A connectionless protocol that runs at the Transport layer and does not use sequencing or acknowledgments
	FTP (File Transfer Protocol)	A file-transfer protocol that runs at the Application layer and is operating-system independent
	SMTP (Simple Mail Transfer Protocol)	A mail-transfer protocol that runs at the Application layer and is responsible for sending e-mail between systems
	NFS (Network File System)	A traditional file-sharing protocol designed for use in Unix networks

The IPX/SPX Protocol Suite

The IPX/SPX protocol suite was designed by Novell for NetWare networks. This protocol stack does self-addressing of hosts and is routable. Table 2.8 lists the protocols in the IPX/SPX protocol suite (see Figure 2.15).

FIGURE 2.15

The IPX/SPX protocol suite compared to the OSI reference model

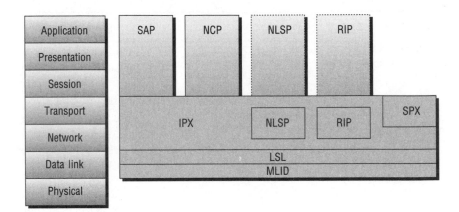

TABLE 2.8	Protocol	Description
Protocols in the IPX/SPX Protocol Suite	IPX (Internetwork Packet eXchange)	A routable protocol that runs at the Network layer and provides connectionless datagram service
	SPX (Sequenced Packet eXchange)	A connection-oriented protocol that runs at the Transport layer and provides end-to-end connection using sequencing and acknowledgments
	NCP (NetWare Core Protocol)	A protocol that provides the interface for file storage and retrieval services between workstations and the server

The AppleTalk Protocol Suite

The AppleTalk protocol suite was designed by Apple for the Macintosh computers. Networking capabilities are built into every Macintosh; the client-side AppleShare software is included with the Apple operating system. The AppleTalk protocol also supports LocalTalk, EtherTalk, and TokenTalk. Table 2.9 lists the protocols in the AppleTalk protocol suite (see Figure 2.16).

FIGURE 2.16

The AppleTalk protocol suite compared with the OSI reference model

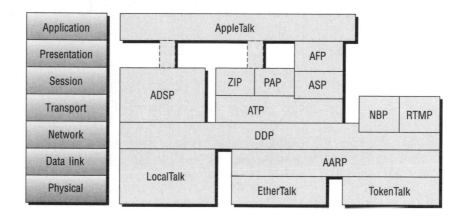

TABLE 2.9

Protocols in the Apple-Talk Protocol Suite

Protocol	Description
AppleShare	A file and print sharing protocol
AFP (AppleTalk Filing Protocol)	A protocol that provides file sharing between Macs and DOS-based computers, provides an interface for communication between AppleTalk and other network operating systems, and is responsible for file-system security
DDP (Datagram Delivery Protocol)	A connectionless protocol that runs at the Network layer and provides datagram service between Macs
ATP (AppleTalk Transaction Protocol)	A connectionless protocol that runs at the Transport layer and provides reliable transmissions, using acknowledgments

Selecting the Appropriate Connectivity Devices

To expand a LAN, you can divide it into separate segments, which can allow you to reduce the number of broadcasts and increase security. Connecting these segments together creates an *internetwork*. There are five connectivity devices that can be used to connect your segments together to create your internetwork:

- Repeaters
- Bridges
- Brouters
- Routers
- Gateways

Repeaters

All transmission media attenuate (weaken) the electromagnetic waves that travel through them. Attenuation limits the distance any medium can carry data. A repeater amplifies the signal so it can travel farther, allowing you to increase the size of the network (see Figure 2.17). Active hubs have repeaters built into them.

Repeaters work at the Physical layer of the OSI reference model.

FIGURE 2.17

A network using a repeater

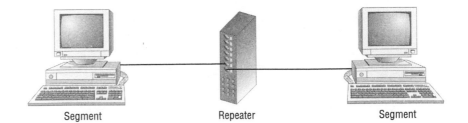

Segment   Repeater   Segment

Repeaters fall into two categories:

- *Amplifiers* simply amplify the entire incoming signal.

- *Signal-regenerating repeaters* create an exact duplicate of incoming data by identifying it amidst the noise, reconstructing it, and retransmitting only the desired information.

Bridges

Bridges connect network segments and are useful for small networks and for protocols that cannot be routed, such as NetBEUI. Unlike a repeater, which simply passes on all the signals it receives, a bridge selectively determines the appropriate segment to which it should pass a signal. It does this by reading the MAC address (sometimes referred to as the hardware address) of all the signals it receives (see Figure 2.18).

Bridges work at the MAC sublayer of the Data-Link layer of the OSI reference model.

FIGURE 2.18

A bridged network

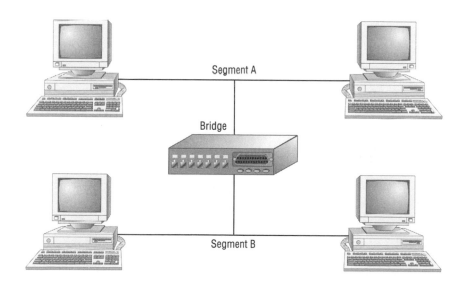

Routers

Routers use logical and physical addressing to connect two or more logically separate networks (see Figure 2.19). They accomplish this connection by organizing a large network into smaller logical network segments. Each of these smaller subnetworks (also know as *subnets*) is given a logical address. Routers use a route-discovery algorithm to determine possible routes through the internetwork.

FIGURE 2.19

A network using routers

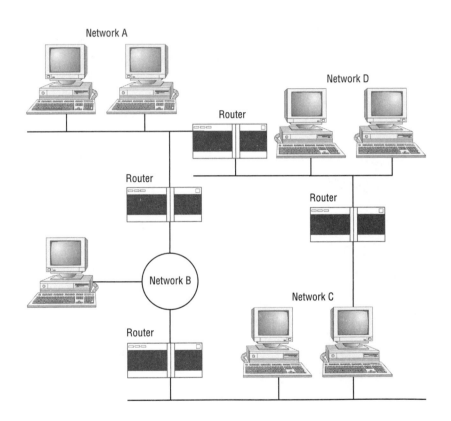

Routers are a combination of both hardware and software. The hardware consists of the physical interfaces to the networks in an internetwork.

Routers work at the Network layer of the OSI reference model.

Routers can be configured in two ways:

- With *static routing*, the administrator configures the routers with the paths to different networks.

- With *dynamic routing*, a routing protocol uses broadcasts to talk to the other routers on the network to determine the routes to different networks. The two common methods of dynamic routing are distance-vector (RIP) and link-state (OSPF).

Brouters

Brouters can perform both routing and bridging. For example, IP can be routed, but NetBEUI must be bridged. Brouters allow you to run both protocols through the same internetwork. A brouter is typically software that runs on a router.

Brouters work at the Network layer of the OSI reference model.

Gateways

Routers can successfully connect networks with protocols that function in similar ways. When the networks that must be connected are using completely different protocols, however, a more powerful and intelligent device is required.

A gateway is a device that can interpret and translate the different protocols that are used on two distinct networks. For example, you might have an e-mail gateway on your network. This will allow you to seamlessly exchange mail between a CCMail server and a Microsoft Exchange mail server.

Gateways function at all layers of the OSI reference model.

Selecting WAN Connection Services

WANs originated to solve the problem of connecting a LAN to a distant workstation or another remote LAN when the distances exceed cable media specifications or when physical cable connections are not possible. WANs can use various telecommunication services for their connections.

Analog versus Digital Signaling

WAN connection services can use either *analog* or *digital* signaling (see Figure 2.20). Analog signaling, which is used for voice communications, for example, is made up of constantly changing analog waveforms.

FIGURE 2.20

Analog and digital signaling

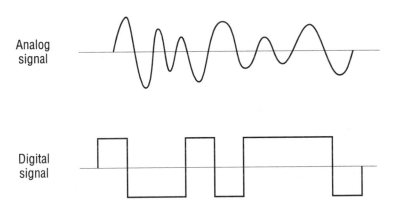

Analog signal

Digital signal

Digital signaling is made up of only ones and zeros. When a digital signal is used to transmit data, this is called *modulating* or *encoding*. For example, a modem modulates the signal from digital to analog, and then demodulates the signal from analog back to digital again. Most WANs use digital signaling.

Dial-up versus Leased Lines

The PSTN (public switched telephone network) offers two types of lines for connections:

- With *dial-up lines*, the subscriber pays for what is used. There is no dedicated path.

- With *leased lines*, the subscriber receives dedicated bandwidth, guaranteed by the provider.

Types of WAN Connection Services

Some of the WAN connection services are listed in Table 2.10 and described in the following sections.

T A B L E 2.10:   WAN Connection Services

Connection Service	OSI Model Layer	Topics and Methods	Comments
X.25	Network	Channel addressing, virtual circuit packet switching with flow and error control	First WAN standard for packet switching
ISDN (Integrated Services Digital Network)	Physical/ Data Link	Time-division multiplexing (TDM)	Standard for voice, video, and data on existing public digital telephone network
Frame Relay	Physical/LLC	Mesh physical topology with a point-to-point connection between sender and receiver, which includes flow and error control	An X.25 upgrade, with a lower error rate
ATM (Asynchronous Transfer Mode)	LLC/Network	Isochronous clocking, with error control and static routing	Uses 53-byte cells instead of packets

X.25

X.25 was the first packet-switching network standard. This standard spans the Physical through Network layer protocols (see Figure 2.21).

FIGURE 2.21

X.25 and the
OSI reference model

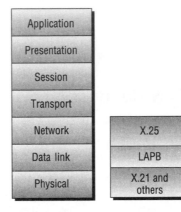

X.25 assumes that the LAPB (Link Access Procedures-Balanced) protocol is being used. LAPB is a full-duplex, bit-oriented, synchronous clocking protocol.

The disadvantage of X.25 is that it is slower than the other WAN connection services because of the flow-control and error-checking techniques it uses. It supports transmission speeds up to only 64Kbps.

Frame Relay

Frame Relay is an upgrade to the X.25 packet-switching network, with fast, variable-length packets. Frame Relay was created to be part of the B-ISDN (Broadband Integrated Services Digital Network).

In this implementation, the overhead from X.25 has been eliminated, and the Frame Relay networks use the higher-layer protocols to provide error control (see Figure 2.22). Because Frame Relay assumes a lower error rate, it transfers data at higher data rates than X.25 (from 56Kbps to 1.544Mbps).

ISDN

ISDN (Integrated Services Digital Network) is an upgrade to the old telephone network (see Figure 2.23). ISDN was created to be a dial-up service rather than a dedicated line.

F I G U R E 2.22

Frame Relay and the
OSI reference model

F I G U R E 2.23

ISDN and the
OSI reference model

Two types of ISDN are commonly in use today:

- *Basic Rate ISDN* (BRI) (also called *2B+D*) consists of three channels: two for data at 64KB each, called B channels, and one 16KB channel used for signaling and link management, called a D channel. BRI has speeds up to 128Kbps.

- *Primary Rate ISDN* (PRI) uses the entire bandwidth of a T1 (23 channels, with the twenty-fourth as the D channel). It has speeds up to 1.544Mbps.

ATM

ATM (Asynchronous Transfer Mode) uses fixed-length, 53-byte cells to transfer data at very fast rates. Cells are 53 bytes long with a 5-byte header. ATM can be used for voice, data, fax, real-time video, CD-quality audio, and imaging.

The *Asynchronous* in ATM means that time-slots don't occur periodically, as with TDM (time-division multiplexing). Instead, time slots are given on a first-come, first-served, or priority, basis. Time-sensitive traffic like video can be given priority time slots over less time-sensitive traffic like data.

The same-size cells allow for a very high efficiency in data transmission, with some equipment achieving speeds up to 2Gbps. The most common ATM data-transmission speeds are 155Mbps and 622Mbps.

Because ATM isn't concerned about the Physical layer specifications, it can run on different hardware platforms (see Figure 2.24).

Because ATM is a relatively new technology compared to Ethernet and Token Ring, only a few companies build ATM hardware.

F I G U R E 2.24

ATM and the OSI reference model

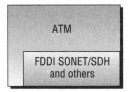

T1 and T3

T1 connection services are available from the PSTN. T1 lines are point-to-point connections across 24 channels, with a speed of 1.544Mbps. Each channel is 64Kbps, and T1 service can be divided to create different sizes of fractional lines.

T3 lines are point to-point connections across 28 T1 lines, with a speed of 44.736Mbps.

Fractional T1 or T3 lines are portions of T1 or T3 lines. You can purchase only the number of channels that you need or can afford.

Switched 56

Switched 56 is a dial-up service, used on demand, that you can lease from the PSTN. It provides 56Kbps connections. Switched 56 leased-line service provides more bandwidth than regular analog modems at less cost than a full T1 leased line.

SONET

SONET (Synchronous Optical Network) is a high-speed, fiber-optic system that can transfer data between two points at speeds of greater than 1Gbps. It can be used as a carrier service for WAN connection services, such as ATM and ISDN.

Selecting the Appropriate Media

1. What are three types of bounded media through which computers can communicate?

_____

_____

_____

2. What are the two most popular types of media?

_____

_____

3. True/False. Wireless media are as fast as cable media.

4. What does bandwidth refer to?

_____

5. What is the bandwidth of Token Ring?

_____

6. True/False. When using broadband technology, only one signal can be present on the media at a time.

7. True/False. Most LANs use baseband technology.

8. What is the bandwidth of 10BaseT?

_____

9. What does the Base in 10Base2 stand for?

_____

10. True/False. When multiplexing, only one digital or analog signal can be on the media at a time.

11. What equipment is used to multiplex the signal on one end of the cable and demultiplex the equipment on the other? At what layer of the OSI reference model does this equipment run?

_____

_____

12. What is attenuation?

_____

13. What is EMI?

_____

14. What causes crosstalk?

_____

STUDY QUESTIONS
---

15. How can crosstalk be eliminated?

_____

16. True/False. The three cable types used in networks are coax, twisted-pair, and ARCnet.

17. True/False. UTP is less expensive than STP.

18. In the spaces below, write the maximum number of nodes per cable type.

UTP: _____

STP: _____

Thinnet: _____

Thicknet: _____

Fiber-optic: _____

19. True/False. Thinnet is more expensive than UTP.

20. True/False. Thicknet is more expensive than STP.

21. In the spaces below, write the maximum distances for each of the cable types:

UTP: _____

STP: _____

Thinnet: _____

Thicknet: _____

Fiber-optic: _____

22. Which is the most expensive cable type?

_____

23. In the spaces below, write the common speed for each of the cable types.

UTP: _____

STP: _____

Thinnet: _____

Thicknet: _____

Fiber-optic: _____

24. Which cable is the most popular of all LAN cable types?

_____

25. List the six categories of UTP cable and what each is used for.

Category type	Use

26. True/False. STP is faster than UTP.

27. What is the difference between STP and UTP?

28. True/False. STP attenuates less rapidly than UTP.

29. Where did the word *coax* come from?

30. Thicknet is also known as _____.

31. Thinnet is also known as _____.

32. RG-59 coax is used for what purpose?

_____

33. True/False. RG-58 is used for Thicknet coax.

34. What is RG-62 used for?

_____

35. ARCnet uses what ohm coax cable?

_____

36. True/False. Coax cable suffers less attenuation than any type of twisted-pair cable.

37. RG-11 is known as what type of coax?

_____

38. What is the ohm on Thinnet coax?

_____

39. What is the speed on an ARCnet network?

_____

40. When speaking of fiber-optic cable, what is the cladding?

_____

41. True/False. Fiber-optic cable attenuates as much as copper wire.

42. True/False. Fiber-optic cable transmits digital and analog signals.

43. True/False. Fiber-optic cable uses light instead of electrical signals to transmit through the cable media.

44. What are two disadvantages of fiber-optic cable?

_____

_____

45. What type of connector is used to connect a UTP cable to a network interface card?

_____

46. List the three main types of wireless media.

_____

_____

_____

47. Why would you use wireless media rather than bounded media?

_____

48. List the three types of radio waves.

_____

_____

_____

49. True/False. High-power, single-frequency radio wave transmission has faster data rates than low-power, single-frequency transmission.

50. In the spaces below, write the data rates for the wireless types.

Low-power, single-frequency: _____

High-power, single-frequency: _____

Spread-spectrum: _____

Microwave: _____

Infrared: _____

51. True/False. The maximum distance for microwave transmissions depends on the weather.

52. What is the electromagnetic spectrum range of radio waves?

_____

53.   True/False. Low-power, single-frequency radio waves can operate on many different frequencies, but only one at a time.

54.   For spread-spectrum radio waves, the signal is encoded with a technique called _____ _____.

55.   True/False. Microwave transmissions use line-of-sight communication.

56.   True/False. Microwave transmissions can go over mountains and around corners.

57.   What are the two types of microwave transmission?

_____

_____

58.   Satellites in geosynchronous orbit are how many miles above the earth?

_____

59.   In microwave transmissions, what type of antenna on Earth is used to communicate with the satellite?

_____

60.   When would you want to use satellite communications?

_____

61. What are the two types of devices used to transmit signals in infrared transmissions?

62. What type of device receives infrared signals?

63. True/False. Infrared media transmit at the terahertz frequency.

Selecting the Appropriate Topology

64. What is the difference between a physical topology and a logical topology?

65. True/False. Bus topologies are typically used for 10Base5 networks.

66. True/False. Bus topologies are typically used for 10Base2 networks.

67. True/False. In a physical bus topology, when one computer sends a signal, all the computers receive the signal.

68. True/False. In a ring topology, each computer is connected to the next computer, with the last one connected to a terminator.

69. True/False. Token Ring is a physical topology.

70. In which type of network will you typically find a physical star topology?

_____

71. True/False. Token Ring is a physical star topology.

72. In which topology is more than one hub connected together?

_____

73. A physical star is run as a logical _____ topology.

74. What is the difference between a passive hub and an active hub?

_____

75. What makes an intelligent hub different from an active hub?

_____

76. True/False. A switch receives a signal and sends it only to the port(s) it is destined for.

77. True/False. The 5-4-3 rule states that an Ethernet network can have five repeaters and four segments with only three segments populated.

78. What is the difference between a true mesh and a hybrid mesh topology?

Selecting the Appropriate Protocols

79. True/False. DLC can be used to communicate between Microsoft hosts.

80. True/False. IPX is a connection-oriented protocol.

81. Which protocol does Windows use for file and print sharing?

82. Which protocol suite was designed for the Apple Macintosh?

83. Which protocol was designed by IBM for small networks and is not routable?

84. Which protocol is an Application layer protocol, created by Sun Microsystems, that provides file and remote-operation services?

85. What does the TDI do in the Windows NT networking structure?

_____

86. True/False. Windows NT, Windows 95, Windows 3.1, and Windows for Workgroups use SMB for file and print sharing.

87. What does NDIS stand for?

_____

88. True/False. IP is a connectionless protocol that runs at the Transport layer.

89. What does ARP do?

_____

90. What are RIP and OSPF used for?

_____

91. True/False. TCP is a connection-oriented protocol that runs at the Transport layer.

92. At which layer of the OSI reference model does UDP reside?

_____

93. What is FTP used for?

_____

94. True/False. SMTP is used to transfer mail to client computers.

95. NFS is used for _____ _____.

96. True/False. IPX/SPX is a self-addressing protocol stack.

97. What is the name of Microsoft's IPX/SPX implementation?

_____

98. True/False. IPX is faster than TCP/IP in smaller networks.

99. True/False. SPX is a connection-oriented protocol.

100. Which Novell NetWare protocol is responsible for file storage and retrieval services?

_____

101. NetBEUI stands for _____.

102. What is an advantage of NetBEUI?

_____

103. True/False. NetBEUI is a routable protocol.

104. True/False. NetBEUI is compatible with all types of operating systems.

105. How can NetBEUI exist with other protocols on the same network?

_____

106. When you are using NetBEUI, how can you divide your network into smaller segments?

_____

107. Which networking protocol comes with every Macintosh computer?

_____

108. Which protocol would you use on a Macintosh if you were running Token Ring?

_____

109. Which Macintosh protocol supports file and print sharing?

_____

110. Which Macintosh-based protocol supports file sharing between Macintosh computers and DOS-based computers?

_____

111. Which Macintosh protocol runs at the Network layer and is a connectionless datagram service?

_____

112. True/False. ATP is a connectionless protocol that runs at the Transport layer.

113. Which protocol is used in a Windows NT environment that includes HP Jet Direct cards with printers?

_____

Selecting the Appropriate Connectivity Devices

114. Which device would you use to connect an Ethernet network with a Token Ring network?

_____

115. You need to connect two computers together that are 400 feet apart. What is the least expensive piece of equipment that will do this in an UTP or STP environment?

_____

116. You have an Ethernet network with 4 repeaters. You need to add another 30 workstations. What should you do?

_____

117. What two types of repeaters can you use?

_____

_____

118. Your network has 200 workstations running NetBEUI. What device can you use to segment your network?

_____

119. Which device removes electrical noise from a signal but otherwise passes it without modification?

_____

120. Bridges work at which layer of the OSI reference model?

_____

121. At which layer of the OSI reference model does a router work?

_____

122. Which device would you use to connect to the Internet?

_____

123. Which type of addressing does a bridge use to filter segment traffic?

_____

124.   Which device forwards data based on logical addresses?

_____

125.   Which two types of routing are available in routers?

_____

_____

126.   What is the difference between a router and a brouter?

_____

127.   What do gateways do?

_____

128.   At which layer(s) of the OSI reference model does a gateway work?

_____

Selecting WAN Connection Services

129.   True/False. Analog signals can take on many values.

130.   True/False. Digital signals can take on many values.

131.   When a digital signal is used to transmit data, this is called _____.

132.   What does PSTN stand for?

_____

133.   Which WAN connection service is well suited for dial-up connections?

_____

134.   Which technology is a packet-switching network that runs at 64Kbps?

_____

135.   Which technology will work on both your LAN and WAN?

_____

136.   At which layers of the OSI reference model is X.25 specified?

_____

137.   What is LAPB?

_____

138. What is a disadvantage of X.25?

139. Which WAN connection service is the most expensive?

140. Which WAN connection service is sometimes referred to as 2B+D?

141. What does the 2B+D refer to?

142. Which WAN connection type can carry real-time video?

143. Why does Frame Relay assume it can carry traffic faster than X.25?

144. What size cells does ATM use?

145. How many T1 lines are in a T3 line?

_____

146. What is the data rate of a T1 line?

_____

147. What is the data rate of T3 line?

_____

148. True/False. SONET systems can transfer data at speeds of 1Gbps or more.

149. What is the data rate of a Switched 56 line?

_____

SAMPLE TEST

2-1 You must connect six computers together in the same room as cheaply as possible. What physical topology should you use?

    A. Bus

    B. Star

    C. Ring

    D. Mesh

2-2 You need to provide a high-speed link between the buildings on your campus. The only available cabling path is alongside the currently installed power cables, which generate a great deal of EMI. Which media should you use?

    A. Copper

    B. Glass

    C. Wireless

    D. Radio

2-3 You are installing a standard IBM Token Ring network with copper media. Which cable type should you use?

    A. UTP

    B. STP

    C. Coaxial

    D. Fiber-optic

2-4   You are building a Windows NT Server network with Microsoft Proxy Server connected to the Internet. Which protocol must be bound on the network interface card going to the Internet?

A. NetBEUI

B. NWLink

C. TCP/IP

D. IP

2-5   Your boss has dictated that you must run all cables through the walls and ceiling of your office building. What kind of cable must you use?

A. Plenum

B. PVC

C. Gel-filled

D. Fire-retardant

2-6   Which device's purpose is to connect two network segments so that the overall length may be longer than the maximum for a single segment? (Choose the most correct answer.)

A. Hub

B. Router

C. Repeater

D. Network adapter

2-7   You have been hired to cable up a very busy automotive shop. The runs will be short, but they will pass several high-powered electrical devices. Your primary concern for these cables should be:

A. Dispersion

B. Attenuation

S A M P L E   T E S T

    C. EMI

    D. Crosstalk

2-8   You are installing a network of 40 computers now, and you expect the network to grow by at least 100% in the next year. You wish to use a network topology that is easy to expand and troubleshoot. Which topology should you use?

    A. Bus

    B. Star

    C. Ring

    D. Mesh

2-9   Which of the following factors do not significantly affect fiber-optic LAN cables? (Choose all that apply.)

    A. Dispersion

    B. Attenuation

    C. EMI

    D. Crosstalk

2-10   You are running a cable from one building to another. The total distance of the cable run will be 400 feet. Which cable types can you use? (Choose all that apply.)

    A. UTP

    B. STP

    C. Coaxial

    D. Fiber-optic

SAMPLE TEST

2-11   You need to link computers in your warehouse and you can't run any new cables. Which radio wave technology best copes with EMI?

  A. Low-power, single-frequency

  B. High-power, single-frequency

  C. Spread-spectrum

  D. Encrypted

2-12   Which network protocol can you use to connect to the Internet?

  A. NetBEUI

  B. NWLink

  C. TCP/IP

  D. AppleTalk

2-13   Your company has a very bursty custom application that you use to stay competitive in the marketplace. It is imperative that the network (and the application) continues to operate even when the network is extremely loaded. Which topology exhibits the graceful degradation under load characteristics that you require?

  A. Bus

  B. Star

  C. Ring

  D. Mesh

2-14   You plan to link the servers in your campus network with a 1.2Gbps backbone. Which type of media is required to support this data rate?

  A. UTP

  B. STP

    C. Coaxial

    D. Fiber-optic

2-15   Which network protocol has the least communications overhead?

    A. NetBEUI

    B. NWLink

    C. TCP/IP

    D. X.25

2-16   Which kind of route discovery can result in excessive network broadcasts?

    A. Distance-vector routing

    B. Link-state routing

    C. Broadcast routing

    D. Static routing

2-17   You need to link three offices together with twisted-pair cable, but the length of the cable will be near the maximum length specified for the cable. Your primary concern for this cable should be:

    A. Dispersion

    B. Attenuation

    C. EMI

    D. Crosstalk

SAMPLE TEST

2-18 You wish to install the cheapest cable that will support data rates of 100Mbps. Which cable type should you choose?

    A. UTP

    B. STP

    C. Coaxial

    D. Fiber-optic

2-19 Which of the following ISDN service levels provides the greatest bandwidth?

    A. A single ISDN B channel.

    B. 2B+D

    C. Basic rate service

    D. Primary rate service

2-20 Which protocol should you use to allow Macintosh clients to access Windows NT file servers?

    A. NetBEUI

    B. NWLink

    C. TCP/IP

    D. AppleTalk

2-21 Which device resides at the center of a star network and links the network cables?

    A. Hub

    B. Bridge

    C. Network adapter

    D. Server

2-22   You are considering installing an ATM network in your organization. Which of the following data-link types will ATM run over? (Choose all that apply.)

    A. FDDI

    B. SONET

    C. T3

    D. Ethernet

2-23   You must connect client computers to both NetWare servers and Windows NT servers. You want to use just one protocol, and you want to use the fastest one possible. Which protocol should you choose?

    A. NetBEUI

    B. NWLink

    C. TCP/IP

    D. DLC

2-24   What process do routers use to determine possible routes through an internetwork?

    A. Network mapping

    B. Route discovery

    C. End-node search

    D. Path search

2-25   Which of the following network devices does not electrically regenerate the network signal?

    A. Passive hub

    B. Active hub

    C. Intelligent hub

    D. Repeater

2-26 You are in charge of a WAN connecting the three San Francisco offices of your company and linking them to the Los Angeles main office. The San Francisco offices are linked together with three leased lines: one linking downtown to Marin, one linking Marin to Daly City, and one linking Daly City to downtown. The primary link between San Francisco and Los Angeles goes to the Marin office, but you also have a slower connection between Los Angeles and downtown for backup in case the main link goes down. Which network topology are you using?

    A. Bus

    B. Star

    C. Ring

    D. Mesh

2-27 Which high-speed network type divides data into small, fixed-sized cells rather than frames or packets?

    A. TCP/IP

    B. FDDI

    C. ATM

    D. PPP

2-28 You need your accounting department to connect to a remote office running an IBM mainframe. Which protocol must the workstations run?

    A. TCP/IP

    B. NWLink

    C. DLC

    D. AppleTalk

SAMPLE TEST

2-29   You have two Ethernet segments in your network with many computers on each segment. You would like to join the segments so that network broadcasts and cross-segment traffic pass between segments, but network traffic within a segment does not. Which device should you use?

   A. Hub

   B. Bridge

   C. Router

   D. Gateway

2-30   Which network protocols cannot be routed? (Choose all that apply.)

   A. NetBEUI

   B. NWLink

   C. TCP/IP

   D. X.25

2-31   You need to set up a network for an emergency disaster center. You must be able to set up a network in hours, and you must be able to place network stations in hard-to-cable locations. Network speed, however, is not terribly important. Which media best fit your needs? (Choose all that apply.)

   A. Copper

   B. Glass

   C. Infrared

   D. Radio

2-32 What is the difference between a router and a brouter?

    A. A brouter routinely broadcasts routing information

    B. A brouter is a basic functionality router

    C. A brouter can function as a bridge as well as a router

    D. A brouter is a router that routes signals on broadband networks

2-33 You can use an appropriately configured router to route data between which of the following data-link types? (Choose all that apply.)

    A. Ethernet

    B. Token Ring

    C. ATM

    D. Frame Relay

2-34 Which of the following network types can be implemented over fiber-optic cable? (Choose all that apply.)

    A. FDDI

    B. ATM

    C. SONET

    D. Ethernet

2-35 What is the difference between baseband and broadband transmission?

    A. One uses TCP/IP; the other uses IPX only

    B. You must use fiber-optic cable for baseband and twisted-pair cable for broadband

    C. Baseband can have multiple signals on the wire at the same time; broadband can have only one

    D. Broadband can have multiple signals on the wire at the same time; baseband can have only one

2-36   You have a Windows NT server running Microsoft Proxy Server to the Internet. The server has two network interface cards: one to the outside network (Internet) running TCP/IP and one to the inside network. You need a protocol on the inside network that is routable but self-addressing. Which protocol could you use to run on the inside network?

    A. NetBEUI

    B. NWLink

    C. TCP/IP

    D. X.25

2-37   Which of the following network protocols establish permanent and switched virtual circuits between end stations? (Choose all that apply.)

    A. X.25

    B. FDDI

    C. ATM

    D. SONET

2-38   You will not be able to use a router to reduce broadcast storms if you use which of the following protocols?

    A. NWLink

    B. TCP/IP

    C. NetBEUI

    D. XNS

2-39 You have a single fiber-optic cable linking two office complexes. You would like to send Ethernet, Token Ring, and telephone signals over the same cable. Which device can you use to do this?

    A. Hub

    B. Router

    C. Multiplexer

    D. Gateway

2-40 Which two link-level protocols are most commonly used to connect to the Internet over dial-up lines?

    A. SLIP

    B. Token Ring

    C. PPP

    D. FDDI

2-41 You must provide a permanent connection for your company to the Internet. You need a faster link than can be provided by a regular analog modem, but bandwidth requirements do not justify a T1 line. What kind of leased line can you use?

    A. T3

    B. Switched 56

    C. ATM

    D. SONET

2-42   Your research department needs more bandwidth. Which cable type will support the highest data rates when cost is no object?

    A. UTP

    B. STP

    C. Coaxial

    D. Fiber-optic

2-43   Which internetworking protocol provides for robust, low-speed packet-switching of dedicated or switched virtual circuits without the use of TCP/IP?

    A. IPX/SPX

    B. ATM

    C. X.25

    D. FDDI

2-44   Windows 95 is the client operating system on your network, and the clients use NetBIOS client software (over NetBEUI) to access your Windows NT servers. You would like your client computers to be able to access resources on NetWare servers, but you do not want to install Client Services for NetWare on each of the client computers. Which network component can give your NetBIOS clients access to the NetWare network?

    A. Bridge

    B. Router

    C. Gateway

    D. CSU/DSU

2-45   Your network uses the NWLink transport protocol, and the Internet uses TCP/IP. Your remote-client computers must be able to make dial-up connections to your network and to the Internet. Which dial-up protocol will support both NWLink and TCP/IP?

A. SLIP

B. CSLIP

C. PPP

D. CHRP

2-46   Which telephone service can provide you with a dial-up digital line to another computer across telephone lines?

A. POTS

B. ISDN

C. SONET

D. X.25

2-47   Which of the following factors can affect fiber-optic LAN cables? (Choose all that apply.)

A. Dispersion

B. Attenuation

C. EMI

D. Crosstalk

2-48   You need to provide a 100Mbps campus backbone over fiber-optic cabling. Which network types will meet your needs? (Choose all that apply.)

A. ATM

B. Token Ring

C. FDDI

D. 100BaseFX

2-49   You need a protocol to run a small network with no routers. Which protocol should you use?

A. NetBEUI

B. NWLink

C. TCP/IP

D. DLC

2-50   Which of the following devices amplifies the network signal but does not interpret the signal or perform path selection or switching?

A. Passive hub

B. Active hub

C. Intelligent hub

D. Router

2-51   You manage the network infrastructure for a marketing firm. You need to link two company sites and the link must support data rates of greater than 1Gbps. Which of the following will meet your needs? (Choose all that apply.)

A. FDDI

B. 100BascFX

C. SONET

D. X.25

2-52 Which of the following are problems that can afflict twisted-pair networks? (Choose all that apply.)

A. Crosstalk

B. Dispersion

C. EMI

D. Improper termination

2-53 You must connect 60 computers together in the same room and cost is an issue. Which topology should you use?

A. Bus

B. Star

C. Ring

D. Mesh

2-54 You need to install a LAN in an industrial building with a lot of large machinery. Which type of media should you install?

A. Copper

B. Glass

C. Infrared

D. Radio

2-55 You need to order cable to extend your existing IBM twisted-pair network. Which cable type should you use?

A. UTP

B. STP

C. Coaxial

D. Fiber-optic

2-56   As your network grows, why should you create an internetwork with routers and gateways rather than extending a single LAN with bridges and hubs? (Choose all that apply.)

A. Too many stations on one LAN can cause broadcast storms

B. LANs have maximum cabling distances that you cannot exceed

C. WANs use slow network links that are not efficiently supported by LAN data-link protocols such as Ethernet

D. Gateways and routers are less expensive than hubs

2-57   You wish to use SNMP software to manage network devices. Which protocol should you use in your network to carry regular network traffic?

A. NetBEUI

B. NWLink

C. TCP/IP

D. AppleTalk

2-58   You need to provide a link between the buildings on your campus. You need it to be as fast as possible, but digging a trench between buildings is not possible. Which media type should you use? (Choose all that apply.)

A. Copper

B. Glass

C. Low-power or high-power, single-frequency

D. Infrared

2-59 You wish to install the cheapest cable that will support data rates of 155Mbps. Which cable type should you choose?

    A. UTP category 6

    B. STP

    C. UTP category 5

    D. Fiber-optic

2-60 You have been hired to cable up a very busy automotive shop. The runs will be long. What should your primary concern for these cables be?

    A. Dispersion

    B. Attenuation

    C. EMI

    D. Crosstalk

2-61 You want to set up satellite transmissions to multiple branches throughout the country. You also need to have security and redundancy. Which type of wireless technology should you use?

    A. Low-power, single-frequency

    B. High-power, single-frequency

    C. Spread-spectrum

    D. Encrypted

2-62 You want to run HP Jet Direct cards in all your printers. Which protocol must you run on your Windows NT Server machines?

    A. NetBEUI

    B. NWLink

    C. TCP/IP

    D. DLC

UNIT

3

Implementation

Test Objectives: Implementation

- Choose an administrative plan to meet specified needs, including performance, management, account management, and security.

- Choose a disaster recovery plan for various situations.

- Given the manufacturer's documentation for the network adapter, install, configure, and resolve hardware conflicts for multiple network adapters in a token-ring or Ethernet network.

- Implement a NetBIOS naming scheme for all computers on a given network.

- Select the appropriate hardware and software tools to monitor trends in the network.

To ensure that a network meets its business requirements and accommodates the needs of its users, you must develop an administrative plan. To avoid data loss due to disaster or human error, you must develop a disaster recovery plan. Also, as a network administrator, you need to resolve any hardware conflicts and implement a naming scheme for the computers on your network. And, finally, to make sure that your network runs smoothly, you should monitor it on a regular basis. All of these topics are addressed in this unit.

Choosing an Administrative Plan

It is important to understand and plan how you are going to administer your network. In your administrative plan, you should consider the following elements of your network:

Resources   Hardware devices, such as hard drives and printers, that can be shared in the network.

Network shares   The areas of a hard drive or printers you have chosen to share.

Permissions   The security assigned to a particular resource. Security can be share-level (or password-protected), with read-only or full-access permissions, or through access permissions, with access rights granted to users or groups through an access control list (ACL).

Users   The accounts for the people who will be connecting to your network.

Groups   The accounts that simplify user and security administration. You can assign rights to groups instead of individual users, and place users who share a common trait or who need access to a common resource in the groups.

Rights   The abilities given to users and groups to manage or use different resources.

Network Configuration

Before you can plan the specifics of administering your network, you need to configure your servers and clients to suit your business requirements, as well as to facilitate managing your network. Your network configuration considerations include the following:

- Network growth and how you will maintain the level of security required as your network expands
- Server applications and how they will integrate into your network
- Client operating systems, including non-Windows clients

Network Growth

One of the biggest challenges in administering a network is planning for network growth. Here, we will outline some ways that you can manage a growing network, including some tools you can use for managing a TCP/IP network regardless of its size.

Document Your Network   Documenting your network will help tremendously when trouble strikes or you need to expand your network. Keeping your documentation up-to-date can be a challenge, but it's worth the effort.

Protect Your Environment   You must protect your network from intentional and accidental damage. A security plan will help you keep your network safe from intruders. You can protect your network from viruses by using scanning software. Both your security plan and anti-virus software should change as your network changes (you should update your virus-scanning software every month). See the "Security Management" section later in this unit for more information about planning your network's security.

Expand Your Network with Routers and Gateways   By building your network with routers and gateways, rather than with repeaters and bridges, you will be better able to handle network growth. However the cost might not justify the means if your network is small or your budget does not allow you to buy expensive routers. Repeaters and bridges can actually hinder network management if your network grows too fast or too large. You do not want to put too many stations on a segment or to exceed cable specifications.

Choose Protocols Carefully   You should choose protocols that will grow with your network. Do not run more protocols than you actually need. Running multiple protocols on a network that needs only one or two will waste precious bandwidth with broadcasts. Here are some points to keep in mind about various protocols:

- NetBEUI is suitable for very small workgroups.

- You should run either NWLink or TCP/IP in large organizations.

- IPX can be very chatty in large organizations, but it is self-addressing and easy to administer.

- TCP/IP probably will be the primary protocol of the future, and it might be a good idea to plan your network accordingly.

Use DHCP to Assign IP Addresses   For a TCP/IP network, you can use DHCP (Dynamic Host Configuration Protocol) to dynamically assign IP addresses for hosts. DHCP was initially created for organizations that had fewer IP addresses than hosts. At that time, IP addresses were not used or needed as often as they are now, and a client could get away with having an IP address when it was available. We know that that is impossible today, but DHCP is still a good option.

If a network uses static IP addresses on all its hosts, duplicate addresses could easily turn up on the network. Then both computers with the same address would not work on the network. If used correctly, DHCP's dynamic assignments can prevent duplicate IP addressing. DHCP can also keep a database of who has which address, which is useful for troubleshooting network problems (the subject of Unit 4).

Use WINS to Resolve NetBIOS Names   Another useful tool for TCP/IP networks is WINS (Windows Internet Naming Service). WINS resolves NetBIOS names to IP addresses. When communicating from host to host, regardless of whether the host is a client or a server, the NetBIOS (computer) name must be resolved to an IP address. There are a couple of ways to do this, but resolving names through WINS is by far the best method.

WINS is dynamic, which means that whenever any user gets a DHCP address, the computer can automatically register its NetBIOS name and IP address with WINS. Then, rather than needing to broadcast a NetBIOS name to get its IP address, the client will ask the WINS server to resolve the name, therefore saving precious bandwidth and time.

Use DNS to Resolve Host Names   DNS (Domain Name Service) is used to resolve host names (not NetBIOS names) to IP addresses. However, you can configure DNS to use WINS to resolve a WINS address, if you are using Windows NT DNS services.

Typically, DNS is used to resolve names on the Internet, but Windows NT 5 will have a dynamic DNS (like WINS). Also, NetBIOS naming is being phased out. So, in the future, WINS will not be used (except to be backward compatible), and DNS will be a standard server in networks.

Use Host Tables   A HOSTS file, typically used in Unix networks, is a table of host names assigned to IP addresses, not unlike DNS or WINS. The only difference is that you need to have one on every client computer. Furthermore, if one name is added or changed, you must add or change it on every machine, which is very inefficient. DNS and WINS were created to solve this problem. HOSTS (the name must be plural) files can be used in all Windows, Unix, and DOS clients.

An LMHOSTS file provides the same service for NetBIOS names that a HOSTS file does for host names, but it can also preload names and IP addresses into RAM to speed up resolution. LMHOSTS can be used on all Microsoft Windows clients, but like HOSTS, it must be updated on all machines.

Server Database Applications

Will your company use a database to store organizational or business-related information? If so, that database will affect your network's configuration.

For certain types of database applications, you store the database files on the server and run the database program on the client. For example, Microsoft Access works this way. The database program manipulates the database files directly and cooperates with other database programs on other computers to keep the database in a consistent state.

In other types of database applications, the database runs on the server and only the user interface runs on the client computers. These are called *client-server databases,* sometimes referred to as *database back-ends*. For example, Microsoft SQL Server runs as a client-server database.

Client-server databases provide better database performance for large networks because they reduce network traffic. The database program running on the server takes over the task of manipulating the database files stored on the file server. The client database program sends requests to the back-end program, which performs the necessary data manipulation and then returns the results to the client.

Client Operating Systems

Windows 95 and Windows NT come with clients for Microsoft and Novell NetWare servers. Microsoft also includes clients that will allow non-Windows devices to communicate with a Windows NT network.

Microsoft Clients   For Microsoft clients to communicate with Windows NT, you must load the Client for Microsoft Networks (see Figure 3.1). For the clients to communicate with a Windows NT Workstation or Server computer, you can use the TCP/IP, NetBEUI, or IPX protocol.

FIGURE 3.1

Loading the Client for
Microsoft Networks

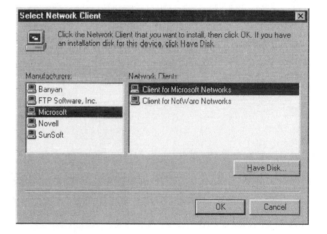

To configure a Windows 95 client to attach to a Microsoft network, the client must join either a workgroup or a domain:

- To join a workgroup in Windows 95, select the Identification tab of the Network dialog box (see Figure 3.2) and enter the computer's name and the name of the workgroup to which the client will belong.

- To join a domain, specify the domain name in the Client for Microsoft Networks Properties dialog box (see Figure 3.3).

FIGURE 3.2

Joining a workgroup in
Windows 95

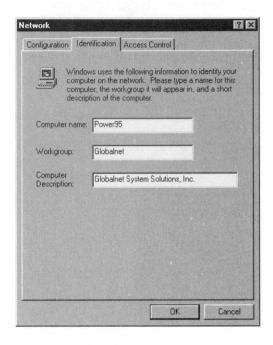

FIGURE 3.3

Joining a domain in
Windows 95

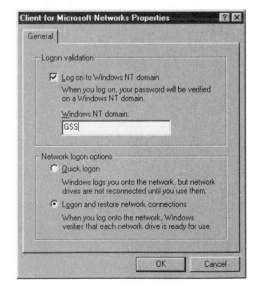

NetWare Clients NetWare servers do not use domains or workgroups, so you do not need to configure the clients to log on to a domain. However, you do need to set the server name the client will log in to. You do this through the client software. In Windows 95, you load the Client for NetWare Networks (see Figure 3.1, shown earlier) or the Novell Client 32 provided by Novell. (The Novell client works better if you are running Novell IntranetWare.)

Clients that want to communicate with Novell NetWare servers must run the IPX protocol, which is named NWLink on Microsoft Windows devices.

You must consider the frame type when connecting to a NetWare server. If your clients are set to the automatic frame type (the default), you should only need to worry about the frame type on the NetWare server (Ethernet 802.2 by default). Always check the frame type first if you are having problems with a client not being able to communicate with a NetWare server.

Account Management

Account management involves managing your network's user and group accounts, as well as your network shares.

User Accounts

User accounts maintain the privacy of information on a shared computer and help users work in ways that are comfortable to them by keeping track of their personal preferences. Every user who uses Windows NT must have a user name and password in order to gain access to the workstation.

Windows NT creates two user accounts by default:

Administrator This user account manages the overall configuration of the computer and can be used to manage the following:

- Security policies

- Users and groups

- Shared directories for networking

- Hardware maintenance tasks

Guest This user account allows one-time users with low or no security access to use the computer in a limited fashion. The Guest account will not save user preferences or configuration changes, so any changes that a guest user makes are lost when that user logs off. The Guest account is installed with a blank password.

Both the Administrator and Guest accounts can be renamed, but they cannot be deleted.

You can add user accounts to your Windows NT workstation in two ways: You can create new user accounts or you can make copies of existing user accounts.

You manage user accounts with the Windows NT Workstation utility called User Manager (you manage user accounts on a Windows NT Server computer with the User Manager for Domains utility). Table 3.1 describes the fields in the User Manager's New User dialog box (see Figure 3.4).

F I G U R E 3.4

The New User dialog box in Windows NT User Manager

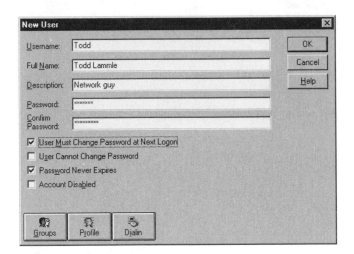

T A B L E 3.1: User Account Properties

Field	Description
Username	A required text field of up to 20 characters. Uses both uppercase and lowercase letters, but it is not case-sensitive. The following characters cannot be used: " / \ [ ]: ;	= , + * ? < >. The user name must be unique among workstation users or among network domain members if attached to a network
Full Name	An optional text field typically used for the complete name of the user

T A B L E 3.1: User Account Properties *(continued)*

Field	Description
Description	An optional text field used to more fully describe the user, his or her position in the firm, etc. This field is limited to 48 characters
Password	A required text field of up to 14 characters. The password is case-sensitive. This field displays asterisks, rather than the characters typed, to keep the password secure
Confirm Password	A required text field used to confirm the entry in the Password field
User Must Change Password at Next Logon	A checkbox used to force a password change at the next logon. Windows NT will not allow you to apply changes to a user account if this field and the User Cannot Change Password field are both checked
User Cannot Change Password	A checkbox that makes it impossible for users to change their own passwords. Typically not used
Password Never Expires	A checkbox that prevents a password from expiring according to the password policy. This setting is normally used for automated software services that must be logged on as a user
Account Disabled	A checkbox that prevents users from logging on to the network with this account
Account Locked Out	A checkbox that is checked if the account is currently locked out due to failed logon attempts. You can clear it to restore access to the account, but it cannot be set
Groups	A button that assigns group membership
Profile	A button that activates the user environment profile information
Dial-In	A button that allows users to dial into this computer using RAS (Remote Access Service)

Group Accounts

Group accounts simplify managing permissions, because the administrator can assign permissions to groups rather than to individual users. Users that belong to a group have all the permissions assigned to that group.

Windows NT has two basic types of groups:

- A *local group* is used to assign rights and permissions to resources on the local machine. These resources consist of drive space and printers on the specific computer, and the local group exists only on that computer.

- A *global group* is a collection of user accounts within the domain. Global groups have no power by themselves—they must be assigned to local groups to gain access to the local resources. You can use a global group as a container of users and then insert the global group into a local group.

Windows NT creates six groups by default:

Administrators   Members of this group can fully administer the workstation.

Power Users   Members of this group have normal user rights and permissions.

Users   Member of this group have Guest user rights and permissions.

Guests   Members of this group can share directories and printers.

Backup Operators   Members of this group can bypass security to back up and restore files.

Replicator   This group supports file replication in a network domain.

You cannot delete any of the six default local groups.

Like user accounts, group accounts on a Windows NT Workstation computer are managed through the User Manager utility in Windows NT. In the New Local Group dialog box, fill in the Group Name, Description, and Members fields (see Figure 3.5). The Group Name field identifies the local group and has the same restrictions as the Username field in the New User dialog box (see Table 3.1).

You cannot rename a local group account. If you delete a local group, all the rights and permissions are also deleted.

Group membership changes will not take effect until the user logs out and then back in to the workstation.

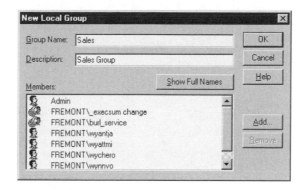

File and Printer Shares

To share files and printers in Windows 95, you must enable sharing (this is the default in Windows NT). To do this, install the File and Printer Sharing service (see Figure 3.6).

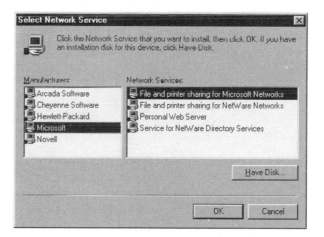

To use either a Windows NT or Windows 95 printer as a network print server, you simply share a printer directly connected to a computer. After the printer is shared on the network, most clients—such as Windows 95, Windows for Workgroups, NetWare, and Windows NT clients—can access the printer.

Print Job Scheduling

By scheduling print jobs, you can specify the times when the printer will be available to service print jobs. You can do this through the Scheduling tab of the printer's Properties dialog box (see Figure 3.7). This way, you can create two printers: one for the regular business day and the other to print after hours. Users could then send low-priority, high-volume jobs to the second printer to print the jobs at night, thus freeing the first printer to do the high-priority jobs during the day.

FIGURE 3.7

Scheduling printers

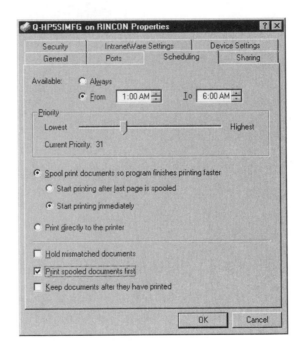

Printer Spooler Settings

To make printer sharing more efficient, you can manage printer spooler settings on a per-printer basis. These options, which are set from the printer's Properties dialog box (see Figure 3.7), are described in Table 3.2.

	Option	Description
T A B L E 3.2 Printer Spooling Options	Spool print documents so program finishes printing faster	Turns on spooling. If you select this option, you can choose one of the two following spooling methods
	Start printing after last page is spooled	Sets the printer not to print until the job is completely spooled
	Start printing immediately	Sets the printer to begin printing before the job is completely spooled
	Print directly to the printer	Turns off spooling. This typically will work only if the printer is shared
	Hold mismatched documents	Holds documents that do not match the configuration of the printer
	Print spooled documents first	Prints a completely spooled document before a partially spooled document, even if it has a low priority
	Keep documents after they have printed	Retains documents in the spooler, even after they print (making the documents available for reprinting)

Security Management

The type of security you use for your network depends on the level of security you require and the operating system's implementation of security.

Windows NT Security

Three types of security are available on Windows NT:

Access permissions   Provides for simple password-protected shares. This type of security allows up to two passwords: one for read access and one for full access.

User-level security Allows administrators to control security by adding user or group permissions to resources. This type of security is more secure than basic access permissions.

File-level security Enables administrators to assign rights to files and directories (folders), including restricting users from gaining access or allowing only limited access to files and directories. This type of security provides more administrative power than access permissions and user-level security, and is more secure than those methods. However, it is available only on NTFS partitions.

Table 3.3 describes share permissions, and Table 3.4 describes NTFS permissions.

	Permission	Folder Access
T A B L E 3.3 Share Permissions	No Access	Users and groups can see the shared folder, but when they try to access the folder, they will be denied
	Read	Users and groups can view files and subfolders and execute programs
	Change	Users and groups can add files or subfolders into the shared folder. Gives the user or group all rights associated with the Read permission
	Full Control	The default permission on a network share. Lets all users have full control, including the Change permission

T A B L E 3.4: NTFS Permissions

Permission	Folder Access	File Access
Read (R)	Users and groups can display the folder and subfolders, permissions, and attributes	Users and groups can display the file and its attributes and permissions
Write (W)	Users and groups can create or add subfolders and files, and display permissions and attributes	Users and groups can change files and attributes of a file

T A B L E 3.4: NTFS Permissions *(continued)*

Permission	Folder Access	File Access
Execute (X)	Users and groups can display attributes and permissions, and make changes to the folder	Users and groups can run programs, and display attributes and permissions
Delete (D)	Users and groups can delete the folder	Users and groups can delete the file
Change Permission (P)	Users and groups can change folder permissions	Users and groups can change file permissions
Take Ownership (O)	Users and groups can take ownership of the folder	Users and groups can take ownership of the file

Windows 95 Security

Windows 95 allows you to implement access-level security, also known as share-level security. It does not support user-level security unless there is a server on your network.

Access-Level Security   You can assign passwords to permit access to each folder or printer share. The share name, access type, and passwords are set through the Sharing tab of the resource's Properties dialog box (see Figure 3.8). Three types of access are available with Windows 95:

Read-only access   Users can read files and subfolders, but not save files to the share or delete files or subfolders.

Full access   Users can read, write, and delete files and subfolders.

Depends on password   Users' access depends on which password is used. This works when two passwords have been created: one for read-only access and one for full access.

User-Level Security   In order to use user-level security on a Windows 95 share, you must have a Windows NT server or a NetWare server on your network to authenticate and manage the users.

FIGURE 3.8

Access-level security in
Windows 95

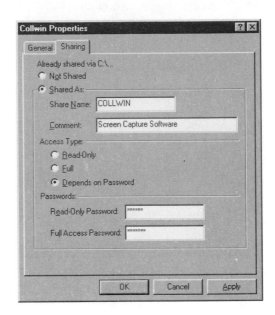

You can grant the following privileges to each user or group to access a
Windows 95 share:

Read-only   Users can read files and subfolders, but not save files to the
share or delete files or subfolders.

Full access   Users can read, write, and delete files and subfolders.

Custom   The administrator can grant one or all of the privileges—Read,
Write, Create, List, Delete, Change File Attributes, and Change Permissions.

Performance Management

Your network is constantly changing. As a network administrator, you need to
keep up with the changes in a proactive way. A primary concern of every network administrator is that the network runs well. Growing networks commonly develop bottlenecks that slow down the system, and it is your job to find
and remove those bottlenecks.

Network Performance Baselines

To start with, you must be able to recognize when your network is running well. You should use the monitoring tools available to you to get a performance baseline for your network. A *baseline* is a record of the response characteristics of your network when it is not heavily loaded or otherwise performing badly. You can later refer to this baseline to recognize anomalous situations.

Each operating system has its own tools to monitor network performance. Windows NT has two tools you will find very useful for managing your network: Performance Monitor and Network Monitor. These are discussed later in this unit, in the "Selecting the Appropriate Tools to Monitor Your Network" section.

Automated Network Management

SMS (Systems Management Server) is a software package that can help you automate the management of your network. SMS can track performance of your network server and client operating systems, such as the amount of free disk space and the peak amount of traffic on your network. SMS provides remote control and monitoring of client and server machines, as well as software distribution and inventory management features.

Choosing a Disaster Recovery Plan

Your disaster recovery plan should include strategies for protecting your data and reducing downtime. You can use a combination of the following to ensure that your network will be able to recover from a disaster:

- Backup system
- UPS (uninterruptible power supply) system
- Fault-tolerant disk scheme
- Backup WAN links

Backup Systems

Your backup system protects your network from data loss. You need to plan a backup schedule, what types of backups you will run, and a backup tape-rotation scheme.

Types of Backups

Windows NT offers the following types of backups:

- *Full backups* create a complete backup.

- *Incremental backups* back up all files modified since the last full backup.

- *Differential backups* back up all the data that has been modified since the last full backup.

Any backup plan should include a combination of full and incremental backups. Differential backups, which take longer than incremental backups, generally are not used in network backup systems.

Backup System Options

You should design a backup system that meets your business requirements. The following are some of your options:

- You could have one backup server that backs up all servers every night. This type of centralized backup system is easy to manage and is effective for small to medium-size networks.

- You could put individual tape units on each server. Note that this system is more difficult to manage than a single backup server.

- You could install a second network interface card in each server and create a backup network. This method is not too popular, but it does keep an enormous amount of data from being transmitted over your production network.

To protect your backup tapes, store them at an off-site location. Then they will not be damaged if there is a fire or other type of disaster at your network site.

UPS Systems

Your UPS system protects your network from power failures. A UPS device supplies electricity to a system after a power failure so that the server or other devices can shut down properly.

A UPS system can communicate with the Windows NT server to send broadcasts to users about the power failure and notify them that the server is about to shut down. For your own UPS system, you need to decide how to set up server-to-UPS communications, as well as how much load you will be carrying on the UPS and how long you want the system to run on battery power. In Windows NT, the settings for UPS configuration, characteristics, and service are on the UPS Control Panel (see Figure 3.9).

Before you purchase a UPS device, make sure that it is compatible with Windows NT.

FIGURE 3.9

UPS settings in Windows NT

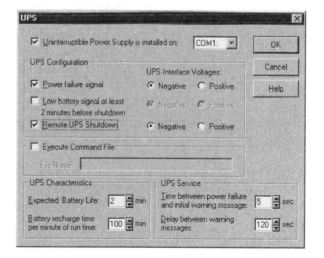

Fault-Tolerant Disk Schemes

Hard drive failure is the most common type of hardware failure in a network. One of the best ways to prevent downtime is to use a fault-tolerant disk scheme. A RAID (Redundant Array of Independent Disks) system combines two or more disks to create a fault-tolerant structure that will continue to function even if one of your hard disks fails.

RAID is software in Windows NT. The RAID software replaces the regular SCSI software and makes the stripe set look like one disk to Windows NT (see Figure 3.10).

FIGURE 3.10

A stripe set volume across three disks

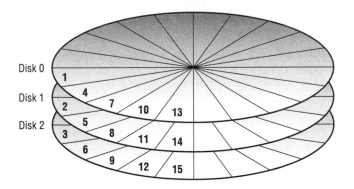

Windows NT supports three levels of RAID:

RAID Level 0   Striping without parity, which provides fast access but does not add fault tolerance.

RAID Level 1   Disk mirroring, which uses two hard drives—one primary and one secondary—that use the same controller card.

RAID Level 5   Striping with parity, which uses three or more disks. One disk is used for parity information only.

Redundant WAN Links

If you have a medium-size to large network that spans multiple sites, you might want to consider setting up redundant WAN links to help ensure the smooth flow of data. Figure 3.11 shows how a network with three sites might be configured to work even if one WAN link fails.

FIGURE 3.11

Redundant WAN links

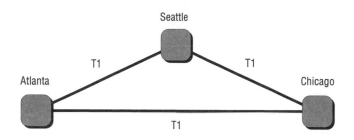

In this example, the main office is in Seattle, and it is connected to Chicago. Chicago is connected to Atlanta, and Atlanta is connected to Seattle. All of these connections are with T1 lines. If the link between Atlanta and Seattle went down, the users in Atlanta would still be able to connect to the Seattle office through the Chicago office. They might experience degradation in service, but slow response is better than no response.

Another possibility is illustrated in Figure 3.12. In this example, there is a T-1 line connection between the New York office and the Los Angeles office, and the service is about 95 percent. You could connect a second T1 line and do load balancing (getting approximately 3Mbps), as well as add redundancy. This would bring the percentage closer to 100 percent. Of course, whether or not this approach is worthwhile for your network depends on its application and if you can afford another T1 line.

The cost of a T1 line depends on the area of the country and the distance involved. For example, a T1 connection between Los Angeles and New York could range between $5,000 to $10,000 a month, depending on your exact locations. In other areas and for shorter distances, a T1 connection could be as cheap as $800.

FIGURE 3.12

Redundant T1 lines to the same office

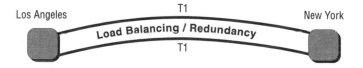

If you cannot afford another T1 line or do not require it, you could install a 56Kbps or ISDN dial-up line. Then you could configure that line to automatically dial-up in case of failure.

Installing and Configuring Multiple Network Adapters

A network adapter, or network interface card (NIC), is a piece of hardware that requires software (a driver) to run it. The NIC also has the hardware address burned into PROM (Programmable Read-Only Memory) on the card. This is sometimes referred to as the *MAC address*, because the MAC sublayer of the Data Link layer is responsible for maintaining hardware addresses. Each MAC address is 6 bytes long—the first 3 bytes are from the IEEE, and the last 3 bytes are assigned by the manufacturer.

A NIC may store card information in the base memory address area of the system's memory.

A NIC coordinates the digital signaling between the PC and the cable. The NIC is responsible for the following tasks:

- Making the connection between the cable and the computer itself.

- Sending ones and zeros over the cable in a logical manner.

- Taking information from the network driver and following the driver's instructions.

Multi-homing Techniques

The Windows NT operating system is capable of handling multiple NICs in the system at the same time (called *multi-homing*). You might consider using multiple NICs to segment your network or to put a computer in more than one network.

Segmenting Your Network

The Windows NT operating system is capable of being an IP router. This will let you cheaply segment your network. Figure 3.13 shows an example of Windows NT Server running as a router.

F I G U R E 3.13

Windows NT Server
running as a router

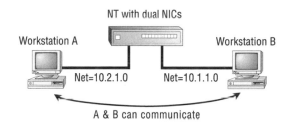

Putting a Computer in Different Networks

If you install a second NIC in your workstation or server, your computer could be in two networks simultaneously (see Figure 3.14).

F I G U R E 3.14

A Windows NT
workstation in two
different networks at
the same time

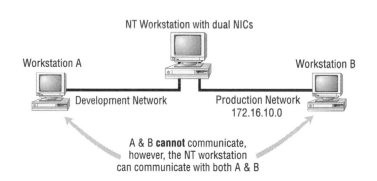

For example, suppose that you had a production network and a development network. You would like to connect your workstation to the production network in order to get e-mail, use file and print services, and so on. You would also like to access the development network from your workstation, but you want to keep your development network independent of the production network to avoid extra traffic on the production network. You could install a second NIC into the development network. Then you would be able to access both networks from the same workstation.

Data Bus Architecture

In the PC environment, there are four different types of computer bus architectures. Each bus is physically different from the other. You should understand the differences between the data bus architectures, so that you don't buy an ISA network interface card when you need a PCI card. Table 3.5 lists the types of bus architectures.

TABLE 3.5 Data Bus Architectures	Architecture	Description
	ISA (Industry Standard Architecture)	The original IBM AT bus architecture. Originally an 8-bit architecture, expanded to 16 bits in 1984. ISA was the standard for all PCs until the EISA bus was developed
	EISA (Extended Industry Standard Architecture)	A 32-bit architecture. Both ISA and EISA cards work in these slots
	MicroChannel	An architecture created by IBM as a replacement for ISA, introduced in PS/2 computers. Runs as either a 16-bit or 32-bit bus and is incompatible with ISA
	PCI (Peripheral Component Interconnect)	A 32-bit local bus in wide use today in both PCs and Power Macs. Provides Plug-and-Play functionality

Network Cabling and Connectors

In order to purchase the correct NIC, you must understand the type of cabling and connectors used in your network.

Many NICs come with more than one connector on the card itself. Choose the connector type you will use by setting either the jumpers of dip switches on the card, or by using a software setting if such an option is available. Today, most PCI cards are 10BaseT or 100BaseT only, which has become the industry standard.

See Unit 2 for the types of connectors used for network cabling.

Network Adapter Installation

If you are not using Plug and Play, or Windows NT did not detect your network interface card, follow these steps to configure and install the card in Windows NT:

- Place the card into the machine after configuring the jumpers and dip switches if needed, or use the software configuration utility that came with the card.

- Install the software driver.

- Add the protocols.

- Add the client software.

- Attach the network cable.

Before you buy a network interface card for Windows NT, check the Hardware Compatibility List (HCL) to make sure that it is compatible with your system.

Hardware Conflicts

IRQs (interrupt request lines) are hardware lines over which devices such as input/output ports, keyboard, disk drives, and network interface cards can send messages or interrupts to the CPU. The interrupts are built into the hardware of the computer and are assigned different levels of priority so that the CPU can understand which requests are the most important requests.

Network adapters are typically preconfigured for a particular IRQ. You will need to make sure that the IRQ settings for your devices do not conflict, particularly if you have multiple NICs in the same server.

To see what resources are available before you install a NIC, check the Resources tab in the Windows NT Diagnostics program.

Table 3.6 lists the IRQs and their typical functions.

	IRQ	Reserved by
T A B L E 3.6	0	Timer
IRQ Functions	1	Keyboard
	2	Hardwired to IRQ 9
	3	COM2 or COM4
	4	COM1 or COM3
	5	LPT2 or MIDI
	6	Floppy disk controller
	7	LPT1
	8	System clock
	9	Linked to IRQ 2 or sound card
	10	Free, NIC, or primary SCSI adapter
	11	Free or secondary SCSI adapter
	12	PS/2, Logitec, or bus mouse
	13	Math processor
	14	Primary IDE hard disk controller
	15	Free or additional IDE controller

Implementing a NetBIOS Naming Scheme

NetBIOS (Network Basic Input/Output System) is the interface that is used in Windows NT, Windows 95, and OS/2. NetBIOS allows applications to interface with lower-layer protocols.

NetBIOS Names

When you're using NetBIOS, all the names on the network must be unique. The computer name must not be longer than 15 characters. NetBIOS names are not case-sensitive and can include almost all alphanumeric characters.

NetBIOS is not a protocol and is not to be confused with NetBEUI (NetBIOS Extended User Interface). Just remember that NetBIOS is the interface and NetBEUI is the protocol.

Universal Naming Convention

To identify resources on networks, Microsoft and IBM created the UNC (Universal Naming Convention) names. UNC paths can consist of the following:

- The NetBIOS computer name where the resource exists followed by two backslashes

- The share name of the resource

- The MS-DOS path of a file or directory

For example, to map a directory called sales from the Sales-Mrkt server, you would type:

Net use g: \\sales-mrkt\sales

Selecting the Appropriate Tools to Monitor Your Network

To ensure that your network runs smoothly and avoid networking problems, you need to monitor trends on a network. This way, you will be able to establish a baseline for "normal" network performance and recognize changes.

There are a number of tools that network administrators can use to monitor trends in a network:

- Network protocol analyzers, such as Network Monitor, which comes with Windows NT. Network Monitor captures packets flowing through the server.

- Network system parameter monitors, such as Windows NT's Performance Monitor. Performance Monitor shows statistics about network objects.

- Values for system settings, such as those shown by the Windows NT's Diagnostics program. The Diagnostics program shows the current values of certain registry entries.

- Event logs, such as those displayed by Windows NT's Event Viewer. Windows NT event logs record error messages, successful and unsuccessful login attempts, and other information.

The following sections describe protocol analyzers and Windows NT's Performance Monitor program. The Windows NT Diagnostics program, Event Viewer, and event logs are covered in Unit 4.

Protocol Analyzers

Protocol analyzer tools can capture frames for later analysis, see bad frames, and help you to isolate which computer is causing the problem. There are dozens of companies that offer protocol analyzers that run on Windows NT or Windows 95, or even in Macintosh environments.

Microsoft's Network Monitor performs packet-capture and decoding and can also do baselining of network performance. The version that comes with Windows NT can analyze frames coming and going from the server on which it runs. The version that comes with SMS can filter packets from any station on the network. Unit 4 provides more information about Network Monitor as a troubleshooting tool.

Performance Monitor

Performance Monitor shows you how your Windows NT Server is performing (see Figure 3.15). Almost any aspect of your Windows NT Server can be graphed or logged using the Performance Monitor. It can present information about your system in charts, logs, and reports so you can view the information in several ways.

You can use Performance Monitor for the following tasks:

- Monitor real-time and historical system performance.

- Identify trends over time.

- Identify bottlenecks.

- Monitor the effects of system configuration changes.

- Determine system capacity.

Windows NT uses *objects* to identify and manipulate system resources. These objects represent individual processes, sections of shared memory, and physical devices. Performance Monitor uses *counters* to measure the performance of the various objects. You specify which counters you want to monitor through the Add to Chart dialog box (see Figure 3.16). Table 3.7 lists the built-in objects for which the Performance Monitor has counters.

FIGURE 3.15

Performance Monitor's display

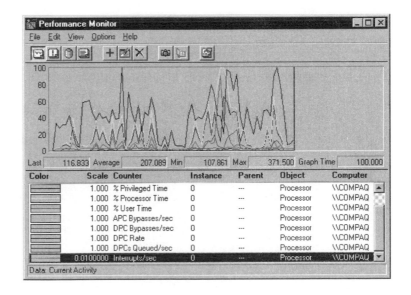

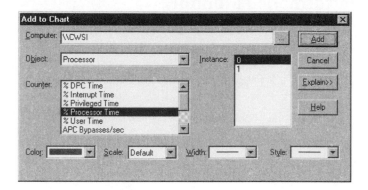

Your system will have other Performance Monitor counters. Each network service you install registers its own Performance Monitor counters.

TABLE 3.7

Windows NT
Performance Monitor
Object Counters

Object	Description
Cache	File system used to buffer physical device data
LogicalDisk	A drive partition, which is assigned a drive letter
Memory	Real and virtual memory
Objects	Miscellaneous system software objects
Paging file	The system used for handling virtual memory
PhysicalDisk	A hard drive as a whole (rather than individual partitions)
Process	A running program
Processor	A CPU that executes instructions
Redirector	A service that redirects requests from a local machine to the network
Server	Server processes that are used for network sharing
System	The Windows NT system as a whole
Thread	An individual thread within a process

Choosing an Administrative Plan

1.   When choosing an administrative plan, what should you keep in mind?

_____

_____

_____

_____

2.   True/False. Only directories and printers can be network resources.

3.   What are the two types of permissions for a particular resource?

_____

_____

4.   True/False. Share-level security is very secure.

5.   User-level security is created by giving access rights to users and groups through an

_____.

6.   True/False. User-level security is easier to manage than share-level security.

7. Which two users are created automatically when you install Windows NT?

_____

_____

8. With Windows NT Workstation, the administrator can create users through the _____ program.

9. With Windows NT Server, the administrator can create users through the _____ program.

10. True/False. Groups are used to simplify assigning file permissions.

11. What is the definition of rights?

_____

12. True/False. Sharing refers to a network resource made available for users to access through the network.

13. True/False. Permissions are used to restrict access to network resources.

14. What security entities are used to simplify user management?

_____

15. True/False. The Guest account is disabled by default.

16.   True/False. The Administrator account cannot be deleted.

17.   List at least four groups that Windows NT creates by default.

_____

_____

_____

_____

18.   What are the two types of groups that you can create in Windows NT?

_____

_____

19.   True/False. Local groups can go into global groups.

20.   True/False. Global groups can go into local groups.

21.   True/False. You can add users and global groups into the Everyone group.

22.   Is the Administrators group a local group or a global group?

_____

23. True/False. In order for the Backup group to back up all files, it must be part of the Administrators group.

24. What are the three types of security available on Windows NT?

_____

_____

_____

25. True/False. NTFS permissions can be set on a FAT volume.

26. What is the easiest way to manage user-level security?

_____

27. Which is more secure: user-level security or share-level security?

_____

28. True/False. Share permissions can be set only on an NTFS partition.

29. On what type of partition can you use file-level security?

_____

30. How does an administrator make user-level security more secure than just basic access permissions?

_____

31. Which type of security is the easiest to administer?

_____

32. True/False. When your network is running only Windows 95, you can support user-level security.

33. True/False. When creating a share within Windows 95, you must provide at least one password.

34. What are the three types of access permissions available within Windows 95?

_____

_____

_____

35. What do full-access permissions within Windows 95 allow?

_____

36. Why would you give Read-Only permissions to a share?

_____

37. How many passwords can you create for a Windows 95 share?

_____

38. What do you need if you want to use user-level security on a Windows 95 share?

_____

39. What are the three types of privileges you can grant to each user or group?

_____

_____

_____

40. Define the privileges you listed above.

_____

_____

_____

41. True/False. When using the Depends on User Name section of Windows 95 permissions, you can assign up to two passwords for the same resource.

42. True/False. It is recommended that you share printers only from Windows NT servers.

43. True/False. Sharing of resources is turned on by default in both Windows 95 and Windows NT Workstation.

44. True/False. When you share a printer through Windows 95, only Windows 95 and Windows NT workstations can use that printer.

Choosing a Disaster Recovery Plan

45. What should you do to prepare for disaster recovery?

_____

46. What are the two best ways to reduce downtime on your servers?

_____

_____

47. Explain the difference between full backups and incremental backups.

_____

48. True/False. You can do backups with a combination of both full and incremental backups.

49. When would you decide to use a differential backup?

_____

50. What is an advantage of using a single centralized backup system?

_____

51. What should your backup strategy be if your network is spread across several buildings?

_____

52. True/False. Backup tapes should be locked in your desk drawer.

53. What does a UPS do?

_____

54. True/False. When using a UPS system, you must install third-party software on your Windows NT server.

55. True/False. If a Windows NT Server computer loses power, a UPS system can notify all the users that the server is about to be shut down.

56. What is the most common type of hardware failure?

_____

57. What does RAID stand for?

_____

58. What are the three types of RAID supported by Windows NT?

59. Define each type of RAID supported by Windows NT.

60. How many disks do you need to run RAID Level 5?

61. What is the difference between mirroring and duplexing?

62. True/False. Disk duplexing is a form of disk mirroring.

63. When would you consider using redundant WAN links?

_____

Installing and Configuring Multiple Network Adapters

64. What does NIC stand for?

_____

65. Explain what a NIC driver does.

_____

66. What does MAC stand for?

_____

67. What is a MAC address?

_____

68. When do you install the MAC address?

_____

69. Where does the MAC layer fit into the OSI reference model?

_____

70. True/False. A NIC is a piece of hardware that requires software to run it.

71. True/False. Base memory address is an area of memory in which the NIC can store card information.

72. What is the responsibility of the NIC?

_____

73. What are two reasons for putting multiple NICs in a computer?

_____

_____

74. What is the most important thing to remember when installing NICs?

_____

75. Before buying a NIC, what should you do to make sure it is compatible with Windows NT?

_____

76. What are the four types of data bus types available?

_____

_____

_____

_____

77. True/False. Microsoft created MicroChannel.

78. What was the first data bus type?

_____

79. What is the best data bus type in use today?

_____

80. True/False. Windows NT supports Plug and Play.

81. List the three types of cable connections used for NICs.

_____

_____

_____

82. You are installing a NIC and you want to see what resources are available. Where would look?

_____

83. Which IRQ shares with IRQ 9?

_____

84. Which device uses IRQ 7?

_____

85. Which IRQs are typically available to use for NICs?

86. Your computer has both a serial mouse and an external modem. Which IRQ should you configure your NIC to use?

_____

87. True/False. You have an additional IDE controller, so you should set the IRQ for the additional IDE controller to 15.

Implementing a NetBIOS Naming Scheme

88. What does NetBIOS stand for?

_____

89. What does NetBEUI stand for?

_____

90. How long can a NetBIOS name be?

_____

91. What is the difference between NetBIOS and NetBEUI?

_____

92. What is the basic purpose of a NetBIOS name?

_____

93. True/False. Each computer name on a network must be unique, except when going through a router because routers don't allow broadcasts to propagate.

94. True/False. NetBIOS names are case-sensitive.

95. You install a router in your large NetBEUI network, and now only the users on the segment in which the server resides can log on. What is the problem?

_____

96.   Which protocol must you run when using the NetBIOS interface?

_____

97.   True/False. You must use the NetBIOS interface to communicate between Windows NT hosts.

98.   What three parts can make up UNC names?

_____

_____

_____

99.   Who created UNC names?

_____

100.   In the line below, map a drive to the Shipping directory located on the FSHQ NT server.

_____

Selecting the Appropriate Tools to Monitor Your Network

101.   List at least three tools provided by Windows NT to help monitor networks.

_____

_____

_____

102. True/False. By monitoring the network, you can get a baseline of the performance of your network.

103. List at least three tasks that you can perform with Windows NT's Performance Monitor.

_____

_____

_____

3-1 Which device or devices can be a network resource? (Choose all that apply.)

    A. Printers

    B. Disk drives

    C. Modems

    D. Scanners

3-2 Which is the actual piece of software a network client uses to help communicate ones and zeros over the network?

    A. Network device driver

    B. Network interface adapter

    C. Networking protocol stack

    D. Network client software

3-3 Which protocols can Windows 95 use to connect to a file server? (Choose all that apply.)

    A. TCP/IP

    B. NWLink (IPX/SPX)

    C. DLC

    D. NetBEUI

3-4 Which of the following files can be used to resolve host names to IP addresses if your DNS server goes down?

    A. LMHOSTS

    B. WINS

    C. HOSTS

    D. CACHE.DNS

3-5 How long can a NetBIOS name be?

    A. 8

    B. 8+3

    C. 15

    D. 255

3-6 Each Token Ring and Ethernet card must be unique from all other cards on the network. How is this accomplished?

    A. Subnet mask

    B. Transceiver setting

    C. MAC address

    D. Frame type

3-7 Which accounts are created by default when you install Windows NT Server? (Choose two.)

    A. Administrator

    B. Supervisor

    C. Guest

    D. Anonymous

3-8 The sales manager has been fired and a new one is starting tomorrow. What is the easiest way to give the new sales manager the same rights to the same directories that the previous manager had?

    A. Delete the old account, and then create a new account for the new manager and give it permissions to all of the same resources

    B. Disable the old account, and then create a new account for the new manager and give it permissions to all of the same resources

C. Rename the account to reflect the user name and password of the new manager

D. Change the password of the old account, give the new manager the new password, and then create another account for the new manager to use

3-9   Which piece of software must be either NDIS or ODI compliant in order to run under Windows 95?

A. Network interface card driver

B. Network interface adapter

C. Networking protocol stack

D. Network client software

3-10   Your computer is running TCP/IP, and WINS is configured on your network. You try to connect to a computer from a command prompt by its computer name to retrieve a file, and you receive an error that the file cannot be found. What could be the problem?

A. Your DNS service is down

B. You have misspelled the computer name you are trying to get a file from

C. You are using a static IP address

D. The name is misspelled in the HOSTS file

3-11   Which global group gives users the rights to administer any computer in the domain?

A. Administrators

B. Domain Admins

C. Domain Users

D. Server Operators

SAMPLE TEST

3-12 Which device can communicate with a Windows NT server to broadcast that the server will be shut down because of a power failure?

    A. TDR

    B. UPS

    C. RAID

    D. No such device

3-13 What does a tape backup unit protect your system from? (Choose all that apply.)

    A. Network intrusion

    B. Hard drive failure

    C. Accidental file deletion

    D. RAM failure

3-14 Which of the following must be installed on the Windows NT server that will allow NetWare clients to access resources on the Windows NT server? (Choose all that apply.)

    A. NWLink

    B. Client Service for NetWare

    C. File and Print Services for NetWare

    D. File and Print Services for Microsoft Networks

3-15 You want to add new users to your existing Windows NT Server network. The users want to use their full names. How long can their names be?

    A. 8 characters

    B. 8.3 characters

    C. 20 characters

    D. 255 characters

SAMPLE TEST

3-16 What is a disadvantage of using broadcasts to resolve NetBIOS names to IP addresses on your network instead of using WINS?

  A. It is slower than WINS

  B. NetBIOS broadcasts are only received by computers on the local subnet

  C. Windows for Workgroups computers cannot respond to NetBIOS name broadcasts

  D. There is no disadvantage

3-17 Which of the following would you use in case of disk failure in Windows NT? (Choose two.)

  A. Disk mirroring

  B. RAID Level 0 (disk striping)

  C. RAID Level 5 (disk striping with parity)

  D. Volume octs

3-18 Which cable would you use to connect an external analog modem to your computer?

  A. A SCSI cable

  B. A parallel cable

  C. RS-232 serial cable

  D. Insert it in an ISA slot

3-19 How long is a MAC address?

  A. 2 bytes

  B. 3 bytes

  C. 5 bytes

  D. 6 bytes

SAMPLE TEST

3-20   A user is going on vacation for two weeks; in the meantime, you don't want anyone to be able to use the account. What should you do?

  A. Disable the account

  B. Delete the account

  C. Rename the account

  D. Change the account's password

3-21   Windows NT client computers use which Application layer protocol to communicate between hosts?

  A. NCP

  B. SMB

  C. NetBEUI

  D. UDP

3-22   Which two operating systems allow you to assign a password to each shared resource?

  A. Windows 95

  B. Windows NT Workstation

  C. Windows NT Server

  D. Windows for Workgroups 3.11

3-23   Which application would you use to see which users have unsuccessful logon attempts when you turn on auditing for logon activities with your Windows NT Workstation?

  A. User Manager

  B. File Manager

  C. Security Manager

  D. Event Viewer

3-24   You have installed WINS for NetBIOS name resolution on your TCP/IP network. Two computers have the same name but different IP addresses. What will happen?

   A. Neither computer will be registered with WINS, but you will be able to ping the IP address of both computers

   B. Only one computer will be registered with WINS, and this will be the only one you can ping by the IP address

   C. Only one computer will be registered with WINS, but you will be able to ping the IP address of both computers

   D. Both computers will be registered with WINS, and you will be able to ping the IP address of both computers

3-25   Which Windows NT group gives users no special privileges?

   A. Administrators

   B. Backup Operators

   C. Users

   D. Server Operators

3-26   Which of the following backup methods backs up files that were created or changed since the last full backup and marks the files as having been backed up?

   A. Differential backup

   B. Incremental backup

   C. Daily backup

   D. Normal backup

3-27 Which of the following are characteristics of user names in Microsoft networks? (Choose all that apply.)

    A. User names are case-sensitive

    B. User names may not contain the '+' character

    C. User names must be unique

    D. User names may be up to 255 characters in length

3-28 Which of the following RAID levels creates a stripe set but does not provide data redundancy?

    A. Level 0

    B. Level 1

    C. Level 2

    D. Level 3

3-29 What piece of hardware must you install in your computer in order to connect to the network?

    A. Network device driver

    B. Network interface adapter

    C. Networking protocol stack

    D. Network client software

3-30 When using Windows 95 computers, which of the following is required to implement user-level security?

    A. A DHCP server

    B. A master browser

C. A Windows NT Workstation computer

D. A Windows NT Server computer

3-31   Which of the following RAID levels creates a stripe set with parity?

A. Level 0

B. Level 1

C. Level 5

D. Level 6

3-32   A user forgot his password. How can you fix this?

A. Edit the user's password by using the Password option in the server's Control Panel

B. Assign the user to the Administrator group

C. Edit the user's profile by using System Policy Editor

D. Change the user's password with User Manager for Domains

3-33   You want your Windows 95 computer to communicate with a NetWare server. You have installed the NetWare client and the IPX/SPX-compatible protocol. Which of the following should you do?

A. Set the frame type

B. Bind the protocol to the LAN driver

C. Set the frame type only if the network uses a single frame type

D. Set the frame type only if the network uses more than one frame type

3-34   Why should you build your growing network with routers and gateways rather than bridges and repeaters? (Choose all that apply.)

    A. Too many stations on one LAN can cause broadcast storms

    B. LANs have maximum cabling distances that you cannot exceed

    C. WANs use slow network links that are not efficiently supported by LAN data-link protocols such as Ethernet

    D. Gateways and routers are less expensive than hubs

3-35   Suppose that you use WINS for NetBIOS name resolution, you do not have an LMHOSTS file on your computer, and the WINS server becomes unavailable. Which computers will you be able to see in your Network Neighborhood browser without generating a NetBIOS broadcast?

    A. Computers on the local subnet only

    B. Computers in the local domain only

    C. All computers on all subnets

    D. No computers

3-36   Which of the following services are provided by Microsoft Systems Management Server (SMS)? (Choose all that apply.)

    A. Virus protection

    B. Network monitoring

    C. Remote control of client machines

    D. Inventory management

3-37   Which of the following is a utility that can help you manage a TCP/IP network when users move from subnet to subnet?

   A. WINS

   B. DHCP

   C. DNS

   D. LMHOSTS

3-38   Which of the following must be loaded on the Windows 95 client computers in order for them to access files on NetWare servers? (Choose all that apply.)

   A. NWLink

   B. Gateway Services for NetWare

   C. Microsoft Client for NetWare Networks

   D. File and Printer Sharing for NetWare

UNIT

4

Troubleshooting

Test Objectives: Troubleshooting

- Identify common errors associated with components required for communications.

- Diagnose and resolve common connectivity problems with cards, cables, and related hardware.

- Resolve broadcast storms.

- Identify and resolve network performance problems.

Exam objectives are subject to change at any time without prior notice and at Microsoft's sole discretion. Please visit Microsoft's Training & Certification website (www.microsoft.com/Train_Cert) for the most current exam objectives listing.

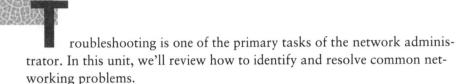

roubleshooting is one of the primary tasks of the network administrator. In this unit, we'll review how to identify and resolve common networking problems.

Identifying Common Communication Errors

To identify errors associated with components required for network communications, you need to know which tool to use and where to look.

Tools for Finding Errors

There are a number of tools that network administrators can use to find the sources of communication errors in the network:

- A *network analyzer*, also called a *protocol analyzer*, can capture and decode packets flowing through your server.

- A *network monitor* can do frame-level analysis and check packet types and errors on the whole network or just part of the network.

- An *event log* records any significant occurrences in the system or in an application.

- Various software is available for finding and resolving communications problems on a TCP/IP network.

We talked about using network analyzers and monitors in Unit 3, and we'll go into a bit more detail about using them for troubleshooting later in this unit, in the "Network Performance Troubleshooting Tools" section. The following sections discuss the TCP/IP tools and the Windows NT event log.

TCP/IP Troubleshooting Tools

For a network that uses the TCP/IP protocol, you can use several software tools to find the causes of communications errors. The main TCP/IP troubleshooting tools are listed in Table 4.1.

	Tool	Description
TABLE 4.1 Tools for Trouble-shooting TCP/IP Problems	Ping	Checks if a host is up and running. Ping (for Packet Internet Groper) does an echo send and reply to an IP address to see if it is alive
	Tracert	Traces a route from a source to a destination. The administrator can use this tool to see the actual packet path through an internetwork
	Nbtstat	Checks the NetBIOS table statistics to see which Windows NT NetBIOS name has been resolved to an IP address (a Windows NT tool)
	NSLookup	Checks the DNS database for name resolution
	ARP	Resolves IP addresses to hardware addresses associated with NICs
	Route	Allows you to view, add, or delete route entries. Route entries are used by a router to route IP packets through an internetwork

The Event Log and Viewer

Windows NT keeps a running log of system events, including warnings and errors from the system. The Event Viewer allows you to access the event log. There are three main log areas:

System   Includes errors and warning messages that describe system events, which typically include service failures, browser elections, and network problems (see Figure 4.1)

Security   Keeps track of events turned on through Windows NT's auditing

Application   Includes specific messages from applications

By default, Windows NT security logging is turned off. To enable security logging, start User Manager for Domains, select Policies ➤ Audit ➤ Audit These Events, and specify which events you want to audit.

FIGURE 4.1

The Event Viewer displaying the System Log

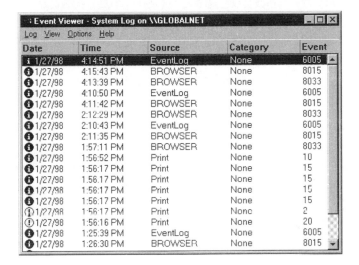

The event log keeps track of five event types, which are listed in Table 4.2.

TABLE 4.2

Event Types Tracked in the Event Log

Event Type	Description
Informational	Denotes a significant event, but one that does not stop NT from loading. Noted by an *i* circled in blue before the message
Warning	Tells of an impending problem, such as low disk space. Noted by an exclamation point before the message
Error	Indicates a component or device in NT has failed or didn't start. Noted by a red stop sign before the message
Success Audit	Indicates an audited security attempt that was successful. A successful logon attempt is logged as a *Success Audit*
Failure Audit	Indicates an audit security access attempt that failed. An unsuccessful attempt to access a network drive is logged as a *Failure Audit*

Common Sources of Communication Errors

Common sources of communication errors include network protocols, network services, modems, and RAS (Remote Access Service).

Network Protocol Failures

Network protocols are a common source of network problems. The following sections describe typical failures related to five protocols: NetBEUI, DLC, TCP/IP, NWLink, and SLIP.

See Unit 2 for more information about network protocols and protocol suites.

NetBEUI This is a nonroutable protocol designed for small networks. Typically, the biggest problem with NetBEUI is that it is "chatty." If there are many workstations on the network, the network can be seriously degraded with broadcasts. Also, since it is not routable, routers will not pass packets to another segment, so servers and workstations on opposite sides of routers cannot communicate. If possible, you should avoid running the NetBEUI protocol on large networks.

DLC This protocol is primarily used to communicate between Windows NT Server computers running as print servers and HP Jet Direct cards in printers. It is also used by an SNA Server computer to communicate with a mainframe or AS/400. The biggest problem with DLC is that it is nonconfigurable. People tend to forget about the protocol and do not load it on the server when they should.

TCP/IP This protocol suite allows addressing of packets for delivery through both the Internet and an intranet. All nodes must have a unique address number, assigned by an administrator or a DHCP server. The following are some typical problems associated with TCP/IP:

Duplicate IP addresses If a host does not have a unique IP address, the network interface of the host will shut down.

Incorrect subnet masks If a host has an incorrect subnet mask, it can think it is on the wrong subnet, and it might not route packets to a router to be sent to another subnet.

Incorrect or missing default gateways   If a host is configured with an incorrect default gateway address or does not have a default gateway configured, the host will stop communicating with other subnets.

Incorrect DNS and WINS information   DNS resolves host names to IP addresses. If a name is incorrectly spelled in DNS, the name cannot be resolved. WINS dynamically resolves NetBIOS names to IP addresses. If a static address is placed in WINS and is misspelled, then the host name cannot be resolved.

DHCP also helps administrators manage a TCP/IP network by keeping a database of used and unused IP addresses.

NWLink   This is an IPX "look-alike" protocol. NWLink is self-addressing and routable. It is probably one of the most resilient protocols of all the protocols discussed here. It does not require any host configuration or maintenance. However, each network segment must have a unique network number. Also, in order for computers running the NWLink (or IPX) protocol to communicate, they must use the same frame type.

The most common problem associated with NWLink is an incorrect frame type. However, this rarely occurs with Windows 95 and NT because they use *auto-sensing*, which means that they can tell which frame type is used on the network and adjust their settings accordingly.

The *frame type* is the format used to put together packet header and data information for transmission on the data link. The 802.2 frame type is the default and most commonly used frame type in Microsoft networks.

SLIP   This older protocol generally has been replaced by the newer PPP. SLIP supports only TCP/IP and static IP addressing. Problems with SLIP occur when hosts try to run multiple protocols, which SLIP does not allow. Also, because you must use static IP addresses, you can easily make a mistake in configuring the host.

Network Service Problems

Windows NT includes Browser, Replication, DNS, DHCP, and WINS, as well as other network services. However, for the Networking Essentials exam, keep these two important services in mind:

- The *Server service* enables a Windows NT Workstation or Server computer to share resources on a network. If the Server service is not started, then the workstation will not be able to share folders and printers on the network.

- The *Workstation service* allows a Windows NT Workstation or Server computer to be a client to a computer running the Server service. If the Workstation service is not started, then the workstation will not be able to gain access to folders or printers that are shared on the network.

Modem Problems

Modems can be the source of many problems (and headaches!). You may have problems with drivers and resource conflicts, and/or you may have trouble connecting to the telephone system. The following are the most common problems associated with modems:

Dialing errors   The dialing feature may not be dialing a "9" to get out of the office telephone system. Check the dialing properties for the dial-up connection.

Connection problems   If you cannot make a connection, the communication settings may be incorrect. Check the speed, data bits, parity, and stop bits settings.

Protocol errors   Incompatible protocols cannot communicate. Check the protocols in use to see if they are compatible.

RAS Problems

RAS can be another source of communications problems. The following are the most common problems:

Invalid user accounts   The user name is misspelled or does not exist on the Windows NT domain.

No permissions   The user does not have the Log On Locally right or does not have Dial-In permissions.

Wrong telephone number   The user has the wrong telephone number or is not typing the number correctly.

Wrong modem cables   The pin connections on the cables are not specified for the modem or port on the computer.

Incompatible modems   The user's modem and the modem on the Windows NT server running RAS are not compatible.

Call-waiting is not disabled   If the call-waiting feature is enabled, the user will be dropped from the telephone call whenever a call is coming in.

Poor telephone line quality   When the telephone line cannot handle the load, data is retransmitted or the connection will timeout.

Windows NT Server is offline or down   If Windows NT is not running, the modem will answer, but the user cannot log on.

The event log can be a good source of information about RAS errors.

Diagnosing and Resolving Common Connectivity Problems

Cabling is the most common cause of network connectivity problems. Other possible sources of these types of problems are connectivity devices (bridges, routers, and repeaters) and network interface cards (NICs). We'll look at the tools and techniques for troubleshooting each of these components, and then focus on some problems specific to Ethernet and Token Ring networks.

Cable Problems

Various tools are available to help you diagnose network cable problems. These tools are listed in Table 4.3.

T A B L E 4.3: Tools for Troubleshooting Cable Problems

Tool	Description	Typical Use
Digital voltmeter (DVM)	A hand-held tool that can check the continuity and voltage of cables	Checks ohmage of cable and terminators and finds a short or an open in the cabling
Time-domain reflectometer (TDR)	A tool that sends sound or light waves down a copper or fiber-optic cable	Finds a break, a short, or an imperfection in a cable, or loss of decibels in a fiber-optic cable
Oscilloscope	A tool that measures fluctuations in signal voltage	Tests the digital signal in a coax cable
Advanced cable tester	A tool that works up to the Transport layer of the OSI reference model. It can test the physical cable as well as frame counts, collisions, congestion, and beaconing	Checks for the presence of a signal

Electrical storms can cause a terminator to become open or terminate at a higher voltage.

The following are items to check when you are troubleshooting cable-related problems:

Cable connections   Make sure that the cable is connected properly.

Cable-run lengths   Make sure that the cable runs are not longer than mandated by the cable specifications.

Termination   If you are using coax, make sure that the cable is terminated properly.

Electrical interference   Check for electrical interference, which can result from power cords, electric motors, or fluorescent lights.

Cable rating   If you are running 10BaseT, make sure that the cable rating matches the speed and distances you are running on your network.

Connectors   Check for loose connectors.

Ohmage   Check for the correct ohm measurements on Thinnet and Thicknet networks.

Continuity   Check for problems that affect the continuity of cables, such as a short or an open terminator.

It is very important to remember your LAN coax ratings and ohmage. Table 4.4 shows Thinnet, Thicknet, and ARCnet network specifications.

T A B L E 4.4 Coaxial Cable Specifications	Connector	Cable Type	Ohmage	Length
	RG-58	Thinnet (10Base2)	50 ohms	185 meters (610 feet)
	RG-8 or 11	Thicknet (10Base5)	50 ohms	500 meters (1650 feet)
	RG-62U	Coax in ARCnet network	93 ohms	6060.6 meters (20,000 feet)

Connectivity Device Problems

No matter which device—a bridge, router, or repeater—is having or causing problems, you should always start with the basics. Check that the unit is plugged in and the power is on. Then make sure that all the cables and connectors are in place.

After checking the basics, check the following items when you are troubleshooting connectivity device problems:

The 5-4-3 rule   If you are using repeaters, remember that you can have up to five segments and four repeaters, and only three segments can be populated.

Dissimilar network types   Repeaters cannot connect dissimilar network types, such as Ethernet to Token Ring, and only expensive bridges can connect dissimilar types of networks. Typically, a router is used to connect dissimilar network types.

NetBEUI and DLC protocols   Routers cannot route NetBEUI and DLC. However, you can purchase bridging software that can bridge NetBEUI and DLC for most major router types.

Dissimilar routing protocols   To connect dissimilar routing protocols, such as IPX to TCP/IP, you must use a gateway. Again, most major routing companies can provide gateway software for their routers.

Bridges and repeaters do not stop broadcast storms.

NIC Problems

The following are items to check when you are troubleshooting NIC-related problems:

NIC drivers   Check that you have the correct drivers for your NICs.

Device conflicts   Check to make sure that there are no device conflicts with IRQ, memory, and DMA addresses.

NIC and software settings   Make sure that the settings on the NIC match the settings on the network software you are using.

Speed setting   Make sure that the NIC is set to the speed that you are running on your network.

Cable connections   Make sure that the cable is properly connected to the NIC.

Active connector   If the NIC has multiple connectors, make sure that the connector for the type of network you are using is active.

You can run the NIC diagnostic program to see if the NIC itself is defective. If you find that the NIC is defective or you cannot resolve the problem, replace the NIC.

In Windows 95, you can use Device Manager to make sure that a network interface card does not have a resource conflict.

Ethernet and Token Ring Connectivity Problems

In general, it is not difficult to isolate and troubleshoot problems on an Ethernet network. After you figure out which hub is causing the problem, you can unplug each device until the problem goes away. Typically, a bad Ethernet card is the cause of Ethernet connectivity problems.

If you are having problems with a Token Ring network, check the following items:

MSAU cable connections Make sure that the cables are connected to the MSAU correctly. MSAUs are connected with the ring-out cable connected to the ring-in port of a different hub (see Figure 4.2).

FIGURE 4.2

Token Ring MSAU connections

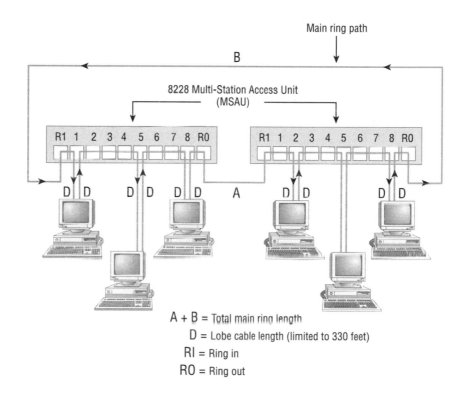

A + B = Total main ring length
D = Lobe cable length (limited to 330 feet)
RI = Ring in
RO = Ring out

MSAUs from different manufacturers If you have MSAUs from different manufacturers in the same network, they may be incompatible, which can cause intermittent (up and down) problems.

Active MSAUs MSAUs that are active hubs require power. These can blow fuses, or their power supply can fail.

Token Ring cards Check that you have not installed a 4Mbps card into a 16Mbps network, because this can bring down the network. Typically, 16Mbps cards can adjust themselves and do not cause the same problem. However, the newer, twisted-pair hubs can shut off a port if they notice a problem.

Resolving Broadcast Storms

Broadcast storms clog the network bandwidth and can cause the computers on the network to run very slowly or to simply timeout.

Common Causes of Broadcast Storms

A common cause of a broadcast storm is a bad NIC that is continually transmitting garbage. When this happens, other users may not be able to transmit (see Figure 4.3).

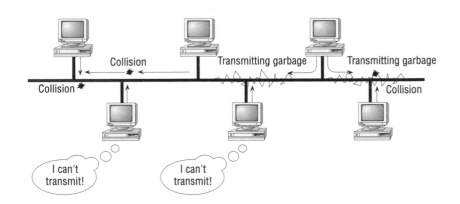

FIGURE 4.3

A bad NIC causing a broadcast storm

Meaningless transmissions sent by a network node, because of a network malfunction or other error, are sometimes called *jabber packets*.

Also, a server that is down or not responding can cause a broadcast storm. A computer trying to contact that server may broadcast a packet destined for the server every millisecond.

Tools for Resolving Broadcast Storms

You can use a protocol analyzer or a network monitor to find out which computer on the network is causing the broadcast storm. The protocol analyzer will give you the IP address and/or MAC address of the workstation. Unfortunately, tracking down a MAC address can be difficult, if not almost impossible.

If possible, you should document hardware addresses for each PC on your network. This can help you resolve broadcast problems quickly.

You should be able to figure out which network segment is causing the problem, and then you can try turning off each workstation on that network segment until the broadcast storm stops.

Although you can't actually prevent broadcast storms from happening, you can stop them from propagating throughout the network by configuring your network with a router or routers. Routers will not propagate broadcast storms through the internetwork (see Figure 4.4).

FIGURE 4.4

Routers stopping a broadcast storm from propagating through a network

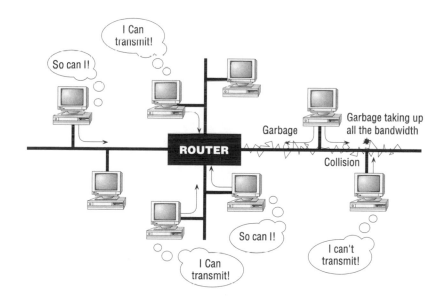

Recognizing a Broadcast Storm

Running a network monitor periodically is a good idea, but you must understand what you are seeing. How can you tell if it is normal data or if the PC is transmitting garbage? The following is part of a display shown by a network monitor catching a broadcast storm in action:

```
Packets Received:    324
Packets Filtered:    324
Packets Processed:   324
Bytes Available:     1,853,900
Bytes Used:          240,652
```

Source	Source Physical	Destination	Destination Physical	Size	Protocol
IP-10.1.1.31	00:60:97:70:82:4e	Ethernet Brdcast	ff:ff:ff:ff:ff:ff	64	ARP Req
IP-10.1.1.31	00:60:97:70:82:4e	Ethernet Brdcast	ff:ff:ff:ff:ff:ff	64	ARP Req
IP-10.1.1.31	00:60:97:70:82:4e	Ethernet Brdcast	ff:ff:ff:ff:ff:ff	64	ARP Req
IP-10.1.1.31	00:60:97:70:82:4e	Ethernet Brdcast	ff:ff:ff:ff:ff:ff	64	ARP Req
IP-10.1.1.31	00:60:97:70:82:4e	Ethernet Brdcast	ff:ff:ff:ff:ff:ff	64	ARP Req
IP-10.1.1.31	00:60:97:70:82:4e	Ethernet Brdcast	ff:ff:ff:ff:ff:ff	64	ARP Req
IP-10.1.1.31	00:60:97:70:82:4e	Ethernet Brdcast	ff:ff:ff:ff:ff:ff	64	ARP Req
IP-10.1.1.31	00:60:97:70:82:4e	Ethernet Brdcast	ff:ff:ff:ff:ff:ff	64	ARP Req

Notice that the network monitor caught the IP address of the workstation creating the broadcasts: 10.1.1.31. It also shows that it is an Ethernet broadcast. But two other pieces of information let you know what is actually going on:

- The destination physical address is all *f*'s. All *f*'s means that it is a broadcast for all computers on the network segment. Remember that routers will not pass these broadcasts to other network segments.

- The protocol is an ARP Request. This means that the source computer is trying to find a hardware address for a computer on the network, but it can't for some reason.

The Broadcast Storm Packets

Let's take a closer look at some packets and see what the computer is actually trying to do.

Here's the first packet:

```
Flags:          0x00
Status:         0x00
Packet Length: 64
Timestamp:      14:18:26.193000  01/30/1998
```
Ethernet Header
```
Destination:    ff:ff:ff:ff:ff:ff  Ethernet Brdcast
Source:         00:60:97:70:82:4e
Protocol Type: 08-06   IP ARP
```
ARP - Address Resolution Protocol
```
Hardware:                   1   Ethernet (10Mb)
Protocol:                   08-00 IP
Hardware Address Length: 6
Protocol Address Length: 4
Operation:                  1   ARP Request
Sender Hardware Address: 00:60:97:70:82:4e
Sender Internet Address: 10.1.1.31
Target Hardware Address: 00:00:00:00:00:00  (ignored)
Target Internet Address: 10.1.89.119
```
Extra bytes (Padding):
```
YwYwYwYwYwYwYwYw  59 77 59 77 59 77 59 77 59 77 59 77 59 77 59 77
Yw                59 77
Frame Check Sequence: 0x00000000
```

The first packet captured includes the sender's hardware address and IP address, and the destination computer's IP address (10.1.89.119), but it does not show the destination computer's hardware address. That is why the source computer is doing an ARP Request. The sending computer is saying to the destination computer, "I have your IP address, but I need your hardware address." This packet almost looks fine—with a normal ARP Request for a hardware address—except for the actual data, shown at the bottom. The data is just *Yw,Yw,Yw...*, which is garbage.

Here's the next packet:

```
Flags:          0x00
Status:         0x00
Packet Length: 64
Timestamp:      14:18:26.194000  01/30/1998
```
Ethernet Header
```
Destination:    ff:ff:ff:ff:ff:ff  Ethernet Brdcast
Source:         00:60:97:70:82:4e
Protocol Type: 08-06   IP ARP
```
ARP - Address Resolution Protocol
```
Hardware:                    1   Ethernet (10Mb)
Protocol:                    08-00 IP
Hardware Address Length: 6
Protocol Address Length: 4
Operation:                   1   ARP Request
Sender Hardware Address: 00:60:97:70:82:4e
Sender Internet Address: 10.1.1.31
Target Hardware Address: 00:00:00:00:00:00  (ignored)
Target Internet Address: 10.1.89.118
```
Extra bytes (Padding):
```
YvYvYvYvYvYvYvYv  59 76 59 76 59 76 59 76 59 76 59 76 59 76 59 76
Yv                59 76
Frame Check Sequence: 0x00000000
```

This packet looks almost identical to the first packet, except that its destination computer's IP address is different (10.1.89.118), and the data is different (*Yv,Yv,Yv*).

There are hundreds of these packets, all with different destination IP addresses but asking for the same thing. The source computer is trying to get a hardware address for every computer on the network. This probably was caused by a program on the computer trying to find a server or by a malfunctioning NIC.

This kind of problem can cause havoc on a busy Ethernet network that is not properly segmented with routers. Remember that even with routers, a broadcast storm could cause problems on the segment on which it is located, but it would not affect the entire network.

The Resolution

So how can you resolve this problem? Since the network monitor gave the IP address of the source computer, you only need to find out who has that IP address.

In this example, the network administrator was running DHCP, so he could look in the DHCP database (DHCP keeps a database of computer names or NetBIOS names to IP addresses) to see who was registered with that IP address. He found that workstation, rebooted the computer, and the problem disappeared. And he knows that if the problem reappears, he should replace the NIC on that computer.

Identifying and Resolving Network Performance Problems

All of the information reviewed so far in this unit pertains to identifying and resolving typical network performance problems. Here, we will review several other problems that can affect network performance, and then look at three tools available with Windows NT.

Common Sources of Network Performance Problems

We've described troubleshooting communication errors and connectivity problems. Three other problems can affect your network:

Down server   Administrators can quickly become unemployed if they have not taken the precautions necessary to guard against data loss if a server crashes. Make sure that you have a regular backup system, and if possible, a fault-tolerant drive array (RAID) system.

Upgrade failure   Be careful when you are upgrading your server to new software if it is running an older operating system version. Make sure that the new software is compatible with the server's existing system. You should test the upgrade in a test environment first, before upgrading a production server.

Power outage   A power outage can happen to anyone—no one is immune. Make sure that all of your important servers and hardware have UPS systems installed. Also, remind users to save their work periodically.

Network Performance Troubleshooting Tools

Windows NT comes with three software tools that can help you diagnose and resolve network performance problems: Performance Monitor, Network Monitor, and Windows NT Diagnostics.

Performance Monitor

We talked about using NT's Performance Monitor for monitoring trends in your network in Unit 3. It can also help you to identify bottlenecks in your network.

When you are troubleshooting network performance problems, check the % Net Utilization counter for your network segments (for each network interface). For the Server object, the following are some useful counters to check:

- Bytes Total/Sec
- Sessions Errored Out

If you're running the NetBEUI and/or NWLink protocol, you should look at the following NetBEUI and NWLink IPX object counters:

- Session Timeouts
- Failures Link
- Resource Local

Network Monitor

As mentioned in Unit 3, Windows NT Server comes with a network protocol analyzer, called Network Monitor. Network Monitor captures, filters, and analyzes frames and packets sent over a network segment. Each packet contains the following information:

- The source and destination hardware addresses of the transmitting station

- The source and destination of the logical address of the transmitting station

- Header and control information from each protocol used in the transmission

- The actual data that is being transmitted

The Network Monitor window displays the packet information in four sections (see Figure 4.5):

Graph Illustrates network utilization, frames per second, and bytes per second broadcast and multicast per second

Session Statistics Shows a summary of packets sent and received between two hosts

Total Statistics Displays statistics for frames captured, utilization, and the network adapter

Station Statistics Shows a summary of network utilization, frames per second, and bytes per second broadcast and multicast per second

F I G U R E 4.5

The Network Monitor window

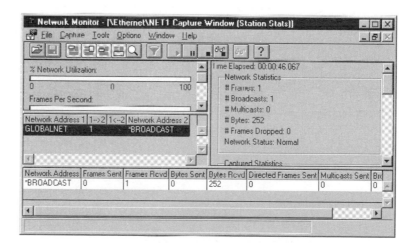

You can easily install Network Monitor on any Windows NT server by adding the service through the Network applet in the Control Panel.

The version of Network Monitor that comes with Windows NT is limited in that it can capture and analyze only the packets flowing into and out of the server. However, the version of Network Monitor that comes with SMS can capture packets that are not addressed to the server. Also, you can purchase other network protocol analyzers from different vendors.

Windows NT Diagnostics

The Windows NT Diagnostics program (WinMSD) shows the computer hardware and operating system data that is stored in the system registry.

To start Windows NT Diagnostics, select Start ➤ Programs ➤ Administrative Tools (common) ➤ Windows NT Diagnostics.

Table 4.4 lists the tabs in the Windows NT Diagnostics window (see Figure 4.6).

TABLE 4.5	Tab	Description
Windows NT Diagnostics Window Tabs	Services	Shows the states of running or stopped services. Lists all the services and devices in CurrentControlSet
	Resources	Lists IRQs, I/O ports, DMA channels, memory allocation, and device drivers that are in use
	Environment	Displays environment variables
	Network	Lists network configurations and current network statistics
	Version	Shows the operating version number, build number, Service Pack information, and the registered owner
	System	Displays BIOS, HAL, and CPU information
	Display	Contains information about the video adapter, driver, and settings
	Drives	Lists all installed drives and their type, including floppy, removable drives, CD-ROMs, and network-connected drivers
	Memory	Shows physical and virtual memory information

FIGURE 4.6

The Network tab of
the Windows NT
Diagnostics program

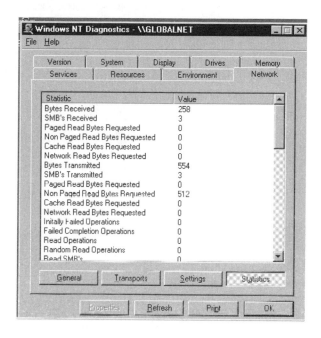

Windows NT Diagnostics gives you a "snapshot" of current statistics for your network. For example, to get a quick look at current network statistics, go to the Network tab and click the Statistics button. Here are some statistics that are useful to watch for troubleshooting network performance problems:

- Session timed out

- Sessions errored out

- Jobs queued

- Server response time

Sources for Troubleshooting Information

Many online and offline sources can provide the information you need to troubleshoot network problems. These include vendor documentation, bulletin board services (BBSs), the Internet, and CD-ROMs from vendors.

For Microsoft network problems, two other sources of information are available:

- Windows NT Books Online is supplied on the Windows NT Server CD (see Figure 4.7).

- Microsoft's TechNet CD contains technical information, product information, articles, and announcements.

Identifying Common Communication Errors

1. List at least three software tools that you can use to find the sources of communication errors on a TCP/IP network.

_____

_____

_____

2. Which types of events are logged in the Windows NT event log?

_____

3. Which protocol is not routable?

_____

4. True/False. The NWLink protocol is used to communicate between Windows NT and Novell NetWare servers.

5. Which protocol is not self-addressing and is used to route packets through the Internet and an intranet?

_____

6. When would you use the DLC protocol?

_____

7. When starting Windows NT Workstation, the LAN driver gives you an error. Where would you look for more specific information?

_____

8. Which two protocols are self-addressing?

_____

_____

9. Which newer protocol has replaced SLIP?

_____

10. A user says that he cannot log in to the NetWare server when he dials in. He is using the SLIP protocol. What could be the problem?

_____

11. A user says he cannot Telnet into the Unix database when dialing into the network. He is using the SLIP protocol. What could be the problem?

_____

12. A user calls and complains that she cannot share any files on her Windows NT workstation. Since NT Workstation has file and print sharing automatically installed when NT is installed, what could be the problem?

_____

13. A user complains that she cannot see any other workstation network shares from her workstation. She tried connecting to a network share from a different workstation, and it worked fine. What could be the problem?

_____

14. Which service within Windows NT allows you to dynamically assign TCP/IP addresses to hosts?

_____

15. You have two computers, A and B. A cannot ping B. Both computers are running TCP/IP. Which items should you check?

_____

16. You have two computers, A and B. Computer A is located on network segment 100, and computer B is located on network segment 200. A router separates the two segments. Computer A is running TCP/IP and NetBEUI. Computer B is running NetBEUI. Why can't A and B communicate?

_____

17. List at least two problems associated with modems.

_____

_____

18. What does RAS stand for?

_____

19. True/False. The event log would be a good source of information for RAS errors.

20. List at least four problems associated with RAS.

_____

_____

_____

_____

Diagnosing and Resolving Common Connectivity Problems

21. Which device looks for breaks in cables by measuring voltage?

_____

22. True/False. A time-domain reflectometer (TDR) sends sound or light waves down a copper or fiber-optic cable to look for problems in the cable.

23. At which layer of the OSI reference model do the most network problems occur?

_____

24. You are troubleshooting a Thinnet network that is not working. It has five repeaters with four segments, and only three are populated. The terminators show 50 ohms. What could be the problem?

_____

STUDY QUESTIONS

25. What does an oscilloscope measure?

_____

26. What is the easiest way to troubleshoot a 10BaseT hub?

_____

27. You have been hired to expand the XYZ company's existing network. The company has one Token Ring network and one Ethernet network, which the managers want to connect together with a repeater. What should you do?

_____

28. True/False. A generator or mechanical device near the network could degrade network performance.

29. True/False. Fluorescent lights can cause electrical interference.

30. True/False. Category 5 UTP cable is specified up to 155Mbps.

31. What ohm terminator is used on both Thicknet and Thinnet networks?

_____

32. What might cause a terminator to become open or terminate at a higher voltage?

_____

33. You install a NIC and install the driver. The cable is secure, but the workstation is not communicating on the network. What could be the problem?

_____

34. List at least three items you should check if you are having problems with a Token Ring network.

_____

_____

_____

35. You have an Ethernet network. Utilization is constantly around 25 to 30 percent. What should you do?

_____

36. You have a cable company install UTP cable through your acoustic tile ceiling. The network has become intermittent (goes up and down). What could be the problem?

_____

37. Category 6 UTP cable is specified to run up to _____ Mbps.

38. You are running a Token Ring network and the utilization is always exceeding 50 percent. What should you do?

_____

39.   What is the maximum distance of your 10Base5 network?

_____

Resolving Broadcast Storms

40.   True/False. A broadcast storm is a large, sudden increase in network traffic.

41.   True/False. Broadcast storms are typically caused by poor administration of the network.

42.   Which tools can you use to help you locate the source of broadcast storms?

_____

43.   If you use a network tool to locate the source of a broadcast storm but cannot find the problem, what should you do?

_____

44.   What are the two most common reasons for broadcast storms?

_____

_____

45.   How do you stop broadcast storms from propagating throughout the network?

_____

Identifying and Resolving Network Performance Problems

46. What are two ways to protect against data loss due to hard drive failure?

_____

_____

47. True/False. Performance Monitor captures, filters, and analyzes frames and packets sent over a network segment.

48. When would you use a network monitor on your network?

_____

49. True/False. Each packet contains the source and destination of the logical address of the transmitting station.

50. True/False. Using a UPS system on your server guarantees your workstation will not lose any data.

51. When using Performance Monitor, you notice that the paging file (pages/sec) statistic is high. What should you do?

_____

52. True/False. Performance Monitor can determine if you have a slow hard disk.

53. Suppose that you're running the NetBEUI and/or NWLink protocol. Which three NetBEUI and NWLink IPX object counters should you monitor with Performance Monitor?

_____

_____

_____

54. For the Server object, what are two useful Performance Monitor counters to watch?

_____

_____

55. What does the Windows NT Diagnostics program (WinMSD) show?

_____

SAMPLE TEST

4-1 You just had a cable company install UTP category 5 cable through your acoustic tile ceiling. Now the network is intermittent (goes up and down). What could be the problem?

   A. Tie wraps are too tight

   B. The punch-down blocks are not the right specification

   C. The cable company ran the cables over fluorescent lights

   D. The NetWare server is causing the problem

4-2 Your Ethernet network is having broadcast storms. What can you do to resolve the problem?

   A. Install a switched hub

   B. Partition the network into two or more segments with a router

   C. Install fiber-optic cabling and 10BaseFL networking components (adapters, hubs, etc.)

   D. Check the Thinnet cable terminators

4-3 When trying to protect against data loss, what should you do? (Choose all that apply.)

   A. Install UPS systems on all important devices

   B. Install and use a tape backup unit

   C. Use data encryption

   D. Install a RAID system

4-4 Which cable tester can provide information about message frame counts, excess collisions, late collisions, error frame count, congestion errors, and beaconing?

   A. Advanced cable tester

   B. Time-domain reflectometer

   C. Oscilloscope

   D. Volt-ohm meter

4-5 You want to eliminate broadcast storms through your intranetwork. Which protocol will not work in this situation?

    A. NWLink

    B. TCP/IP

    C. NetBEUI

    D. DLC

4-6 Which of the following tasks cannot be performed with a protocol analyzer?

    A. Packet-level analysis

    B. Time-based monitoring

    C. Creation of network activity logs

    D. Protocol reconfiguration

4-7 When should you use a time-domain reflectometer?

    A. When installing network protocols

    B. When analyzing your network at the packet level

    C. When trying to identify faulty network cables

    D. When changing IRQ settings

4-8 What is the term used to describe when computers timeout on the network because all the broadcasts are taking up all the bandwidth?

    A. A broadcast storm

    B. A massive broadcast

    C. Crosstalk

    D. Beaconing

SAMPLE TEST

4-9   You need to test the network to see if there are problems without shutting down the network. Which of the following devices can help you do this?

    A. Advanced cable tester

    B. Time-domain reflectometer

    C. Protocol analyzer

    D. Voltmeter

4-10   When should you use a router? (Choose all that apply.)

    A. When you want to transmit packets through a large internetwork

    B. When you want to manage flow control

    C. When you want to manage broadcasts

    D. When you want to multiplex

4-11   Which dial-up protocol cannot provide automatic IP addressing?

    A. DLC

    B. SLIP

    C. SMB

    D. PPP

4-12   Which of the following devices can you use to examine packets captured on the network?

    A. SNMP management interface

    B. Protocol analyzer

    C. Time-domain reflectometer

    D. Advanced cable tester

SAMPLE TEST

4-13 You are running Windows 95 and you want to make sure that a NIC does not have a resource conflict. Which tool can you use?

    A. Device Manager

    B. Protocol analyzer

    C. Performance Monitor

    D. None of the above

4-14 Your Windows 95 computer is not communicating with the NetWare server on your network. Which of the following probably needs to be reconfigured?

    A. The protocol stack

    B. The frame type on the client machine

    C. The frame bindings on the client

    D. The frame bindings on the server

4-15 Which of the following devices would determine which station on a network is broadcasting jabber packets?

    A. A time-domain reflectometer

    B. A digital voltmeter

    C. A protocol analyzer

    D. A terminator

SAMPLE TEST

4-16   You install a NIC in your computer and then notice that the CD-ROM has stopped working. Which of the following is most likely the cause of the problem?

A. There is a memory error

B. The wrong bus slot is being used

C. The NIC is using bus mastering

D. There is an IRQ or I/O setting conflict

4-17   You want to see if there is a short on each of the conductors in a twisted-pair cable by using a volt-ohm meter. Which of the following settings should you use?

A. Resistance measured in ohms

B. Impedance measured in ohms

C. Voltage measured in volts

D. Voltages divided by resistance

4-18   You just put a new NIC in your PC, but the operating system does not detect the card. Which of the following is the most likely cause of the problem?

A. Incorrect MAC address

B. Incorrect IRQ setting

C. Incorrect protocol setting

D. Incorrect transceiver setting

SAMPLE TEST

4-19   You have just been hired as an administrator and are asked to solve problems that have come up since the previous administrator had new category 5 UTP cable installed. Only one of the four new computers installed in the sales department works. The four computers are located in the back of the building. Computer A is located 520 feet from the hub. Computer B is located 650 feet from the hub. Computer C is located 480 feet from the hub. Computer D is located 275 feet from the hub. What could be the problem? (Choose all that apply.)

    A. The distance from computer A to the hub exceeds the maximum cable length specified for 10BaseT.

    B. The distance from computer B to the hub exceeds the maximum cable length specified for 10BaseT.

    C. The distance from computer C to the hub exceeds the maximum cable length specified for 10BaseT.

    D. The distance from computer D to the hub exceeds the maximum cable length specified for 10BaseT.

4-20   You want to replace your old Windows NT Server computer with new hardware. Which tools can you use to gather performance data for your new server? (Choose all that apply.)

    A. TDR

    B. Spread-spectrum

    C. Network monitor

    D. Windows NT Performance Monitor

4-21 Which of the following statements about network troubleshooting are true? (Choose all that apply.)

    A. Advanced cable testers can be used to identify a wide range of problems including congestion errors and beaconing

    B. Most network problems occur at the Physical layer of the OSI model

    C. Network monitors work at the Physical layer because that is where most network problems occur

    D. Windows NT Performance Monitor can be used to identify trends over time and establish a baseline for troubleshooting

4-22 Which of the following can an administrator use to gather information about different system components and functions? (Choose all that apply.)

    A. Task Manager

    B. Performance Monitor

    C. SNMP

    D. SMS

4-23 What is the problem with having a high number of broadcasts on your network?

    A. Broadcast messages are processed by every computer on the network

    B. Broadcast messages are automatically routed to every LAN segment

    C. Routers send broadcasts to all network segments

    D. Broadcast messages require acknowledgment packets from every computer on the network

4-24   Your PC cannot communicate on the network, but all the other computers can. Which of the following is most likely the cause of the problem?

    A. Faulty cable terminator

    B. The server is down

    C. A bad NIC in your PC

    D. A faulty hub

4-25   Which tools can you use to view the contents of network packets?

    A. Protocol analyzer

    B. TDR

    C. Packet generator

    D. Oscilloscope

UNIT

5

Final Review

FINAL REVIEW

Do you think you're ready for the exam yet? Here's a good way to find out. Grab your watch and take note of the time. The real exam will have 58 questions with a 90-minute time limit. Here are 58 questions. Get ready, get set, GO!

1.   Which of the following devices work at the Data Link layer of the OSI reference model?

   A. Routers

   B. Bridges

   C. Repeaters

   D. Gateways

2.   Which device resides at the center of a star network and links all of the network cables together?

   A. Hub

   B. Bridge

   C. Network adapter

   D. Server

3.   You must run an Ethernet network cable between two buildings. The buildings are 350 meters apart. Which Ethernet cable types can you use? (Choose all that apply.)

   A. 10BaseT

   B. 10Base2

   C. 10Base5

   D. 10BaseFL

4. Which device does not electrically regenerate the network signal?

    A. Passive hub

    B. Active hub

    C. Intelligent hub

    D. Repeater

5. Which of the following ISDN service levels provides the greatest bandwidth?

    A. A single ISDN B channel

    B. 2B+D

    C. Basic Rate ISDN service

    D. Primary Rate ISDN service

6. You want to join two Ethernet segments together so that network broadcasts and cross-segment traffic pass between segments but network traffic within a segment does not. Which device should you use?

    A. Hub

    B. Bridge

    C. Router

    D. Gateway

7. What does a time-domain reflectometer allow you to do?

    A. Install network protocols

    B. Analyze your network at the packet level

    C. Identify faulty network cables

    D. Change IRQ settings

8.   You would like to send Ethernet, Token Ring, and telephone signals over the same cable. Which device can you use to do this?

   A. Hub

   B. Router

   C. Multiplexer

   D. Gateway

9.   What is the difference between a router and a brouter?

   A. A brouter routinely broadcasts routing information

   B. A brouter is a basic functionality router

   C. A brouter can function as a bridge as well as a router

   D. A brouter is a router that routes signals on broadband networks

10.   What can you do to resolve broadcast storms on an Ethernet Thinnet network?

   A. Install a switched hub

   B. Partition the network into two or more segments with a router

   C. Install fiber-optic cabling and 10BaseFL networking components (adapters, hubs, etc.)

   D. Check the Thinnet termination

11.   How do routers build route maps that will help determine possible routes through an internetwork?

   A. They use network mapping

   B. They use route discovery

   C. They use end-node search

   D. They use path search

12. Which protocols are used to connect to the Internet over dial-up lines? (Choose all that apply.)

    A. SLIP

    B. Token Ring

    C. PPP

    D. FDDI

13. You need to install a WAN that connects three offices: one in New York, one in Los Angeles, and one in San Francisco.

Required Result: Each site must be able to communicate with each other.

Desired Result: Connections must be 1Mbps or greater, and communications between all sites must continue even if one WAN line fails.

Solution: Connect New York to Los Angeles with a T1, connect Los Angeles to San Francisco with a T1, and connect San Francisco to New York with a T1.

    A. The solution meets the required result and both of the desired results

    B. The solution meets the required result and one of the desired results

    C. The solution meets the required result but neither of the desired results

    D. The solution does not work and does not meet the required results

14. Which of the following are problems that can afflict twisted-pair networks? (Choose all that apply.)

    A. Crosstalk

    B. Dispersion

    C. Electromagnetic interference

    D. Improper termination

15.   Which troubleshooting device would you use to determine which station on a network is broadcasting jabber packets? (Choose the most correct answer.)

    A. A time-domain reflectometer

    B. A digital voltmeter

    C. A protocol analyzer

    D. A terminator

16.   What does T1 technology offer? (Choose all that apply.)

    A. Transmission speeds up to 1.544Mbps

    B. Transmission speeds up to 45Mbps

    C. Point-to-point, full-duplex transmission

    D. Two 64Kbps B channels and one 16Kbps D channel per line

17.   You are installing an Ethernet 10Base5 network. Which type of cable will you use?

    A. Twisted-pair

    B. Thinnet coax

    C. Thicknet coax

    D. Fiber-optic

18.   What do you use to connect a transceiver to the conductor of a Thicknet (10Base5) cable?

    A. A terminating resistor

    B. A DIX connector

    C. A BNC T connector

    D. A vampire tap

19. How many repeaters can you place in series in a 10Base5 or 10Base2 network?

    A. Two

    B. Three

    C. Four

    D. Five

20. LocalTalk uses which of the following media-access control protocols?

    A. CSMA/CD

    B. CSMA/CA

    C. Token passing

    D. Time-division multiplexing

21. Your network has grown to encompass 153 computers. You provide SQL database service, e-mail exchange through the Internet, and network printing, as well as centralized file storage on your network. You would like to optimize the performance of your network. What kind of network best fits your needs?

    A. Peer

    B. Single-server

    C. Multi-server

    D. Enterprise

22. You must run the same protocol on your LAN and WAN. Which of the following protocols allows you to do this?

    A. ISDN

    B. X.25

    C. ATM

    D. Frame Relay

23. Which TCP/IP setting must be unique for each computer on the network?

    A. Default gateway

    B. IP address

    C. Network address

    D. Subnet mask

24. How many print drivers do you need to install on your computer if you have three different printers on your network?

    A. One

    B. Two

    C. Three

    D. None

25. Which of the following computing models has one or more computers do the processing and returns the results to a client PC?

    A. Centralized computing

    B. Client computing with central file storage

    C. Client-server computing

    D. Stand-alone computing

26. Which of the following protocols uses cells instead of packets?

    A. Token Ring

    B. Frame Relay

    C. ATM

    D. ISDN

27. You must link together 60 computers on four floors of an office building. What kind of network should you install?

    A. LAN

    B. WAN

    C. MAN

    D. CAN

28. Which of the following network topologies is the slowest?

    A. Spread-spectrum

    B. Microwave

    C. Low-power, single-frequency

    D. Infrared

29. You need file, print, message, database, and application services on your 420-computer network. How many servers do you need?

    A. One

    B. Two

    C. Three

    D. Four

30. You must connect five computers together in the same room as cheaply as possible. Which topology should you use?

   A. Bus

   B. Star

   C. Ring

   D. Mesh

31. You need to install a high-speed connection between your two offices. The only connection is electric power poles that run for over 1000 feet. Which media should you use?

   A. Twisted-pair cable

   B. Fiber-optic cable

   C. Microwave

   D. Copper

32. Which RF technology best copes with EMI?

   A. Low-power, single-frequency

   B. High-power, single-frequency

   C. Spread-spectrum

   D. Encrypted

33. Your network device driver cannot find your network adapter. Your adapter is set to IRQ 4 and port 320. You are using the twisted-pair transceiver of the card. What is the problem?

   A. The network cable is improperly terminated

   B. The first serial port (COM1) is conflicting with the adapter's interrupt setting

   C. The floating-point processor is conflicting with the adapter's interrupt setting

   D. There is another adapter in the network with the same Ethernet MAC address

34. At which layer of the OSI reference model are MAC addresses defined?

    A. Physical

    B. Data Link

    C. Network

    D. Transport

35. What is the specification for Ethernet over fiber-optic cable?

    A. 802.1

    B. 802.5

    C. 802.8

    D. 802.12

36. Which of the following specifications allow several network protocols to run simultaneously on one NIC? (Choose all that apply.)

    A. NDIS

    B. ODI

    C. OSI

    D. TCP/IP

37. Which network protocols cannot be routed? (Choose all that apply.)

    A. NetBEUI

    B. NWLink

    C. TCP/IP

    D. X.25

38. Which protocol is loaded when you install Services for Macintosh on your Windows NT Server?

    A. NetBEUI

    B. NWLink

    C. TCP/IP

    D. AppleTalk

39. You plan a network that will span several cities and cross state boundaries. Which protocol best fits this kind of network?

    A. NetBEUI

    B. NWLink

    C. TCP/IP

    D. DLC

40. You want to upgrade your computer but have several older DOS programs that are essential in running your business. Which operating system should you choose?

    A. MS-DOS

    B. Windows 95

    C. Windows NT Workstation

    D. Unix

41. Which piece of hardware must you install for your PC to communicate on a LAN?

    A. Network device driver

    B. Network interface adapter

    C. Networking protocol stack

    D. Network client software

42. Which of the following protocols can you use to connect Windows 95 to a file server? (Choose all that apply.)

    A. TCP/IP

    B. NWLink (IPX/SPX)

    C. NetBEUI

    D. DLC

43. Which address must be unique on each NIC on your network?

    A. Subnet mask

    B. MAC address

    C. Transceiver setting

    D. Frame type

44. You want a second NIC in your Windows NT Server computer. That computer has been working for two months with one NIC installed. When you install the second NIC, neither NIC will work. What is the problem?

    A. The adapters do not work because they are not the same type; they must be of the same type (such as both Ethernet or both Token Ring)

    B. The adapters do not work because they are the same type; they must be of different kinds (such as one Ethernet and one Token Ring)

    C. The adapters do not work because they do not each have a unique IRQ, DMA (if used), port, and/or MAC address; network adapters in a computer require these settings to be unique

    D. The adapters do not work because they are faulty—replace them

45. What is the definition of attenuation?

    A. Signal crossover in the wires

    B. Signal disruption from another wire

    C. Loss of signal strength as the data signal travels down the wire

    D. Gain in signal distortion as the data signal travels down the wire

46. Which of the following provides fault tolerance in Windows NT Server computers? (Choose all that apply.)

    A. Disk mirroring

    B. RAID Level 0 (disk striping)

    C. RAID Level 5 (disk striping with parity)

    D. Novell IntranetWare

47. What is the data-transfer rate of the B channel of Basic Rate ISDN service?

    A. 33.6Kbps

    B. 64Kbps or 56Kbps

    C. 128Kbps + 16Kbps

    D. 1.5Mbps

48. You set up RAS on your Windows NT Server computer. How many simultaneous incoming connections will RAS support on that server?

    A. 1

    B. 10

    C. 256

    D. 65,536

49.   Which device should you use to segment your network if you are using the IPX protocol?

    A. Router

    B. Gateway

    C. Time-domain reflectometer

    D. Hub

50.   You need to dynamically assign TCP/IP addresses to all the hosts on your network. Which service should you load on your Windows NT Server?

    A. DNS

    B. WINS

    C. DHCP

    D. IPConfig

51.   Which of the following devices runs at all seven layers of the OSI reference model?

    A. Router

    B. Bridge

    C. Repeater

    D. Gateway

52.   Which of the following devices works at the Network layer of the OSI reference model?

    A. Router

    B. Bridge

    C. Repeater

    D. Hub

53. You need to make sure that your clients can communicate with TCP/IP across subnets. Which configuration must you set on each client computer?

    A. Default gateway

    B. IP address

    C. Network address

    D. Subnet mask

54. Which of the following cable types is the least expensive?

    A. 10Base5

    B. 10Base2

    C. 10BaseT

    D. Fiber-optic

55. You wish to use a network topology that is easy to expand and troubleshoot. Which topology should you use?

    A. Bus

    B. Star

    C. Ring

    D. Mesh

The next three questions use the following scenario:

Situation: You need to design a network with the following business requirements:

- Ten users are located on the same floor of an office building, and they are less than 100 meters apart.

- No dedicated network wiring is installed in the building.

- The telephone wire is category 3, with open pairs that can be used.

- The users need to share files and printers.

- All the users use Windows 95 and do not want a file server.

- You have a very limited amount of money.

56. Which network operating system should you use?

    A. Windows NT

    B. Novell NetWare

    C. Windows 95 peer-to-peer

    D. LANtastic peer-to-peer

57. Which network cabling scheme should you choose?

    A. Twisted-pair

    B. Coax

    C. Wireless

    D. Infrared

58.   Which type of network equipment should you buy?

A. Hub

B. Router

C. Bridge

D. Transmitter

APPENDIX

Study Question and
Sample Test Answers

Unit 1 Answers

Study Questions

Defining Networking Terms

1. A network is defined as a group of interconnected computers that share resources and information.

2. False

   Explanation: Transmission media is the cabling or wireless signal used in networks. Also, typically, digital signaling is used rather than analog signaling.

3. Stand-alone

4. A group of computers interconnected within a building or campus.

5. WAN (wide area network)

6. Ethernet

7. Wide area network

8. Network topology is the physical cabling or transmitters on the network.

9. Telephone lines, fiber-optic cable, satellite, and microwave

10. Bus

11. All computers connected with a single cable with a terminator on each end

12. Ring

13. Star

14. Ring

15. A set of rules that allows computers to communicate

16. True

17. False

    Explanation: TCP/IP represents only two of the protocols in the Internet protocol suite.

18. IPX (Internetwork Packet eXchange)

19. NetBIOS Extended User Interface

20. HTTP (HyperText Transfer Protocol)

21. False

    Explanation: IBM created the NetBEUI protocol for use in small workgroups.

22. False

    Explanation: WINS (Windows Internet Name Service) is a network service for Microsoft networks that resolves NetBIOS names. *DNS (Domain Name Service)* is the service that translates Internet host names into IP addresses.

Comparing File, Print, and Application Servers

23. File service

24. Print service

25. One server

26. Spooling a job means that when a user sends a print job to the printer, the print server stores the job in a directory called a queue or spool. When the printer is available, the print server sends each print job in the spool to be printed. This allows the client to continue working without needing to stop and wait for the job to finish printing.

27. False

Explanation: Windows NT and NetWare print servers can run up to 255 printers.

28. False

Explanation: The print spooler runs on the print server.

29. True

30. True

Explanation: Even when running applications from a server, you still must have a license for every connection to the application. However, if you have 100 users, but only 50 users use the application at a time, you can buy a 50-user license.

31. False

Explanation: The SQL Server computer processes requests for a client. A file server does file storage.

32. When you want to offload processing from the clients

33. False

Explanation: Depending on your application, typically, the application server needs more power, memory, and storage.

34. File and print servers do not do processing for the client computers. Application servers offload work from the client by running programs for the client and sending the results back to the client.

Comparing Client-Server and Peer-to-Peer Networks

35. False

    Explanation: Clients request services from service *providers*.

36. Password-protected shares, also known as share-level security

37. The rule of thumb is around 10 computers.

38. Peer-to-peer

39. requestor

40. True

    Explanation: Dedicated servers run file, print, application, and other services. They do not request services from other service providers.

41. Peer

42. False

    Explanation: In a peer-to-peer network, *all* of the computers are equal and therefore are known as peers.

43. Client, server, and peer-to-peer combined

Comparing User-Level Security with Access Permissions

44. Share-level, file-level

45. True

46. Server-based

47. Share-level security

48. File-level security

49. True

50. False

Explanation: In share-level security, the user only needs to enter a password to gain access to a network resource. However, in file-level security, the user must be authenticated with both a user name and a password.

Comparing Connection-Oriented with Connectionless Communications

51. Connectionless

52. False

Explanation: Because connectionless methods do not guarantee delivery, they are *faster* than connection-oriented methods (which do guarantee delivery).

53. **IP:** Connectionless

    TCP: Connection-oriented

    SPX: Connection-oriented

    IPX: Connectionless

54. You cannot decide.

    Explanation: The *application developer* decides when and if to run connectionless and/or connection-oriented protocols.

Distinguishing between SLIP and PPP

55. Serial Line Internet Protocol

56. Point to Point Protocol

57. False

    Explanation: SLIP has *less* overhead than PPP.

58. True

    Explanation: SLIP can use only TCP/IP. PPP can use IPX, AppleTalk, and other protocols.

59. True

60. Login and password

Defining Communications at the OSI Model Levels

61. 7

62. Data Link

63. Router

64. Gateway

65. Data Link, MAC sublayer

66. Data Link, bridge

67. Physical

68. Data Link

69.

Layer	Function
Application	File, print, message, database, and application services
Presentation	Data translation
Session	Dialog control
Transport	End-to-end connection
Network	Routing
Data Link	Framing
Physical	Sending 1s/0s across the wire

70. Transport

71. Physical

72. Application

73. Physical

74. Data Link (MAC)

75. Gateway

76. Presentation

Defining the Media Used in IEEE 802.3 and IEEE 802.5 Standards

77. False

Explanation: Project 802 has that name because it was created in February 1980.

78. True

79. Logical Link Control

80. CSMA/CD

81. False

Explanation: 802.4 is known as Token *Bus* LAN.

82. False

Explanation: 802.5 is know as Token *Ring* LAN.

83. 802.6

84. True

85. Integrated Voice/Data Networks

86. False

Explanation: The 802.8 specifications are for the Fiber-Optic Technical Advisory Group.

87. 802.8

88. 802.10

89. True

90. 100BaseVG-AnyLAN

91. True

92. **CS (Carrier Sense):** Check the cable to see if there is a digital signal present before transmitting.

MA (Multiple Access): Every computer uses the same cable, or wire.

CD (Collision Detect): Detect collision, retransmit.

93. 10Base5 or Thicknet

94. 10Base2 or Thinnet

95. 100 meters, or 330 feet

96. 3, 5, and 6

97. Because it uses a *logical* ring

98. True and False!

Explanation: Token Ring can be faster than 10BaseT if it is running at 16Mbps. 10BaseT Ethernet is faster than 4Mbps Token Ring on small, bursty networks.

99. 4, 16

100. 5

101. Tokens

Explanation: Tokens are passed to each workstation. Only the workstation with the token can transmit data.

102. False

Explanation: *Unshielded* twisted-pair (UTP) is the most popular type of cable used for LANs.

103. 8 wires, or 4 pairs

104. Type 9

Understanding NDIS and Novell ODI Standards

105. Microsoft and 3Com in 1989

106. Apple and Novell in 1989

107. Data Link

108. Workstations can run multiple protocols with one network interface card.

Sample Test

1-1 A

Explanation: A LAN links computers in the same general location (such as an office building).

1-2 B

Explanation: Peer-to-peer networks are less expensive for small networks that do not require central administration.

1-3 B

Explanation: Server-based security requires a password and user name at logon and evaluates all share access on the basis of account information.

1-4 A

Explanation: One Windows NT Server computer can perform all of these roles in a small network.

1-5 A

Explanation: Termination is a Physical layer issue.

1-6 A

Explanation: Server-based or client-server networks provide central administration and data backup by locating all the files in one location.

1-7 C

Explanation: A router operates at the Network layer of the OSI reference model.

1-8 C

Explanation: The Fiber-Optic Technical Advisory Group produced 802.8.

1-9 B

Explanation: The MAC sublayer of the Data Link layer is responsible for bridging.

1-10   A, B

Explanation: NDIS and ODI allow one adapter to be used with many network protocols, and vice versa.

1-11   B

Explanation: UDP is a faster protocol because it is not required to guarantee reliable or in-order delivery of datagrams, nor does it require an acknowledgment.

1-12   B

Explanation: A WAN links computers that are geographically separated.

1-13   B, C, D

Explanation: Token Ring, ARCnet, and FDDI use token-passing media access.

1-14   A

Explanation: The Physical layer is concerned with sending ones and zeros (1s and 0s) and synchronizing bits between hosts.

1-15   A

Explanation: Peer-to-peer networks are the least expensive solution and are appropriate for small networks that do not require centralized user administration.

1-16   B

Explanation: Single-server or client-server networks centralize administration and backup and provide cost-effective support for networks from 10 to 50 computers.

1-17   A

Explanation: If you are putting together a network linking a floor or floors of a building, you are installing a LAN. This could also be considered multiple LANs or subnets.

1-18   B

Explanation: By itself, Windows 95 supports only share-level security. For user-level security, you must have a Windows NT or NetWare server on the network.

1-19 B

Explanation: The MAC address is a responsibility of the LLC (Logical Link Control) sublayer, which is a part of the Data Link layer.

1-20 D

Explanation: PPP provides error checking for each and every frame transmitted. This means that PPP has more overhead than SLIP and therefore is slower than SLIP.

1-21 C, D

Explanation: WINS resolves NetBIOS names to IP addresses dynamically. However, it also allows you to put static NetBIOS addresses in the WINS database.

1-22 A

Explanation: NetBEUI (NetBIOS Extended User Interface) was created by IBM and Microsoft as an interface for OS/2. Microsoft used it for Windows NT. However, Windows NT 5 will see the end of the NetBIOS interface. The Winsock interface, which is much more efficient, will be the standard.

1-23 C

Explanation: DNS (Domain Name Service) is a static database of host names to IP addresses. Dynamic DNS will be the standard in Windows NT 5.

1-24 A

Explanation: The Physical layer is responsible for the specification of the physical topology, which includes the cabling.

1-25 C

Explanation: A hybrid network combines features of server-based networks (which provide central administration and data backup) and features of peer-to-peer networks (which allow users to share files and peripherals from their own computers).

1-26 B

Explanation: FDDI is physical ring, and the signal passes through each computer in the ring.

1-27 D

Explanation: The Application layer is responsible for file, print, application, message, and database services.

1-28 B, C, D

Explanation: Switches, intelligent hubs, and bridges function at the MAC sublayer of the Data Link layer. Multiplexers work at the Physical layer.

1-29 D

Explanation: Both UDP and TCP are specified at the Transport layer of the OSI reference model.

1-30 C

Explanation: Ethernet uses CSMA/CD. The CD stands for "collision detect."

1-31 C

Explanation: You must have a 50-ohm terminator on both ends of the network, or the network will be either very intermittent or will not work at all.

1-32 A

Explanation: 10Base5 stands for 10Mbps, baseband technology at 500 meters.

1-33 B

Explanation: There can only be one token on any given ring at one time.

1-34 C

Explanation: HTTP (HyperText Transfer Protocol) is the method by which Web pages are transmitted.

1-35 A

Explanation: In a physical star network, each computer can talk one at a time, so logically it runs like a bus.

1-36 D

Explanation: Password-supported shares, also called share-level security, is the type supported by Windows for Workgroups.

1-37 D

Explanation: File-level access networks have passwords for users and permissions for resources.

1-38 C

Explanation: SLIP does not support dynamic host configuration.

1-39 B

Explanation: The Data Link layer has two sublayers: MAC and LLC.

1-40 C

Explanation: Windows 95 uses peer-to-peer networking.

1-41 D

Explanation: Token Ring uses a physical star network, but because of the way the signal travels (logical ring), it is called Token Ring.

1-42 C

Explanation: The Network layer is responsible for creating packets (also referred to as *datagrams*).

1-43 D

Explanation: IBM created the MSAU (Multi-station Access Unit), also called an MAU.

1-44   B

Explanation: The MAC sublayer of the Data Link layer is concerned with framing.

1-45   C

Explanation: A Thinnet network can travel up to 185 meters between nodes without repeaters.

Unit 2 Answers

Study Questions

Selecting the Appropriate Media

1. Twisted-pair, coax, and fiber-optic

2. Coax and twisted-pair

3. False

   Explanation: Even though speeds in wireless networks are improving, they are still far behind the speeds of bounded media.

4. Bandwidth is the difference between the highest and lowest frequencies in a given range. The greater the bandwidth, the faster the data-transfer capabilities.

5. 4Mbps or 16Mbps

6. False

   Explanation: Broadband allows multiple channels to be present on the cable media at one time.

7. True

8. 10Mbps

9. Baseband

10. False

    Explanation: Multiplexing allows many frequencies to transmit over the media at one time.

11. Multiplexer (mux), Physical

12. Attenuation is the loss of signal as it goes down the transmission medium, measured in decibels.

13. EMI (electromagnetic interference) is electrical background noise that disturbs or distorts a signal as it travels down the transmission media.

14. Crosstalk is a form of EMI that is caused by wires next to each other interfering with the signals as they travel through the transmission media.

15. The twists in twisted-pair cable decrease crosstalk because the radiated signals from the twisted wires tend to cancel each other out.

16. False

    Explanation: The three cable types are coax, twisted-pair, and fiber-optic.

17. True

18. **UTP:** 1024

    STP: 270

    Thinnet: 30

    Thicknet: 100

    Fiber-optic: No limit

19. False

20. True

21. **UTP:** 100 meters

    STP: 100 meters

    Thinnet: 185 meters

    Thicknet: 500 meters

    Fiber-optic: 20 kilometers

22. Fiber-optic

23. **UTP:** 10 or 100Mbps

    STP: 4 or 16Mbps

    Thinnet: 10Mbps

    Thicknet: 10Mbps

    Fiber-optic: 100Mbps

24. UTP

25.

Category type	Use
Category 1	Voice grade; very low data rates
Category 2	Voice grade; very low data rates
Category 3	Up to 10Mbps; four twisted pairs
Category 4	Up to 16Mbps; four twisted pairs
Category 5	Up to 100Mbps; four twisted pairs
Category 6	Up to 155Mbps; four twisted pairs

26. False

    Explanation: STP only adds shielding from interference. It cannot run at faster data rates.

27. STP has more protection (the shielding) from interference.

28. False

29. Coax has two conductors that share the same axis.

30. 10Base5

31. 10Base2

32. Cable TV

33. False

34. ARCnet

35. 93

36. True

37. Thicknet

38. 50

39. 2.5Mbps

40. Cladding is a layer of glass that reflects the light back into the core. It surrounds the inner core.

41. False

42. False

Explanation: Fiber-optic cable can only transmit digital signals.

43. True

44. Installation and costs

45. RJ-45

46. Radio, microwave, and infrared

47. If you cannot wire into an area or if you have users who move around a lot

48. Low-power, single-frequency; high-power, single-frequency; and spread-spectrum

49. False

Explanation: High-power, single-frequency can go farther distances and through objects, but the data rates are the same.

50. **Low-power, single-frequency:** 2–10Mbps

    High-power, single frequency: 2–10Mbps

    Spread-spectrum: 2–6Mbps

    Microwave: 2–10Mbps

    Infrared: 115Kbps–2Mbps

51. True and False

    Explanation: The maximum distance of microwave transmissions depends on the power used in the transmitters, but it can also be affected by bad weather.

52. 10KHz to 1GHz

53. True

54. chips

55. True

56. False

    Explanation: Microwave transmissions use line-of-sight transmissions. However, you can put repeaters on buildings and mountains that can help transmissions go over mountains and around corners

57. Terrestrial and satellite

58. 22,300

59. Parabolic

60. You would use satellite transmission for locations that wires cannot reach. You also would use satellite transmission if you have many, many locations worldwide.

61. LED (light-emitting diode) and ILD (interjection-laser diode)

62. Photodiode

63. True

Selecting the Appropriate Topology

64. The physical topology is the actual cable layout. The logical topology is the signal path throughout the physical topology.

65. True

66. True

67. True

68. False

Explanation: In a ring topology, each computer is connected to the next computer, with the last one connected to the first.

69. False

70. 10BaseT and Token Ring

71. True

72. Tree or hierarchical

73. bus

74. Active hubs regenerate or amplify the signal.

75. An intelligent hub has a management card that has an IP address.

76. True

77. False

Explanation: You can have 5 segments with 4 repeaters and only 3 segments populated.

78. Hybrid mesh networks have some redundant links rather than all redundant links.

Selecting the Appropriate Protocols

79. False

80. False

81. SMB (Server Message Blocks)

82. AppleTalk

83. NetBEUI

84. NFS (Network File System)

85. TDI (Transport Driver Interface) is an interface that enables the server, redirector, and file system drivers to remain independent of the transport protocol.

86. True

87. Network Driver Interface Standard

88. False

89. ARP (Address Resolution Protocol) is used when a host knows the destination IP address but not the hardware address of the destination computer.

90. RIP (Routing Information Protocol) and OSPF (Open Shortest Path First) are routing protocols that can find and select the best routes for routing packets through an internetwork.

91. True

92. Transport

93. File transfer

94. False

    Explanation: SMTP (Simple Mail Transfer Protocol) is used to transfer mail between mail servers or hosts.

95. File transfer in Unix hosts

96. True

97. NWLink

98. True

99. True

100. NCP (NetWare Core Protocol)

101. NetBIOS Extended User Interface

102. It has low overhead.

103. False

104. False

105. NetBEUI can exist with other protocols on the same network because of the NDIS standards.

106. When running NetBEUI, you can divide your network into segments by using bridges.

107. AppleTalk

108. TokenTalk

109. AppleShare

110. AFP (AppleTalk Filing Protocol)

111. ATP (AppleTalk Transaction Protocol)

112. False

113. DLC (Data Link Control)

Selecting the Appropriate Connectivity Devices

114. Either a bridge or a router will work, depending on the type and the cost.

115. A repeater is the least expensive way to connect two computers together that are 400 feet apart.

116. You have reached the maximum allowed with repeaters. You need to either bridge or route at this point.

117. Amplifiers and signal-regenerating repeaters

118. Bridge

119. Signal-regenerating repeater

120. Data Link

121. Network

122. Router

123. Hardware or MAC addressing

124. Router

125. Dynamic and static

126. Routers use logical addressing to route packets. Brouters can perform both routing and bridging. A brouter is typically a router with bridging software.

127. Gateways interpret and translate the different protocols that are used on two different types of networks.

128. All seven layers

Selecting WAN Connection Services

129. True

130. False

131. Encoding or modulating

132. Public Switched Telephone Network

133. ISDN (Integrated Services Digital Network)

134. X.25

135. ATM (Asynchronous Transfer Mode)

136. Physical through Network layers

137. LAPB (Link Access Procedures-Balanced) is a full-duplex, bit-oriented, synchronous clocking protocol.

138. X.25 is slower than the other WAN connection services.

139. ATM

140. ISDN

141. Two basic data channels and one management channel

142. ATM

143. Frame Relay uses the upper-layer protocols for error corrections, so it assumes a lower error rate.

144. 53-byte cells with a 5-byte header

145. 28

146. 1.544Mbps

147. 44.736Mbps

148. True

149. 56Kbps

Sample Test

2-1   A

> **Explanation:** The bus topology is the least expensive to install, especially for small networks.

2-2   B

> **Explanation:** Glass (fiber-optic cable) is immune to interference and supports high data rates.

2-3   B

> **Explanation:** Standard Token Ring specifies STP cable.

2-4   C

> **Explanation:** You must be running TCP/IP on the outside network interface card. However, you do not need to run TCP/IP on the inside card.

2-5 A

Explanation: A plenum cable is rated to produce a minimum of carcinogens and other poisons when burned.

2-6 C

Explanation: A repeater allows you to connect two network segments together.

2-7 C

Explanation: High-powered electrical devices can interfere with copper cabling.

2-8 B

Explanation: Star networks are the easiest to expand and troubleshoot.

2-9 B, C, D

Explanation: Fiber-optic cables are not significantly affected by attenuation (although they are still subject to some attenuation, like all cable types), EMI (electromagnetic interference), or crosstalk.

2-10 C, D

Explanation: Modern UTP and STP cable lengths should not exceed 100 meters for best performance.

2-11 C

Explanation: Spread-spectrum hops frequencies to achieve greater resistance to interference.

2-12 C

Explanation: TCP/IP is used to transfer packets through an intranetwork or the Internet.

2-13 C

Explanation: Ring networks commonly use token passing to guarantee fair access to the network and to avoid loss of service due to excessive collisions.

2-14   D

Explanation: Fiber-optic cables can support gigabit data-transfer rates.

2-15   A

Explanation: Much of NetBEUI's speed comes from the simplicity of the protocol.

2-16   A

Explanation: Distance-vector routing can result in excessive network broadcasts.

2-17   B

Explanation: Electrical signals on copper cables experience attenuation at longer distances.

2-18   A

Explanation: UTP category 5 cable is the least expensive type of cable that supports 100Mbps data rates.

2-19   D

Explanation: Primary rate (PRI) service provides dial-up bandwidth almost as great as T1.

2-20   D

Explanation: AppleTalk is the protocol developed by Apple for Macintosh network communications.

2-21   A

Explanation: The hub links the network cables and rebroadcasts received network communications so that all of the computers on the network can communicate.

2-22   A, B, C

Explanation: ATM has been specified to be encapsulated in FDDI, SONET, and T3, among other data-link implementations.

2-23 B

Explanation: NWLink is Microsoft's implementation of IPX/SPX, which is the native protocol of NetWare.

2-24 B

Explanation: Routers use a route-discovery algorithm to determine possible routes through the internetwork.

2-25 A

Explanation: Passive hubs do not regenerate a network signal.

2-26 D

Explanation: Redundant links are a characteristic of mesh networks.

2-27 C

Explanation: In order to be able to provide guaranteed quality of service, ATM divides data into 53-byte cells.

2-28 C

Explanation: DLC (Data Link Control) is used mostly to connect to HP Jet Direct cards, and also to connect from Windows workstations to IBM mainframes.

2-29 B

Explanation: A bridge will transfer broadcasts or communications meant for a station on the other side of a network segment.

2-30 A

Explanation: NetBEUI cannot be routed; it can only be bridged.

2-31 C, D

Explanation: Infrared and radio are quick to set up and allow you to get to hard-to-cable places.

2-32 C

Explanation: A brouter can bridge networks as well as route between them.

2-33 A, B, C, D

Explanation: A router can route data over almost any data-link type.

2-34 A, B, C, D

Explanation: All of the network types listed can be implemented over fiber-optic cable.

2-35 D

Explanation: Broadband transmission allows multiple signals on the wire at the same time, both digital and analog. Baseband (which is used in almost all LANs) can have only one signal present at a time, and it uses only digital signaling.

2-36 B

Explanation: NWLink (IPX) is both routable and self-addressable; TCP/IP is not.

2-37 A, C

Explanation: Both X.25 and ATM establish virtual circuits between communicating end stations. X.25 routes variable-sized packets along the virtual circuit, and ATM routes fixed-sized cells.

2-38 C

Explanation: NetBEUI is not a routable protocol, so if you are experiencing broadcast storms on a network that uses NetBEUI, you should consider using another protocol, such as NWLink or TCP/IP.

2-39 C

Explanation: A multiplexer (or *mux*) allows you to send several different signals over the same network cable.

2-40 A, C

Explanation: SLIP and PPP are serial communications protocols that are used to connect clients to the Internet over telephone lines.

2-41 B

Explanation: Switched 56 leased-line service provides you with more bandwidth than regular analog modems at a price less than the cost of a full T1 leased line.

2-42 D

Explanation: Fiber-optic cables support the highest data rates.

2-43 C

Explanation: X.25 is a robust protocol that establishes dedicated and switched circuits between communicating devices.

2-44 C

Explanation: A gateway can translate between different network environments such as that of NetWare servers and Windows NT domains.

2-45 C

Explanation: PPP is a logical-link layer protocol that can support TCP/IP, NWLink, or NetBEUI.

2-46 B

Explanation: An ISDN telephone line is a digital line that you can use to dial-up and establish a connection over the telephone company's network of telephone lines.

2-47 A, B

Explanation: Fiber-optic cable can be affected by chromatic dispersion, when different wavelengths of light travel through glass differently. Also, although fiber-optic cable has much lower attenuation than copper media, it is still subject to some degree of attenuation.

2-48 A, C, D

Explanation: ATM, FDDI, and 100BaseFX can support the data rates that you require.

2-49 A

Explanation: NetBEUI is a fast protocol for small, nonrouted networks.

2-50 B

Explanation: An active hub amplifies the network signal but does not otherwise interpret the signal.

2-51 C

Explanation: SONET is a high-speed protocol that can be used to transfer data between two points at speeds of greater than 1Gbps.

2-52 A, C

2-53 A

Explanation: Ethernet networks use a logical bus topology, which is cheap and easy to install and upgrade.

2-54 B

Explanation: Glass does not suffer from interference.

2-55 B

Explanation: The specification for true IBM cable is STP.

2-56 A, B, C

Explanation: Gateways and routers are expensive pieces of equipment; they cost considerably more than most hubs.

2-57 C

Explanation: SNMP (Simple Network Management Protocol) is part of the TCP/IP suite of protocols.

2-58 C, D

Explanation: You need to use a wireless network, either low-power or high-power, single-frequency radio or infrared.

2-59 A

Explanation: Category 6 UTP cable is specified to 155Mbps.

2-60 B

Explanation: All types of cable suffer from attenuation (loss of signal over distance, measured in decibels).

2-61 C

Explanation: Spread-spectrum transmits over two or more frequencies, which provides both security and redundancy.

2-62 D

Explanation: You must run the DLC protocol on your Windows NT servers to be able to communicate with the HP Jet Direct cards.

Unit 3 Answers

Study Questions

Choosing an Administrative Plan

1. Users, resources, sharing, and permissions

2. False

   Explanation: Almost any hardware can be a network resource.

3. Share-level and user-level

4. False

   Explanation: Share-level security is not as secure as user-level security.

5. Access Control List (ACL)

6. True

7. Administrator and Guest

8. User Manager

9. User Manager for Domains

10. True

11. Rights are permissions assigned to users and groups to control their access to resources.

12. True

13. True

14. Groups

15. True

16. True

17. Any four of the following:

Administrators

Domain Admins

Everyone

Domain Users

Power Users

Backup Operators

18. Local and global

19. False

Explanation: Global groups can go into local groups only.

20. True

21. False

Explanation: You cannot add users to or delete users from the Everyone group.

22. Local

Explanation: The Domain Admins group is global. Administrators is a local group.

23. False

Explanation: The purpose of the Backup Users group is to allow members of that group to back up files, without needing to be members of the Administrators group.

24. Access permissions, user-level security, and file-level security

25. False

    Explanation: Only NTFS partitions allow file-level security.

26. The easiest way to manage user-level security is to put users into groups.

27. User-level security

28. False

    Explanation: You can create shares on both FAT and NTFS partitions.

29. NTFS

30. An administrator adds user or group permissions to resources.

31. Share-level security is the easiest to administer.

32. False

    Explanation: When you are running only Windows 95, you can support only share-level security.

33. False

    Explanation: You can supply up to two passwords for Windows 95, but a password is not required.

34. Read-Only, Full Access, Depends on Password

35. Read, Write, and Delete permissions

36. You would give only Read-Only permissions to a share so that users could access files and subfolders but could not save files to the share or delete files.

37. Two passwords: one for Read-Only access and one for Full access.

38. You need a server that can support user-level security (Windows NT or NetWare). Windows 95 itself does not support user-level security.

39. Read-Only, Full Access, and Custom

40. **Read-Only:** Users can access files and subfolders but cannot save files to the share or delete files.

    Full Access: Users can read, write, and delete files.

    Custom: One or all of the privileges can be granted. The privileges are Read, Write, Create, List, Delete, Change File Attributes, and Change Permissions.

41. False

    Explanation: There is no such thing as Depends on User Name permissions.

42. False

    Explanation: You can easily share printers from any workstation or server.

43. False

    Explanation: In Windows 95, sharing is not turned on by default. However, sharing is turned on by default in Windows NT.

44. False

    Explanation: Almost any type of client can use a shared resource, including a printer.

Choosing a Disaster Recovery Plan

45. To prepare for disaster recovery, you should protect data and prepare for downtime.

46. Implement RAID technology and use UPS systems

47. Full backups perform a complete back up of all files. Incremental backups back up only the files that have been created or changed since the last full backup.

48. True

49. You would use a differential backup when you want to back up all data that has changed since the last full backup (without marking the files as backed up).

50. A centralized tape backup system is easy to manage.

51. You should have single tape units on each server and possibly a separate, redundant backup network.

52. False

Explanation: Backup tapes should be locked up, but they should be stored off site in case of a fire or other disaster.

53. A UPS (uninterruptible power supply) device supplies electricity to a system after a power failure. This can help the server or other devices to shut down properly.

54. False

Explanation: Windows NT comes with UPS software.

55. False

Explanation: This notification is actually part of the Windows NT operating system, not the UPS system.

56. Hard drive failure

57. Redundant Array of Independent Disks

58. Windows NT supports RAID Levels 0, 1, and 5.

59. **RAID Level 0:** Stripping without parity

RAID Level 1: Disk mirroring—two hard drives, one primary and one secondary that use the same controller card.

RAID Level 5: Striping with parity—uses three or more disks. One disk is used for parity information only.

60. RAID Level 5 requires a minimum of three disks.

61. Mirroring is two disks on one hard disk controller. Duplexing is one or more disks, each on its own hard disk controller.

62. True

Explanation: Disk duplexing is mirroring, except it mirrors disk sets rather than two disks on the same hard disk controller.

63. You might use redundant WAN links if you have a medium-size or large network that spans multiple sites.

Installing and Configuring Multiple Network Adapters

64. Network interface card

65. A NIC driver is the software that runs the hardware. It does framing of the data and relays the frame to the NIC to be sent out on the network.

66. Media access control

67. A MAC address is a hardware address that is 6 bytes long and burned into the NIC by the manufacturer.

68. You don't install MAC addresses. The manufacturers do this when they produce the card. However, the hardware (MAC) address can be overwritten with a software configuration.

69. The MAC layer is the bottom sublayer of the Data Link layer.

70. True

   Explanation: A NIC requires a driver to run it.

71. True

72. The NIC is responsible for transmitting ones and zeros from one computer to another.

73. You might put multiple NICs in a computer to segment your network or to put a computer in more than one network.

74. Remember to check to make sure that your resources are free and you do not have any conflicts.

75. Look in the Hardware Compatibility List (HAL).

76. ISA, EISA, MicroChannel, and PCI

77. False

   Explanation: IBM created MicroChannel.

78. ISA

79. PCI

80. False

81. BNC, AUI, and RJ-45

82. The Windows NT Diagnostics program, Resource tab

83. IRQ 2

84. LPT1

85. IRQs 10, 11, and 12

86. IRQ 10

87. True

Implementing a NetBIOS Naming Scheme

88. Network Basic Input/Output System

89. NetBIOS Extended User Interface

90. A NetBIOS name can be up to 15 characters.

91. NetBIOS is an application interface. NetBEUI is a nonroutable protocol.

92. The purpose of a NetBIOS name is to identify a computer and/or resources on the network.

93. False

Explanation: Computer names (NetBIOS names) must be unique on the *entire* network, regardless of your communication devices.

94. False

95. NetBEUI is not routable. Change to TCP/IP or NWLink.

96. It doesn't matter which protocol you run. You could use TCP/IP, NWLink, NetBEUI, AppleTalk, etc.

97. True

98. A NetBIOS computer name preceded by two backslashes, the share name of the resource, and optionally, the MS-DOS path of a file or directory located on the share

99. IBM and Microsoft

100. net use F: \\FSHQ\Shipping

Selecting the Appropriate Tools to Monitor Your Network

101. Any three of the following:

Performance Monitor

Network Monitor

Windows NT Diagnostics program

Event log

102. True

103. Any three of the following:

Monitor real-time and historical system performance

Identify trends over time

Identify bottlenecks

Monitor the effects of system configuration changes

Determine system capacity

Sample Test

3-1   A, B, C, D

Explanation: Printers, disk drives, and modems are some of the resources typically shared on a network. However, other types of devices, such as scanners, also can be shared.

3-2   C

Explanation: The networking protocol stack provides the means for the client software to establish communications sessions over the network.

3-3   A, B, D

Explanation: TCP/IP, NWLink, and NetBEUI are three networking protocol stacks that are commonly used in Microsoft networks.

3-4   C

Explanation: HOSTS is a local text file that contains a mapping of computer names to IP addresses. A HOSTS file maps DNS names to IP addresses (just like a DNS server does). An LMHOSTS file maps NetBIOS names to IP addresses (just like a WINS server does). However, HOSTS and LMHOSTS are not dynamic; each computer's HOSTS or LMHOSTS file must be updated anytime there is a change.

3-5   C

Explanation: You may give your computer a name of up to 15 characters.

3-6   C

Explanation: The MAC address uniquely identifies the network interface cards in the Ethernet collision domain. If two cards have the same MAC address, they will not be able to communicate on the network.

3-7   A, C

Explanation: The Administrator and the Guest accounts are created automatically when you install Windows NT Server.

3-8   C

Explanation: A renamed account retains all of the access permissions of the account but may be given a new account name and password.

3-9   A

3-10   B

Explanation: WINS and LMHOSTS files are used to resolve NetBIOS names to IP addresses. HOSTS files are used to resolve host names to IP addresses. If WINS or LMHOSTS cannot resolve the NetBIOS name, then you will receive an error, probably because the name is misspelled.

3-11   B

Explanation: Domain Admins have full administrative privileges on all computers in the domain.

3-12   B

Explanation: A UPS (uninterruptible power supply) will protect your file server from power loss and can be configured to tell the Windows NT server to broadcast that it will be shutting down.

3-13 B, C

Explanation: A tape backup unit records files on your hard drive and allows you to restore them if the files are deleted or if the hard drive fails.

3-14 A, C

Explanation: Windows NT Server must have the NWLink protocol and File and Print Services for NetWare installed to allow NetWare clients to access resources on that server.

3-15 C

Explanation: A user name in a Microsoft network may be up to 20 characters long.

3-16 B

Explanation: Broadcasts cannot cross routes to get to other subnets. WINS and/or LMHOSTS are necessary for a network with routers.

3-17 A, C

Explanation: Disk mirroring and RAID Level 5 provide redundancy so that in case one hard drive fails, the data can be reconstructed from the other drive(s).

3-18 C

Explanation: Regular external analog modems are connected to your computer via a serial cable.

3-19 D

Explanation: Each MAC address is six bytes long. Three bytes are purchased from the IEEE. The manufacturer then assigns the last three bytes.

3-20 A

Explanation: If you disable a user's account, when the employee returns, you can enable the account again.

3-21 B

Explanation: SMBs (Server Message Blocks) are standard formatted packets that contain instructions required by the Windows NT Server service. SMBs are passed to a transport layer like NetBEUI or NetBIOS over TCP/IP for transmission across a network link.

3-22 A, D

Explanation: Under Windows 95 and Windows for Workgroups 3.11, File Manager or Explorer provides you with the ability to assign a password for each shared resource. With Windows NT, all permissions are assigned to users and groups. When sharing a resource under Windows NT, you cannot specify an access password for that particular resource. Instead, you must specify the users and groups who can access the resource.

3-23 D

Explanation: After you enable Windows NT logon auditing, you can see a report of logon activities in the Security Log by using Windows NT's Event Viewer.

3-24 C

Explanation: You cannot have duplicate computer (NetBIOS) names on your Windows NT network. Only the first one to request registration with WINS will succeed; the other will be NAK'D (receive a negative acknowledgment). However, you can always ping an IP address of a host, because Ping.exe does not care about the computer name.

3-25 C

Explanation: By default, accounts you create are made members of the Users group. You can assign access privileges that everyone should have to the Users group.

3-26 B

Explanation: An incremental backup backs up files that were created or changed since the last normal or incremental backup. It marks files as having been backed up.

3-27   B, C

Explanation: User names may not contain the '+' character, and they must be unique. User names are not case-sensitive, and they may only contain up to 20 characters.

3-28   A

Explanation: RAID Level 0 is commonly known as disk striping and uses a disk file system called a *stripe set*. Data is divided into blocks and spread in a fixed order among all the disks in the array. Disk striping offers the best overall performance among all the Windows NT Server disk-management strategies. However, like volume sets, it does not provide fault tolerance. If any partition in the set fails, all the data is lost.

3-29   B

Explanation: The network interface card, or NIC, is the device that provides the physical connection to the network.

3-30   D

Explanation: User-level security allows you to grant access to Windows 95 resources for users and groups defined in a Windows NT domain security accounts database. When using this configuration under Windows 95, you can see the domain accounts and groups by clicking the Add Users button on the Sharing tab in the resource's Properties dialog box.

3-31   C

Explanation: RAID Level 5 is commonly known as disk striping with parity. It provides redundancy and can recover from one lost drive. However, RAID Level 5 will not recover if you lose the parity drive. Make sure to combine RAID technology with an effective backup system.

3-32   D

Explanation: As the administrator, you can use the account management utility (User Manager for Domains in Windows NT) to change or delete the password so that the user can log on and create a new password.

3-33   D

Explanation: If your IPX/SPX network uses more than one frame type, you will want to tell the driver which frame type to anticipate. You can specify a frame type for the IPX/SPX-compatible protocol by choosing the Advanced tab on its property sheet.

3-34   A, B, C

Explanation: You do not want to put too many stations on a segment or exceed cable specifications. However, gateways and routers are expensive pieces of equipment, and they cost considerably more than most hubs.

3-35   D

Explanation: If you do not have an LMHOSTS file and the WINS server becomes unavailable, you will not be able to browse any computers without generating a Net-BIOS broadcast. This is true even when the computer being queried is on the local subnet.

3-36   B, C, D

Explanation: SMS provides remote control and monitoring of client and server machines for troubleshooting, network monitoring, software distribution, and inventory management features.

3-37   B

Explanation: DHCP (Dynamic Host Configuration Protocol) is a mechanism that automates the assignment and reassignment of IP addresses to network computers.

3-38   A, C

Explanation: You must install NWLink (or any IPX compatible protocol) and the NetWare client software in order for the Windows 95 computers to communicate with NetWare servers.

Unit 4 Answers

Study Questions

Identifying Common Communication Errors

1. Any three of the following:

   Ping

   Tracert

   Nbtstat

   NSLookup

   ARP

   Route

2. The Windows NT event log keeps track of informational, warning, error, success audit, and failure audit events.

3. NetBEUI is not routable.

4. True

   Explanation: NWLink is a Windows NT transport protocol that can be used to connect to NetWare servers through Client Services for NetWare. However, you can run NWLink even if you do not have any Netware servers on your network. Windows NT can use NWLink to communicate between hosts.

5. TCP/IP is not self-addressing and is used to route packets through the Internet and an intranet.

6. The DLC protocol can be used to communicate with HP Jet Direct cards and IBM mainframes.

7. You would look in the event log for more information about a driver error.

8. NWLink and NetBEUI are self-addressing.

9. PPP has replaced SLIP.

10. SLIP cannot be configured to use IPX; therefore, the user cannot log in to a NetWare server.

11. SLIP does not dynamically assign IP addresses to hosts. The user must assign the correct IP address, subnet mask, default gateway, and DNS server (if available to the user's workstation).

12. The Server service failed to start. Check the event log for more information.

13. The Workstation service failed to start. Check the event log for more information.

14. DHCP

    Explanation: DHCP is a server service used to dynamically assign TCP/IP addresses to hosts. It can prevent duplicate IP addresses if used correctly.

15. If one computer cannot ping another, you should check the IP addresses, the subnet mask, the default gateway, and the protocol bindings.

16. NetBEUI is a not a routable protocol. You need to install a different protocol on computer B if you want the computers to be able to communicate.

17. Any two of the following:

    Dialing problems

    Connection problems

    Protocol problems

18. Remote Access Service

19. True

20. Any four of the following:

Invalid user accounts

No permissions

Wrong telephone number

Wrong modem cables

Incompatible modems

Call-waiting is not disabled

Poor telephone line quality

Windows NT Server is offline or down

Diagnosing and Resolving Common Connectivity Problems

21. A digital voltmeter (DVM)

22. True

23. The Physical layer

24. There are too many repeaters.

Explanation: Using the 5-4-3 rule for Thinnet networks, you can have five segments and four repeaters, and only three segments can be populated with computers.

25. An oscilloscope measures fluctuations in signal voltage.

26. The easiest way to troubleshoot a 10BaseT hub is to disconnect attached workstations one at a time.

27. You cannot connect dissimilar networks together with a repeater. The company will need to buy a bridge or a router.

28. True

29. True

30. False

Explanation: Category 6 is specified up to 155Mbps. Category 5 is specified up to 100Mbps.

31. A 50 ohm terminator

32. Electrical storms

33. You may have the wrong NIC driver installed. Also, there may be IRQ, MEM, or DMA address conflicts that could stop the workstation from communicating.

34. Any three of the following:

Check that the cables are connected to the MSAU correctly.

If you have MSAUs from different manufacturers, check that they are compatible.

If the MSAUs are active hubs, make sure that they have power.

Check that you have not installed a 4Mbps card into a 16Mbps network.

35. Segment your network.

Explanation: Ethernet can slow down when reaching a constant utilization of 25 to 30 percent.

36. The cable installer put the cables over the florescent lights. The cabling should be redone.

37. 155

38. Nothing

Explanation: Token Ring actually runs better at higher utilization percentages.

39. 500 meters

Resolving Broadcast Storms

40. True

41. False

Explanation: A bad NIC typically causes broadcast storms.

42. A protocol analyzer, such as Windows NT's Network Monitor, can help you find the source of broadcast storms.

43. Remove the computers from the network one at a time.

Explanation: You can continue disconnecting computers from the network until the broadcast storm stops. However, in a large network, this could be very difficult. A protocol analyzer will give you an IP or MAC address of the workstation that is broadcasting. If you have good documentation for your network, you should be able to find the computer that has that address.

44. The two most common reasons for broadcast storms are a bad NIC and a host looking for a different host that does not respond.

45. To stop broadcast storms from propagating throughout the network, isolate the network segment with routers.

Identifying and Resolving Network Performance Problems

46. Regular backups

RAID Level 1 or 5

47. False

Explanation: Performance Monitor shows statistics about network objects. Network Monitor is the tool that captures, filters, and analyzes frames and packets sent over a network segment.

48. You would use a network monitor when you need to do frame-level analysis and also need to check packet types and errors on the whole or just part of the network.

49. True

50. False

Explanation: To make sure that the workstation does not lose data, you need a UPS on that workstation also.

51. Increase the RAM in the systems.

52. True

53. Session Timeouts

Failures Link

Resource Local

54. Bytes Total/Sec

Sessions Errored Out

55. Windows NT Diagnostics shows computer hardware and operating system data that is stored in the system registry.

Sample Test

4-1   C

Explanation: Fluorescent lights can cause interference on UTP cables. Move the cables away from the lights.

4-2   B

Explanation: Partitioning the network will reduce the impact of broadcast storms on the network at the price of a more complex network architecture.

4-3   A, B, D

Explanation: The UPS gives your computer time to shut down in case of power failure. A tape backup unit allows you to restore data that has been backed up. A RAID system can regenerate information that was stored on a failed hard drive.

4-4   A

Explanation: Advanced cable testers are testers that go beyond the Physical layer of the OSI reference model. Advanced cable testers can also indicate if a particular network adapter card is causing problems.

4-5   C

Explanation: NetBEUI is not a routable protocol. If you are experiencing broadcast storms on a network that uses NetBEUI, you should consider using another protocol, such as NWLink or TCP/IP.

4-6   D

Explanation: Protocol analyzers can help you determine the cause of a network fault. However, they do not reconfigure your network for you.

4-7   C

Explanation: A time-domain reflectometer inspects the physical characteristics of the cable.

4-8   A

4-9   C

Explanation: Protocol analyzers can help you avoid having to shut down servers and routers when troubleshooting problems such as broadcast storms.

4-10   A, B, C

Explanation: Routers understand about choosing the most optimal route when multiple delivery paths are available. Routers also provide flow control, which is the ability to regulate the number of packets flooding a network segment. While a bridge will send broadcast messages out of all ports, a router will not transmit broadcasts.

4-11   B

Explanation: TCP/IP packets can be sent over serial lines using either SLIP or PPP. PPP can provide a way to obtain an IP address automatically, so that remote computers can connect to the workstation at any point. SLIP does not provide automatic IP addressing.

4-12   B

Explanation: A protocol analyzer is a device used to capture and decode network packets.

4-13   A

Explanation: In Windows 95, you can use Device Manager to make sure that a network interface card does not have a resource conflict.

4-14 B

Explanation: Two computers using the IPX (or NWLink) protocol must use the same frame type in order to communicate. If only one computer on the network is affected, then it would almost always be more appropriate to change its frame type rather than to change the frame type of the server and all of the other computers on the network.

4-15 C

Explanation: Protocol analyzers record and analyze data that is transferred over the network cable.

4-16 D

Explanation: If the network adapter card is also configured to use the same IRQ as the CD-ROM drive, it could cause the CD-ROM drive to fail.

4-17 A

Explanation: Short circuits are mostly detected by measuring resistance in ohms between two conductors. A short circuit should measure zero resistance between two conductors; an open circuit should measure high or infinite resistance.

4-18 B

Explanation: Interrupt lines (IRQs) are used by devices to send requests to the computer's CPU. Before installing a network interface card, you should note which interrupts are available on your computer and check the card to make sure that the desired IRQ is set.

4-19 A, B, C

Explanation: The distances for computers A, B, and C to the hub exceed the maximum cable length of 328 feet (100 meters) specified for 10BaseT.

4-20   C, D

Explanation: A network monitor (also called a protocol analyzer) can generate performance statistics on the network's cabling, software, servers, and clients. Windows NT Performance Monitor can also be used to measure a computer's efficiency and identify possible problems.

4-21   A, B, D

Explanation: Network monitors work at all levels of the OSI reference model, not just at the Physical layer.

4-22   B, C, D

Explanation: Performance Monitor; SNMP, and SMS can help a network administrator identify bottlenecks, get a large-scale picture of network performance, and provide centralized total system management.

4-23   A

Explanation: Every computer on the network must look at each packet on the network and decide if that packet is for itself. This can cause slowdowns on networks if a large number of broadcasts are sent out on the network. Routers will not forward broadcasts.

4-24   C

Explanation: Since all other computers can communicate with the network, the cable, hub, and server are probably fine. Check your NIC.

4-25   A

Explanation: A protocol analyzer can capture and decode packets transmitted over a network. It can also generate statistics based on the network traffic to help you monitor and optimize the network.

Unit 5 Answers

Final Review

1. B

    Explanation: Routers work up to the Network layer, bridges only work to the Data Link layer, and repeaters are only at the Physical layer. Gateways work at all seven layers of the OSI reference model.

2. A

    Explanation: The hub links the network cables and rebroadcasts received network communications so that all of the computers on the network can communicate.

3. C, D

    Explanation: 10Base5 cables can be up to 500 meters long. 10BaseFL cables can be up to 2000 meters long.

4. A

    Explanation: Passive hubs do not regenerate a network signal.

5. D

    Explanation: Primary Rate ISDN (PRI) service provides dial-up bandwidth almost as great as a T1 line.

6. B

    Explanation: A bridge will transfer broadcasts or communications meant for a station on the other side of a network segment.

7. C

Explanation: A time-domain reflectometer inspects the physical characteristics of the cable.

8. C

Explanation: A multiplexer allows you to send several different signals over the same network cable.

9. C

Explanation: If you run network protocols that cannot be routed, installing a router that also acts as a bridge—a brouter—will allow you to run routing protocols as well as bridging protocols.

10. B

Explanation: Partitioning the network with a router will reduce the impact of broadcast storms on the network at the price of a more complex network architecture.

11. B

Explanation: Routers use a route-discovery algorithm—either OSPF or RIP—to determine possible routes through the internetwork.

12. A, C

Explanation: SLIP and PPP are serial communications protocols that are used to connect clients to the Internet over telephone lines.

13. A

Explanation: This solution meets the required result and also both of the desired results. The connectivity, speed, and redundancy goals are met.

14. A, C

Explanation: Twisted-pair networks can be affected by crosstalk and electromagnetic interference (EMI). They also suffer from attenuation.

15. C

Explanation: Protocol analyzers record and analyze data that is transferred over the network cable.

16. A, C

Explanation: T1 lines can have transmission speeds up to 1.544Mbps and allow point-to-point, full-duplex transmissions.

17. C

Explanation: Ethernet 10Base5 uses Thicknet coaxial cable.

18. D

Explanation: You use a vampire tap to connect a transceiver to a 10Base5 cable.

19. C

Explanation: The Ethernet 5-4-3 rule specifies that an Ethernet network may have 5 segments connected by 4 repeaters and with 3 of the segments populated by Ethernet devices (such as computers).

20. B

Explanation: LocalTalk uses the CSMA/CA (Carrier Sense Multiple Access with Collision Avoidance) media-access protocol.

21. C

Explanation: You can increase performance on your network by spreading the network load over several server computers.

22. C

Explanation: ATM (Asynchronous Transfer Mode) can run on a LAN and on WANs simultaneously.

23. B

Explanation: Each computer must have a unique IP address.

24. C

Explanation: You need a print driver for each kind of printer on your network.

25. A

Explanation: With centralized computing, a central computer does all of the work and the clients (dumb terminals or PCs running terminal-emulation software) merely display data and accept input from the user.

26. C

Explanation: ATM uses fixed-size cells to transfer data, voice, video, and more on a LAN or WAN.

27. A

Explanation: A LAN links computers in the same general location (such as an office building).

28. D

Explanation: Infrared is by far the slowest, with speeds up to 115Kbps or less.

29. A

Explanation: One Windows NT Server computer can perform all of the above roles in a small network.

30. A

Explanation: The bus topology is the least expensive to install, especially for small networks.

31. B

Explanation: Fiber-optic cable is immune to interference and supports high data rates.

32. C

Explanation: Spread-spectrum transmits on two or more frequencies. If one frequency had interference or failed, data could still be transmitted over the other frequencies.

33. B

Explanation: COM1 also uses IRQ 4.

34. B

Explanation: The MAC address is a feature of the MAC (Media Access Control) sublayer, which is a part of the Data Link layer.

35. C

Explanation: 802.8 was produced by the Fiber-Optic Technical Advisory Group.

36. A, B

Explanation: NDIS and ODI allow one adapter to be used with many network protocols, and vice versa.

37. A

Explanation: NetBEUI cannot be routed.

38. D

Explanation: AppleTalk is the protocol developed by Apple for Macintosh network communications and is loaded automatically when Services for Macintosh is loaded on Windows NT Server.

39. C

Explanation: TCP/IP is the protocol that most easily scales to handle the largest networks.

40. B

Explanation: Windows 95 can use most device drivers written for DOS. However, many of these device drivers have been rewritten for Windows and Windows 95. You should use a Windows 95 driver if there is one available.

41. B

Explanation: The network interface adapter is the device that provides the physical connection to the network.

42. A, B, C

Explanation: TCP/IP, NWLink, and NetBEUI are three networking protocol stacks that are commonly used in Microsoft networks. DLC is used to connect Windows to HP Jet Direct cards and mainframes.

43. B

Explanation: The MAC address uniquely identifies the network interface cards on the Ethernet collision domain. If two cards have the same MAC address, they will not be able to communicate correctly on the network.

44. C

Explanation: Adapter cards (including network interface cards) must have unique settings in order for the computer to communicate with them.

45. C

Explanation: Attenuation is the loss of digital signal as it travels down the wire, measured in decibels. All types of cables suffer from attenuation.

46. A, C

Explanation: Disk mirroring (also known as RAID Level 1) and RAID Level 5 provide redundancy so that in case one hard drive fails the data can be reconstructed from the other drive(s).

47. B

Explanation: An ISDN B channel is 64Kbps or 56Kbps, depending on your location and how much you want to pay.

48. C

Explanation: RAS (Remote Access Service) on Windows NT Server supports up to 256 incoming connections.

49. A

Explanation: Routers are often used to segment networks that would otherwise grow too large for a single collision domain.

50. C

Explanation: DHCP can assign IP addresses, subnet masks, default gateways, WINS information, DNS information, and other information to hosts in a network.

51. D

Explanation: Routers work up to the Network layer. Bridges work to the Data Link layer. Gateways are generally considered to work at the Network layer, but can work at all seven layers of the OSI reference model. An example of a gateway is an SNA gateway.

52. A

Explanation: Routers work up to the Network layer.

53. A

Explanation: The default gateway is where communications are directed when the destination computer does not reside on the local subnet.

54. B

Explanation: 10Base2, or Thinnet, is the least expensive cable type.

55. B

Explanation: The star topology is the easiest to upgrade. You can simply install another cable into the hub or connect another hub to the existing hub. Troubleshooting is easier because you can disconnect each cable until you find the problem.

56. C

Explanation: The business requirements are light (file and print sharing), and each user already has Windows 95, so a Windows 95 peer-to-peer network would be the most cost-effective solution.

57. A

Explanation: Because the users are less than 100 meters apart, the fastest and cheapest solution would be to use the already existing category 3 (twisted-pair) wiring.

58. A

Explanation: For a twisted-pair network, you must purchase a hub.

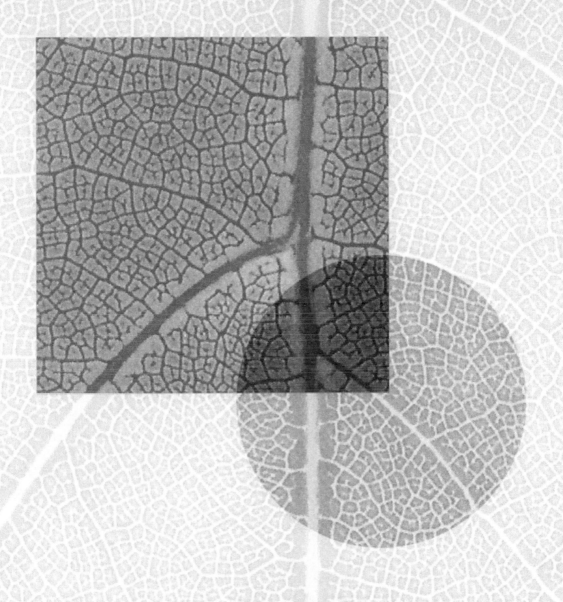

Glossary

2B+D   See *Basic Rate ISDN*.

10Base2   A standard for transmitting Ethernet over Thinnet (RG-58) cable.

10Base5   A standard for transmitting Ethernet over Thicknet (1/2 inch round, 50-ohm coaxial) cable.

10BaseFL   A standard for transmitting Ethernet over fiber-optic cable.

10BaseT   A standard for transmitting Ethernet over twisted-pair cable.

100BaseT   A standard for transmitting Ethernet over twisted-pair cable for speeds up to 155Mbps.

100BaseVG-AnyLAN   An extension of 10BaseT Ethernet that supports transmissions of up to 100Mbps over voice-grade (category 3) twisted-pair cable.

access permissions   A network security model in which rights to access network resources are determined on the basis of security policies stored in a user-access database on a server. A user logs on to a network. After that user has been allowed onto the network, the network security system determines access privileges in accordance with the security policies stored in the user-access database.

active hub   A hub that amplifies transmission signals and sends them to all the computers connected to it. This type of hub is often called a *multiport repeater*.

active monitor   A device on a Token Ring network (usually the device that has been operating on the network for the longest time) that periodically checks the status of the network and monitors for network errors.

Address Resolution Protocol   See *ARP*.

advanced cable tester   A tool that works up to the Transport layer of the OSI reference model. It can test the physical cable as well as frame counts, collisions, congestion, and beaconing.

AFP (AppleTalk Filing Protocol)   A protocol that provides file sharing between Macintosh and DOS-based computers, provides an interface for communication between AppleTalk and other network operating systems, and is responsible for file-system security.

amplifier   A type of repeater that simply amplifies the entire incoming signal. Unfortunately, it amplifies both the signal and the noise.

amplitude   In communications, the distance between the highest and lowest points in a wave. The amplitude controls the strength, or volume, of the signal.

analog data   Data that has an infinite number of possible states, rather than the simple ones and zeros of a digital signal. Audio, video, and voice telephone signals, for example, can all be represented using analog data.

AppleShare   A file and print sharing protocol for Macintosh computers.

AppleTalk   A protocol suite developed by Apple for use with Macintosh computers. The software for AppleTalk connectivity is built into the Macintosh operating system (MacOS and System 7).

AppleTalk Filing Protocol   See *AFP*.

AppleTalk Transaction Protocol   See *ATP*.

Application layer   In the OSI reference model, the layer that provides services that directly support user applications, such as database access, e-mail, and file transfer.

application server   A server that allows client PCs to access and use extra computing power and software applications that reside on a shared computer. Application servers offload work from the client by running programs for the client and sending the results back to the client.

ARCnet   A network topology, created by Datapoint Corporation in 1977, that can connect up to 255 nodes on coaxial, twisted-pair, or fiber-optic cable. ARCnet uses a token-passing scheme and typically reaches speeds up to 2.5Mbps. Some newer generations of ARCnet can reach a speed of 100Mbps.

ARP (Address Resolution Protocol)   A protocol that maps IP addresses (network-based) to data-link addresses (hardware-based).

asynchronous   A type of communication that sends data using flow control rather than a clock to synchronize data between the source and destination.

Asynchronous Transfer Mode   See *ATM*.

ATM (Asynchronous Transfer Mode)   A network transfer method that transmits data in 53-byte packets, called *cells*. ATM is most frequently used on WANs but is sometimes used for LANs and MANs. ATM can reach speeds of up to 2.488Gbps. ATM is frequently called *cell relay*.

ATP (AppleTalk Transaction Protocol)   A connectionless protocol that runs at the Transport layer and provides reliable transmissions, using acknowledgments.

Attachment User Interface connector   See *AUI connector*.

attenuation   A communications term referring to a signal decreasing in volume (and amplitude) over a distance. The length of the cable and its resistance can affect the amount of attenuation.

AUI (Attachment User Interface) connector   Specifies how a transceiver is attached to an Ethernet device. Also called a *DIX* connector.

backbone   The main cabling for a network. In a bus topology, each node on the network is attached either directly or over a shorter cable to the backbone cable.

back end   The server component of a client-server system. It provides services to the front end (the client component).

bandwidth   In network communications, the amount of data that can be sent across a wire in a given time. Each communication that passes along the wire decreases the amount of available bandwidth.

baseband   A transmission technique in which the signal uses the entire bandwidth of a transmission medium. Computers can transmit across the medium only when the channel is not busy.

Basic Rate ISDN (BRI)   An ISDN service, also called *2B+D*, that consists of three channels: two for data at 64KB each, called B channels, and one 16KB channel used for signaling and link management, called a D channel. BRI has speeds up to 128Kbps.

baud rate   The per-second rate of state transitions (that is, from 1 to 0 and vice versa) of a signal. Baud rates of modems define the speed at which they make state transitions. Because state transitions can represent more than a single bit each, this rate is different from the bits per second (bps) rate.

beaconing   The process on a Token Ring network by which a device, in the event of a cable fault, determines the state of the network and the location of the fault.

binary   The numbering system used in computer memory and in digital communications. All characters are represented as a series of ones and zeros. For example, the letter *A* might be represented in a translation code as 01000001.

binding   The process of linking a protocol to a network interface card or device driver.

bits   In binary data, each unit of data is a bit. Each bit is represented by either 0 or 1 and is stored in memory as an on or off state.

bits per second (bps)   The amount of data transferred in a second.

bottleneck   A condition in which network data transfer is slowed significantly because of a problem with a network device.

BRI   See *Basic Rate ISDN*.

bridge   A network interconnectivity device that selectively determines the appropriate segment to which it should pass a signal. Through address filtering, bridges can divide busy networks into segments and reduce network traffic.

broadband   A network transmission method in which a single transmission medium is divided and shared simultaneously.

broadcast storm   A network condition in which a malfunctioning network interface card or some other problem overwhelms a network with message broadcasts. You can use routers to limit broadcast storms.

brouter   A network interconnectivity device that can provide both bridge and router services.

brownout   A temporary decrease in the voltage level of power supplied to network devices. Brownouts are frequently called *sags*.

buffer   In communications, an area of memory used as temporary storage for data being sent or received. The term *buffer* can refer to any area of memory in a computer.

bus (linear bus)   A network topology in which all computers are connected by a single length of cabling with a terminator at each end. The bus is the simplest and most widely used network design.

byte   The unit of data storage and communication in computers. In PC systems, a byte is usually 8 bits, or an 8-digit binary number. A single byte can represent numbers between 0 and 255.

carrier sense multiple access with collision detection   See *CSMA/CD*.

category 1 cable   A type of UTP (unshielded twisted-pair cable) that is for voice-grade transmissions and has very low data rates.

category 2 cable   A type of UTP (unshielded twisted-pair cable) that is specified for voice-grade transmissions and has very low data rates.

category 3 cable   A type of UTP (unshielded twisted-pair cable) that is specified for four-twisted pairs and has data rates up to 10Mbps.

category 4 cable   A type of UTP (unshielded twisted-pair cable) that is specified for four-twisted pairs and has data rates up to 16Mbps. Category 4 cable is not commonly used in networks.

category 5 cable   A type of UTP (unshielded twisted-pair cable) that is specified for four-twisted pairs and has data rates up to 100Mbps.

category 6 cable   A type of UTP (unshielded twisted-pair cable) that is specified for four-twisted pairs and has data rates up to 155Mbps.

cell relay   See *ATM*.

cells   The data blocks used by ATM. Cells are exactly 53 octets long.

channel service unit/digital service unit   See *CSU/DSU*.

chip creep   A situation in which integrated circuits gradually lose contact with their sockets because of temperature changes.

chromatic dispersion   A condition that applies to fiber-optic cables. Chromatic dispersion occurs when light enters the core at different angles and spreads apart slightly as it travels to the destination.

circuit   A communications channel established between two network devices.

circuit switching   A type of data transmission in which a circuit is established between endpoints and data is sent in a stream through a network.

cladding   In fiber-optic cabling, a layer of glass that surrounds the inner core and reflects light back into the core.

client   A workstation used only to request services from a network service provider, such as a dedicated server or another workstation.

client-server architecture   A network architecture in which clients request data, programs, and services from servers. The servers then provide the data, programs, and services to the clients. Applications written for the client-server architecture typically have different components for the server and for the client. Client-server architecture allows clients to exploit the processing power of the server.

client-server network   A server-centric network in which some network resources are stored on a file server, while processing power is distributed among workstations and the file server.

coaxial cable   One type of cable used in network wiring, also called *coax*. Typical coaxial cable types include RG-58 and RG-62. The 10Base2 system of Ethernet networking uses coaxial cable. Coaxial cable is usually shielded. The Thicknet system uses a thicker coaxial cable.

collision   A situation that occurs when two or more network devices transmit at the same time, through the same channel. The two signals transmitted meet and cause data to be destroyed.

collision domain   A network segment in an Ethernet network.

concentrator   See *hub*.

congestion   A condition in which a network transmission medium is over-whelmed with network traffic, causing network performance to decline.

connectionless communications   Methods that do not guarantee delivery of messages. Examples of protocols that use connectionless communications are IP (Internet Protocol), UDP (User Datagram Protocol), and IPX (Internetwork Packet eXchange). Connectionless methods are faster than connection-oriented communications methods.

connection-oriented communications   Methods that do guarantee delivery of messages. Examples of protocols that use connection-oriented communications include TCP (Transmission Control Protocol), SPX (Sequenced Packet eXchange), and X.25. Connection-oriented methods are slower than connectionless methods.

contention   A method for devices to share a media channel. With contention, all devices attached to the network can transmit whenever they have something to communicate. Ethernet is an example of a contention network.

CRC (cyclic redundancy check)   An error-detection method based on a transformation of the bit values in a data packet or frame. The sender computes a CRC value and adds the value to the data packet. The receiver computes a CRC value based on the data portion of the received packet and compares the result with the transmitted CRC value. If the two match, the receiver assumes that the packet has been received without any errors.

crosstalk   Interference, or noise, created on a network transmission medium by another physically adjacent medium. This interference can corrupt data.

CSMA/CD (carrier sense multiple access with collision detection)
The protocol by which Ethernet devices share access to an Ethernet network. *Carrier sense* means that before transmitting, the devices listen for a signal; if none is found, it is okay to transmit. *Multiple access* means that all computers share the same cable and signaling techniques. *Collision detection* means that the devices detect collisions, wait, and retransmit.

CSU/DSU   A network interconnectivity device that connects a network to the public telephone network. CSUs/DSUs translate signals and shield networks from noise and high voltage on the public network.

cyclic redundancy check   See *CRC*.

datagram   See *packet*.

Datagram Delivery Protocol   See *DDP*.

datagram packet-switched network   A type of network on which messages are divided into a stream of separately addressed packets. Each packet is routed independently. The packets are reassembled at the destination address.

Data Link Control   See *DLC*.

Data Link layer   In the OSI reference model, the layer that provides for the flow of data over a single link from one device to another. The Data Link layer is composed of the LLC (Logical Link Control) and MAC (Media Access Control) sublayers.

DDP (Datagram Delivery Protocol)   A connectionless protocol that runs at the Network layer of the OSI reference model and provides datagram service between Macintosh computers.

decoding   The process of translating a message from a transmittable standard form to the native form of the recipient.

dedicated line   A transmission medium that is used exclusively between two locations. Dedicated lines are also known as *leased lines* or *private lines*.

dedicated server   A computer that functions only as a server and is not used as a client or workstation.

default gateway   A method used in packet-switching networks (Ethernet, Token Ring, etc.) to send packets to a remote destination if the recipient is not found on the local network. The default gateway typically is a router. On a TCP/IP network, each client must be configured with a default gateway to communicate with computers not on the local segment or on the Internet.

demarcation point   The point inside your building (or on the campus premises) at which the telephone company (or other service provider) is no longer responsible for network cabling or service.

DHCP (Dynamic Host Configuration Protocol)   A method for automatically assigning IP addresses to client computers on a network.

dial-up connection   A connection made via a modem over regular telephone lines. The term *dial-up* refers to temporary connections, as opposed to leased telephone lines, which provide permanent connections.

digital data   Data that uses ones and zeros to store information.

digital line   A data or voice network interconnectivity medium that supports digital signaling.

digital signaling   Data transmission in the form of discrete units (on or off, 1 or 0, and so on).

digital voltmeter (DVM)   A hand-held tool that can check the continuity and voltage of cables.

disk mirroring   See *mirroring*.

disk striping   See *striping*.

dispersion   See *chromatic dispersion*.

distance-vector routing   A method of route discovery in which each router on the network broadcasts the information contained in its routing table. The other routers then update their routing tables with the broadcast information they receive.

DIX connector   See *AUI connector*.

DLC (Data Link Control)   An IBM SNA (Systems Network Architecture) protocol, analogous to the Data Link layer of the OSI reference model, where channels are specified. DLC is used in Windows NT environments that include HP Jet Direct cards with printers. This protocol is used as a connectivity protocol for IBM mainframes, but it cannot be used as a communication protocol between Microsoft hosts.

DNS (Domain Name Service)   A TCP/IP network service that resolves host names to IP network addresses.

domain   In Windows NT Server systems, a group of computers that share the same security and logon authentication database.

Domain Name Service   See *DNS*.

duplexing   A method of using a second hard drive with a second hard drive controller to provide fault tolerance.

DVM   See *digital voltmeter*.

Dynamic Host Configuration Protocol   See *DHCP*.

dynamic route selection   A method of route discovery in which the router uses the cost information that is continually being generated by routing algorithms and placed in routing tables to select the best route for each packet. As network conditions change, the router can select the best path.

EISA (Extended Industry Standard Architecture)   A 32-bit bus architecture, which remains compatible with 16-bit ISA.

electromagnetic interference (EMI)   A type of low-voltage, low-current, high-frequency signal that interferes with normal network transmission. EMI is typically caused by improper insulation or insufficient grounding.

electrostatic discharge (ESD) An electric shock created by a buildup of static electricity. ESD frequently damages computer components.

EMI See *electromagnetic interference.*

encoding The process of translating a message from the native form of the sender to a transmittable standard form.

encryption The encoding of messages for security reasons. Also called *ciphering.*

ESD See *electrostatic discharge.*

Ethernet The most popular network specification. Developed by Xerox in 1976, Ethernet offers a transfer rate of 10Mbps. Ethernet uses a bus topology and thick (Thicknet) or thin (Thinnet) coaxial, fiber-optic, or twisted-pair cabling.

EtherTalk The driver used to communicate between a Macintosh and an Ethernet network interface card.

Extended Industry Standard Architecture See *EISA.*

FAT (File Allocation Table) The file system used by MS-DOS and available to other operating systems such as Windows, OS/2, and the Macintosh.

fault tolerance Any method that prevents system failure by tolerating single faults, usually through hardware redundancy.

FDDI (Fiber Distributed Data Interface) A network specification that defines the transmission of information packets using light produced by a laser or light-emitting diode (LED). FDDI uses fiber-optic cable and equipment to transmit data packets. It has a data rate of up to 100Mbps and allows very long cable distances.

Fiber Distributed Data Interface See *FDDI.*

fiber-optic cable   One medium type used for network communications. Fiber-optic cable uses a tiny glass or plastic fiber and sends a light signal through it.

file server   A server that offers services that allow network users to share files. File services include storing, retrieving, and moving data.

File Transfer Protocol   See *FTP.*

fractional T1/T3 line   A portion of a T1 or T3 line.

frame   A unit of data, often called a *packet* or *block,* that can be transmitted across a network or internetwork. The term *frame* is most frequently used regarding Ethernet networks.

Frame Relay   An upgrade to the X.25 packet-switching network, with fast, variable-length packets. Because Frame Relay assumes a lower error rate, it transfers data at higher data rates than X.25 (from 56Kbps to 1.544Mbps).

frequency   The repetition rate, usually of a signal, usually reported in cycles per second, or hertz (Hz).

frequency-division multiplexing (FDM)   A form of multiplexing in which the output channel is divided into multiple, smaller bandwidth channels, each defined in a different frequency range.

front end   The client component of a client-server system. A front-end application works with a back-end component stored on a server.

FTP (File Transfer Protocol)   A TCP/IP protocol that permits the transferring of files between computer systems. Because FTP has been implemented on numerous types of computer systems, files can be transferred between different computer systems (for example, a personal computer and a minicomputer).

gateway   A network interconnectivity device that translates communications protocols.

groupware   Applications that involve group interaction across a network. Lotus Notes and Microsoft Exchange are two popular groupware packages.

guaranteed state changes   A type of synchronous timing coordination, used by synchronous modems, in which the clock information is embedded in the data signal.

handshaking   The exchange of codes between two devices in order to negotiate the transmission and reception of data.

hardware address   A unique numerical value assigned to a network interface card (NIC), also known as a *MAC address* or *physical address*.

high-power, single-frequency radio   A type of radio wave transmission that operates at only one frequency but can cover large distances and go through and around objects.

hop   In routing, a server or router that is counted in a hop count.

hop count   The number of routers a message must pass through to reach its destination. Routers use hop counts to determine the most efficient network route.

host   In remote access, the computer that provides data to the RAS (Remote Access Service) client and hosts its connection to the remote network.

HTTP (Hypertext Transfer Protocol)   The WWW (World Wide Web) protocol used to transfer Web pages across the Internet.

hub   A network connectivity device that brings media segments together in a central location. The hub is the central controlling device in some star networks. The two main types are active hubs and passive hubs. See also *active hub, intelligent hub,* and *passive hub.*

hybrid network   A combination client-server/peer-to-peer network. Typically, hybrid networks are client-server networks that also include some peers.

Hypertext Transfer Protocol   See *HTTP*.

IEEE (Institute of Electrical and Electronic Engineers)   A professional organization that defines standards related to networking and other areas.

IEEE 802.*x*   A series of standards, recommendations, and informational documents related to networks and communications. IEEE 802.1 is the standard for internetworking and management. IEEE 802.2 is the standard for logical link control. IEEE 802.3 is the standard for Ethernet networks. IEEE 802.4 is the standard for Token Bus networks. IEEE 802.5 is the standard for Token Ring networks. IEEE 802.6 is the standard for MANs (metropolitan area networks). IEEE 802.7 is the standard for the broadband technical advisory group. IEEE 802.8 is the standard for the fiber-optic technical advisory group. IEEE 802.9 is the standard for integrated voice/data networks. IEEE 802.10 is the standard for network security. IEEE 802.11 is the standard for wireless networks. IEEE 802.12 is the standard for demand-priority access and 100BaseVG-AnyLAN networks.

Industry Standard Architecture   See *ISA*.

infrared transmission   A form of wireless media that uses infrared light to transmit signals. LEDs (light-emitting diodes) or ILDs (interjection-laser diodes) transmit the signals, and photodiodes receive the signals. Infrared signals are in the terahertz (higher frequency) range.

Institute of Electrical and Electronic Engineers   See *IEEE*.

Integrated Services Digital Network   See *ISDN*.

intelligent hub   A hub that provides network management and intelligent path selection in addition to signal regeneration.

interconnectivity devices   Devices that connect independent networks. They include routers, brouters, gateways, and CSUs/DSUs.

Internet Protocol   See *IP*.

Internet protocol suite   The protocol suite developed along with the Internet. These protocols have become the de facto standard because of the success of the Internet. The entire protocol suite is sometimes referred to as *TCP/IP*.

internetwork   Two or more independent networks that are connected and yet maintain independent identities. Internetworks are joined by interconnectivity devices.

Internetwork Packet Exchange   See *IPX*.

InterNIC   The organization responsible for assigning IP addresses to networks that connect over the Internet.

interprocess communications (IPC)   A generic term describing any manner of client-server communication protocols, specifically those operating in the Application layer. IPC mechanisms provide a method for the client and server to trade information.

interrupts   Inputs to the CPU in a PC that allow devices to get the CPU's attention—to interrupt it—if it is performing another task. Interrupts are also called *IRQs* (for interrupt requests).

intranet   A company network that uses Internet technology, such as Web servers and clients.

IP (Internet Protocol)   The Internet protocol suite's protocol for defining and routing datagrams.

IP address   A four-byte (32-bit) number that uniquely identifies a computer on an IP internetwork. InterNIC assigns the first bytes of Internet IP addresses and administers them in hierarchies. Organizations that do not connect to the Internet can assign IP addresses as they please.

IPC   See *interprocess communications*.

IPX (Internetwork Packet Exchange)   Novell's main Network layer protocol, which deals with addressing, route selection, and connection services.

IPX/SPX (Internetwork Packet Exchange/Sequenced Packet Exchange)   Routable protocols created by Novell for NetWare networks.

ISA (Industry Standard Architecture)   The original IBM AT bus architecture, originally an 8-bit architecture but expanded to 16 bits in 1984. ISA was the standard for all PCs until the EISA bus was developed.

ISDN (Integrated Services Digital Network)   A CCITT standard for digital communications. ISDN allows voice, video, and data transfer on the same line. See also *Basic Rate ISDN* and *Primary Rate ISDN*.

ISDN modem   An interconnectivity device that connects a computer to an ISDN line.

jabber packet   A meaningless transmission generated by a network node because of a network malfunction (such as a bad network interface card) or other error.

LAN (local area network)   A group of computers interconnected within a building or campus. For example, a LAN may consist of computers located on a single floor of a building or it might link all the computers in a small company.

leased line   A communications circuit permanently established for a single customer. Also called a *private line*.

link-state routing   A type of routing in which routers broadcast their complete routing tables only at startup and infrequent intervals.

LLC (Logical Link Control) sublayer   In the Data Link layer of the OSI reference model, the top sublayer. The LLC sublayer establishes and maintains links between communicating devices. This sublayer is also responsible for frame error correction and hardware addresses.

local area network   See *LAN*.

LocalTalk   Apple's proprietary network architecture for networks that run AppleTalk.

Logical Link Control sublayer   See LLC *sublayer*.

logical topology   Refers to the logical path of the signal as it travels through the physical topology in a network.

low-power, single-frequency radio   A type of radio wave transmission that operates at only one frequency with very low power.

MAC address   See *hardware address*.

MAC (Media Access Control) sublayer   In the Data Link layer of the OSI reference model, the bottom sublayer. The MAC sublayer controls how devices share a media channel.

MAN (metropolitan area network)   A network larger than LAN but smaller than a WAN. MANs span a single city or metropolitan area.

Media Access Control sublayer   See *MAC sublayer*.

media access protocol   A specification for arbitrating access to physical network media among all devices that wish to transmit on the network. CSMA/CD is a media access protocol.

mesh   A network topology distinguished by redundant links between devices. Most mesh topology networks are not true mesh networks. Instead, they are hybrid mesh networks, with some redundant links rather than all redundant links.

message switching   The process of transmitting messages over a network, where each message is routed through the network independently.

metropolitan area network   See *MAN*.

MicroChannel   A bus architecture that was created by IBM as a replacement for ISA and was introduced in PS/2 computers. MicroChannel runs as either a 16-bit or 32-bit bus and is incompatible with ISA.

microwave   A type of unbounded network transmission medium. Microwaves are most often used to transmit data across satellite links and between earth-based equipment, such as telephone relay towers. Microwave transmission is commonly used to transmit signals when bounded media, such as cable, cannot be used. See also *satellite microwave* and *terrestrial microwave*.

mirroring   Also called RAID Level 1, the process of keeping a constant backup of the server data on another server. Every change to the data made to the primary server is immediately communicated to the backup mirror server so that if the primary server fails for any reason, the mirror can take over instantly.

modem   A device that converts the digital communications of a computer into analog signals that can be carried over a regular telephone line.

modulation   The process of modifying a carrier signal to transmit information.

MSAU (Multiple Station Access Unit)   The hub in a Token Ring network, also called *MSU*.

multi-homing   Installing multiple network interface cards in a single computer.

multimode fiber-optic cable   A type of fiber-optic cable with a wider core, which allows a beam of light to follow multiple paths through the core. See also *single-mode fiber-optic cable*.

Multiple Station Access Unit   See *MSAU*.

multiplexer   A device that multiplexes signals for transmission over a segment and reverses this process for multiplexed signals coming in from the segment. Frequently shortened to *mux*.

multiplexing   A method of sharing a single medium segment by combining several channels for transmission over that segment using a multiplexer. Multiplexed signals are later separated at the receiving end in a process called *demultiplexing*. See also *frequency-division multiplexing*, *time-division multiplexing*, and *wavelength-division multiplexing*.

multiport repeater   See *active hub*.

mux   See *multiplexer*.

NCP (NetWare Core Protocol)   A protocol that provides the interface for file storage and retrieval services between workstations and the server.

NDIS (Network Driver Interface Standard)   A driver interface for Microsoft Windows systems that allows multiple cards to be bound to multiple transport protocols.

NetBEUI (NetBIOS Extended User Interface)   A nonroutable protocol designed by IBM for small networks.

NetBIOS (Network Basic Input/Output System)   A method of communication between two computers via a virtual connection (a *session*) across a network, developed by IBM. Windows NT uses NetBIOS for file and print services.

NetWare Core Protocol   See *NCP*.

network   A group of interconnected computers that share resources and information.

network address   A unique address that identifies each node, or device, on the network. The network address is generally hardcoded into the network card on both the workstation and server. Some network cards allow you to change this address, but there is seldom a reason to do so.

network analyzer   See *protocol analyzer*.

Network Driver Interface Standard   See *NDIS*.

network interface card (NIC)   A Physical layer adapter device that allows a computer to connect to and communicate over a LAN.

Network layer   In the OSI reference model, the layer that makes routing decisions and forwards packets (also known as *datagrams*) for devices that could be farther away than a single link.

network monitor   A tool that can do frame-level analysis and check packet types and errors on the whole network or just part of the network.

New Technology File System   See *NTFS*.

NFS (Network File System)   An Application layer protocol, designed for use in Unix networks, that provides file and remote-operation services.

NIC   See *network interface card*.

node   Any network device (such as a server, workstation, or router) that can communicate across the network.

noise   A low-voltage, low-current, high-frequency signal that interferes with normal network transmissions, often corrupting data.

NTFS (New Technology File System)   A secure, transaction-oriented file system developed for Windows NT that incorporates the Windows NT security model for assigning permissions and shares.

NWLink   The Windows NT compatible implementation of Novell's IPX/SPX.

octet Exactly 8 bits of data. Bytes are usually, but not always, 8 bits. Octets are always 8 bits.

ODI (Open Data Link Interface) A driver interface developed by Apple and Novell that allows multiple cards to be bound to multiple transport protocols. Similar to NDIS, ODI allows Novell NetWare drivers to be written without concern for the protocol that will be used on top of them.

Open System Interconnection model See *OSI reference model*.

oscilloscope A tool that measures fluctuations in signal voltage.

OSI reference model A model defined by the International Standards Organization (ISO) to conceptually organize the process of communication between computers in terms of seven layers, called *protocol stacks*. The seven layers of the OSI model provides a way for you to understand how communications across various protocols take place.

OSPF (Open Shortest Path First) A routing protocol that performs route discovery by using calculations based on bandwidth (not hops).

oversampling A type of synchronous communication in which the receiver samples the signal at ten times the data rate. One of the ten samples provides the data; the other nine provide clocking information.

packet The basic division of data sent over a network, also known as a *datagram*. Each packet contains a set amount of data along with a header containing information about the type of packet and the network address to which it is being sent. The size and format of a packet depends on the protocol and frame types used.

packet switching A type of data transmission in which data is divided into packets, each of which has a destination address. Each packet is then routed optimally across a network. An addressed packet may travel a different route than packets related to it. Packet sequence numbers are used at the destination node to reassemble related packets.

parity checking   A simple form of error checking employed by asynchronous modems. Extra bits added to data words can indicate when data transmission has been flawed.

partition   A section of a hard disk that can contain an independent file system volume.

passive hub   A hub that simply combines the signals of network segments, with no signal processing or regeneration.

password-protected shares   A network security model in which passwords are required for gaining access to each shared resource on a network.

PCI (Peripheral Component Interconnect)   A 32-bit local bus in wide use today in both PCs and Power Macs. PCI architecture provides Plug-and-Play functionality.

peer   A computer on a network that both requests and provides network services.

peer-to-peer network   A network in which each computer is equal (peer) in the sharing of resources. A peer-to-peer network does not have a dedicated server, and there is no hierarchy among the computers. Each peer is responsible for its own security.

Peripheral Component Interconnect   See *PCI*.

permissions   Security constructs used to regulate access to resources by user name or group affiliation. Permissions can be assigned by administrators to allow any level of access.

physical address   See *hardware address*.

Physical layer   In the OSI reference model, the layer that handles sending bits (ones and zeros) from one computer to another.

physical topology   Refers to the actual layout of the physical cabling or transmission media in a network.

Ping A TCP/IP network tool that checks if a host is up and running. Ping (Packet Internet Groper) does an echo send and reply to an IP address to see if it is alive.

plant The wires that connect computers together in a LAN.

plenum The space between the ceiling of an office and the floor above. Usually, fire codes require that only special, plenum-grade cable be used in this space.

point-to-point connection Network communication in which two devices have exclusive access to a network medium. For example, a printer connected to only one workstation would be using a point-to-point connection.

Point-to-Point Protocol See *PPP*.

POTS (Plain Old Telephone System) The standard analog telephone service used by many telephone companies.

PPP (Point-to-Point Protocol) A communications protocol that allows the sending of IP packets on a dial-up (serial) connection. It supports compression and IP address negotiation.

Presentation layer In the OSI reference model, the layer that translates data between the formats the network requires and the formats the computer expects.

Primary Rate ISDN (PRI) An ISDN service that uses the entire bandwidth of a T1 (23 channels, with the twenty-fourth as the D channel). It has speeds up to 1.544Mbps.

print server A server that manages and controls a single printer or a group of printers on a network. The print server controls the queue or spooler, which allows clients to send print jobs to the print server, and the print server uses the spooler to hold the jobs until the printer is ready.

proprietary   Describes a system that is defined by one vendor and typically not supported by others. ARCnet started as a proprietary protocol, as did Token Ring.

protocol   A language, or a set of rules, that the computers in a network need to follow in order to communicate with each other.

protocol analyzer   Also called a *network analyzer*, a tool that can capture and decode packets flowing through a server.

protocol stack   Also called a *protocol suite*, a collection of protocols that are associated with and implement a particular communication model (such as the DOD networking model or the OSI reference model).

PSTN   See *public switched telephone network*.

public switched telephone network (PSTN)   A term that includes the network used to make ordinary telephone calls and modem communications, as well as dedicated lines that are leased by customers for private, exclusive use. Commercial service providers offer numerous services that facilitate computer communication across a PSTN.

radio frequency (RF)   The range of the electromagnetic spectrum between 10KHz and 1GHz.

radio frequency interference (RFI)   Noise created in the radio-frequency range.

radio wave transmission   A form of wireless media that has frequencies between 10 kilohertz (KHz) and 1 gigahertz (GHz). See also *high-power, single-frequency radio*; *low-power, single-frequency radio*; and *spread-spectrum radio*.

RAID (Redundant Array of Independent Disks)   A technique for achieving fault tolerance on a network by using several hard disks (also Redundant Array of Inexpensive Disks). If one or more drives fail, network data can be saved. Windows NT supports RAID Levels 0 (striping), 1 (mirroring), and 5 (striping with parity).

RAS (Remote Access Service)   A service that allows network connections to be established over public switched telephone network lines with modems. The computer initiating the connection is called the *RAS client*; the answering computer is called the *RAS host*.

redirector   Software loaded onto a workstation that can forward or redirect requests away from the local bus of the computer onto a network. These requests are then handled by a server. This type of software is often called a *shell, requester,* or *client*.

Redundant Array of Independent/Inexpensive Disks   See *RAID*.

registry   A database of operating system settings required and maintained by Windows NT and Windows 95.

relative expense   A measure of the actual monetary cost when a given link is used during routing.

Remote Access Service   See *RAS*.

Remote Procedure Calls   See *RPC*.

repeater   A network connectivity device that amplifies network signals to extend the distance they can travel.

requester   See *redirector*.

resource   Any network service that is shared, such as a shared network directory or printer.

RFI   See *radio frequency interference*.

RG-58 connector   A coaxial BNC connector used to connect Thinnet or 10Base2 cables.

ring   A network topology in which computers are arranged in a circle. Data travels around the ring in one direction, with each device on the ring acting as a repeater. Ring networks typically use a token-passing protocol.

RIP (Routing Information Protocol)   A routing protocol that performs route discovery by using hop counts.

RJ-45 connector   A connector with eight conductors used to connect UTP (unshielded twisted-pair) cables.

routable protocols   Protocols that support internetwork communication.

route discovery   The process a router uses to find the possible routes through the internetwork and then build routing tables to store that information.

router   An intelligent internetwork connectivity device that routes using logical and physical addressing to connect two or more logically separate networks. Routers use algorithms to determine the best path by which to send a packet.

Routing Information Protocol   See *RIP*.

RPC (Remote Procedure Calls)   A network interprocess communication mechanism that allows an application to be distributed among many computers on the same network.

RS-232   The most common serial communications system in use.

sag   See *brownout*.

satellite microwave   A type of microwave transmission that uses communication satellites that operate in geosynchronous orbit (rotate with the Earth) at 22,300 miles above the Earth. Parabolic antennas are used to communicate with the satellite.

SCSI (Small Computer Systems Interface)   A high-speed, parallel-bus interface that connects hard disk drives, CD-ROM drives, tape drives, and many other peripherals to a computer.

segmentation   The process of splitting a larger network into two or more segments linked by bridges or routers.

separate clock signal   A method of synchronous communication in which a separate channel carries clocking information.

Serial Line Internet Protocol   See *SLIP*.

server   A computer that provides services to service requestors. A *dedicated* server functions only as a server; it is not used as a client or workstation. Although you can dedicate a server to a particular network service, such as having a computer that serves only as a print server, you do not need a different server for each type of service. One server can function as a file, print, and application server. See also *file server*, *print server*, and *application server*.

server-based network   A network in which a dedicated server is used to provide services to clients, also called *client-server*. For example, the server might provide file, print, message, database, and application services to the clients in the network.

Session layer   In the OSI reference model, the layer that allows applications on separate computers to share a connection (called a *session*).

shielded twisted-pair (STP)   A type of wiring that includes a pair of conductors inside a metal or foil shield. This type of medium can support faster speeds than non-shielded wiring. See also *twisted-pair, unshielded twisted-pair*.

signal-regenerating repeater   A type of repeater that eliminates noise by creating an exact duplicate of incoming data by identifying it amidst the noise, reconstructing it, and retransmitting only the desired information.

signaling   The process of sending information over media.

Simple Network Management Protocol   See *SNMP*.

single-mode fiber optic   A type of fiber-optic cable with a narrow core, which allows a beam of light to follow only a single path through the core. See also *multimode fiber-optic cable*.

SLIP (Serial Line Internet Protocol)   A protocol that permits the sending of IP packets on a dial-up (serial) connection. It does not by itself provide support for compression or for IP address negotiation.

SMB (Server Message Blocks)   A protocol used by Windows systems for file and print sharing.

SMS (Systems Management Server)   A Microsoft software package that helps automate network management.

SMTP (Simple Mail Transfer Protocol)   A mail-transfer protocol that runs at the Application layer and is responsible for sending e-mail between systems.

SNMP (Simple Network Management Protocol)   An Internet protocol that manages network hardware such as routers, switches, servers, and clients from a single client on the network.

SONET (Synchronous Optical Network)   A high-speed, fiber-optic system that can transfer data between two points at speeds of greater than 1Gbps. It can be used as a carrier service for WAN connection services, such as ATM and ISDN.

source-routing bridge   A type of bridge that requires a predefined route to be included with the addresses of signals it receives. IBM Token Ring networks use this type of bridge.

spike   See *transient*.

spooler   A software program that stores documents until they can be printed and coordinates how print jobs are sent to a printer.

spread-spectrum radio   A type of radio wave transmission that signals over a range of frequencies. The available frequencies are divided into *channels* or *hops*. The adapters tune into a specific frequency for a predetermined length of time and then switch to a different frequency.

SPX (Sequenced Packet Exchange)   Novell's main Transport layer protocol. SPX is a connection-oriented protocol that provides end-to-end connection using sequencing and acknowledgments.

stand-alone computer   A computer that is not connected to a network.

standby monitor   A device on a Token Ring network that monitors the network status and may become the active monitor in the case of failure of the active monitor.

star   A network topology in which all the cables run from the computers to a central location, where they are connected by a hub.

start bit   A bit that is sent as part of a serial communication stream to signal the beginning of a byte or packet.

static routing   A type of routing in which the data path is determined in advance rather than on the fly by the router.

stop bit   A bit that is sent as part of a serial communications stream to signal the end of a byte or packet.

STP   See *shielded twisted-pair*.

striping   Also called RAID Level 0, a single volume created across multiple hard disk drives and accessed in parallel for the purpose of optimizing disk-access time. Striping increases disk performance but does not provide fault tolerance for the server.

striping with parity   Also called RAID Level 5, information stored across several hard disk drives, including error-correction information. If one of the striped disks fails, the operating system can recover the information that was on the disk from the other disks in the stripe set.

subnet   A logical segment of a network, also known as a *subnetwork*, which facilitates internetwork packet transmission. Each subnet or subnetwork is given a logical address.

subnet mask   A number mathematically applied to IP addresses to determine which IP addresses are part of the same subnetwork as the computer applying the subnet mask.

switch   A network connectivity device that brings media segments together in a central location; a type of hub. Unlike the other types of hubs, switches receive a signal and send it only to the port(s) it is destined for. The other types of hubs (active, passive, and intelligent) receive the signal and pass it along to all other ports.

Switched 56   A leased-line service that provides 56Kbps connections.

switching   In a LAN environment, switching provides each network transmission with an independent path through the network free of collisions with other network transmissions.

synchronous modem   A connectivity device that uses careful timing and coordination between modems to send large blocks of data without start and stop bits.

synchronous transmission   A type of transmission that uses a clock to control the timing of bits being sent.

Systems Management Server   See *SMS*.

T1 line   A point-to-point connection across 24 channels, with a speed of 1.544Mbps. Each channel is 64Kbps. T1 service can be divided to create different sizes of fractional lines.

T3 line   A point to-point connection across 28 T1 lines, with a speed of 44.736Mbps.

T-carrier   A type of multiplexed, high-speed, leased line. T-carrier service levels include T1, T2, T3, and T4. T-carriers offer transmission rates of up to 274Mbps.

TCP (Transmission Control Protocol)   The Internet protocol suite's transport service protocol.

TCP/IP (Transmission Control Protocol/Internet Protocol)   The best-known protocols that make up the Internet protocol suite; generally used as shorthand for that protocol suite.

TDI (Transport Driver Interface)   In the Windows NT networking architecture, an interface that enables the server, redirector, and file system drivers to remain independent of the transport protocol.

TDM   See *time-division multiplexing*.

TDR   See *time-domain reflectometer*.

terminator   A device at the end of a cable segment that indicates that the last node has been reached. In the case of Ethernet cable, a 50-ohm resistor (a terminator) at each end of the cable prevents signals from reflecting back through the cable.

terrestrial microwave   A type of microwave transmission that uses Earth-based transmitters and receivers in the low gigahertz range of frequencies. Communications are line-of-sight and cannot go around corners or through buildings.

Thicknet   Also known as 10Base5 or RG-8 coaxial, a type of cable used in Ethernet networks. Thicknet carries signals up to 500 meters (1640 feet) at 50 ohms.

Thinnet   Also known as 10Base2 or RG-58 coaxial, a type of cable used in Ethernet network. Thinnet carries signals 185 meters (607 feet) at 50 ohms.

throughput   The amount of data that has been sent over a given time. For example, 10BaseT Ethernet has a theoretical maximum throughput of 10Mbps. In practice, the throughput depends on the quality and length of wiring and is usually slightly less than 10Mbps.

tick count   A term used to quantify routing costs. A tick count refers to the amount of time required for a message to reach its destination.

time-domain reflectometer (TDR)   A tool that sends sound or light waves down a copper or fiber-optic cable.

time-division multiplexing (TDM)   A type of multiplexing in which a channel is divided into time slots that are allocated to each communicating device.

token   A small frame with a special format that designates that its holder (a network device) may transmit. When a node needs to transmit, it captures a token and attaches a message to it, along with addressing information.

Token Bus   A network architecture that uses token passing as the media access method. Token Bus is not commonly used for LANs in offices, but it has been widely used in manufacturing operations.

token passing   A network access method used by FDDI, Token Ring, and Token Bus networks. A short message (token) is passed around the ring. To transmit, a node must be in possession of a token. This prevents multiple nodes from transmitting simultaneously and creating collisions.

Token Ring A network that uses a token-passing protocol in a logical ring. Token Ring transmits at 4Mbps or 16Mbps.

TokenTalk Apple's implementation of the token-ring network architecture for AppleTalk environments.

topology A type of network connection or cabling system. Networks are usually configured in bus, ring, star, or mesh topology. See also *physical topology* and *logical topology*.

transceiver The device that performs both the transmission and reception of signals on a given medium.

transient A high-voltage burst of electric current, usually lasting less than 1 second, occurring randomly. Transients are often referred to as *spikes*.

transmission media The physical pathway on which the computers are connected. Cable and wireless media can connect the computers in a network.

transparent bridge A type of bridge that determines where to send data based on a table of addresses stored in memory.

Transport Driver Interface See *TDI*.

Transport layer In the OSI reference model, the layer that ensures that packets are delivered error-free, in sequence, and without losses or duplication.

Trojan horse A dangerous or destructive program that is designed to disguise itself as something harmless.

twisted-pair cable A type of wiring used for network communications that uses copper wires twisted into pairs, also known as 10BaseT. See also *shielded twisted-pair* and *unshielded twisted-pair*.

UDP (User Datagram Protocol)   A connectionless protocol that runs at the Transport layer and does not use sequencing or acknowledgments.

UNC (Universal Naming Convention)   A multivendor, multiplatform convention for identifying shared resources on a network.

Universal Naming Convention   See *UNC.*

unshielded twisted-pair (UTP)   A type of cable usually containing four pairs of wire, each pair twisted to reduce interference. Commonly used in telephone and LAN cabling.

user name   A user's account name in a logon-authenticated system.

UTP   See *unshielded twisted-pair.*

vampire tap   A specific type of Ethernet transceiver on a Thicknet network. The vampire tap does not break the Thicknet cable, but instead pierces the jacket of the cable to contact the center conductor.

VFAT   An extension of the FAT file system. VFAT allows long filenames up to 255 characters. Windows 95 and Windows NT use the VFAT file system.

virtual circuit   A logical connection made between two devices across a shared communications path. There is no dedicated physical circuit between the devices, even though they are acting as though there is one.

virtual circuit packet switching   An internetwork transmission technique in which all packets travel through a logical connection established between the sending device and the receiving device.

virus   A dangerous or destructive program that alters stored files or system configuration and copies itself onto external disks or other computers.

WAN (wide area network)   A network consisting of computers or LANs connected across a distance. WANs can cover small to large distances using different physical topologies, such as telephone lines, fiber-optic cabling, satellite transmissions, and microwave transmissions.

wavelength-division multiplexing (WDM)   A form of multiplexing in which the output channel is divided into multiple, smaller bandwidth channels. Different signals are transmitted at different wavelengths along the same cable.

WDM   See *wavelength-division multiplexing*.

wide area network   See *WAN*.

Windows Sockets   An interprocess communications protocol that delivers connection-oriented data streams used by Internet software and software ported from Unix environments.

WINS (Windows Internet Name Service)   A network service for Microsoft networks that provides computers with Internet numbers for specified NetBIOS names, facilitating browsing and intercommunication over TCP/IP networks.

wireless media   Network media that do not use an electrical or optical conductor. In most cases, the Earth's atmosphere is the physical path for the data. Wireless media is therefore useful when distances or obstructions make bounded media difficult (or impossible) to install.

wiring closet   An area in which cables are gathered. These cables connect the various areas in an office or building to the central wiring, and from there to the telephone or power company wiring.

word   The standard unit of data manipulated by a computer. A word typically consists of 8, 16, 32, or 64 bits.

workgroup   A group of computers linked together to share resources. A workgroup is less sophisticated than a domain in that workgroups lack the central administrative capacities of a domain.

World Wide Web (WWW)   The collection of computers on the Internet running HTTP (Hypertext Transfer Protocol) servers. The WWW allows for text and graphics to have hyperlinks connecting users to other servers. By using a Web browser, such as Netscape or Internet Explorer, a user can cross-link from one server to another at the click of a button.

worm   A destructive or dangerous program that can spawn another fully working version of itself.

X.25   The first packet-switching network standard. It uses virtual circuit packet switching with flow and error control. This standard spans the Physical through Network layer protocols and supports speeds up to 64Kbps.

Index

Note to the Reader: First-level entries are in **bold**. Page numbers in **bold** indicate the principal discussion of a topic or the definition of a term. Page numbers in *italic* indicate illustrations.

Numbers

10Base2 Ethernet cable, 17, 314
10Base5 Ethernet cable, 17, 314
10BaseT Ethernet cable, 17, 314
100BaseT Ethernet cable, 17, 314
100BaseVG-AnyLAN Ethernet cable, 16, 314
802.x standards, **15–18**. *See also* network standards
    802.3 Ethernet networks, 16–17
    802.5 Token Ring networks, 16, 17–18
    defined, 15, 328
    overview of, 15–16

A

access control lists (ACLs), 125
access permissions security, 10, 125, 314
accessing multiple networks, 147, *147*
account management
    of group accounts, 125, 133–134, *135*
    of user accounts, 125, 131–133, *132*
active hubs, 66, 314
active monitors, 18, 314
Address Resolution Protocol (ARP), 71, 186, 316
addresses
    IP addresses
        assigning with DHCP, 7, 127, 323
        defined, 330
        resolving NetBios names to, 6, 127, 189, 349
        troubleshooting, 188
    MAC (hardware) addresses, 146, 327
    network addresses, 334
    physical addresses, 327
administrative plans, **125–141**. *See also* network configuration; network implementation
    for account management, 131–134, *132*, *135*
    client operating systems and, 129–131, *129*, *130*
    database applications and, 128–129
    for file and printer shares, 135–137, *135*, *136*
    for group accounts, 125, 133–134, *135*
    network configuration and, 126–131, *129*, *130*
    for network growth, 126–128
    overview of, 125
    for performance management, 140–141
    for security management, 126, 137–140, *140*
    study questions on, 155–161
    for user accounts, 125, 131–133, *132*
Administrator user accounts, 131
Administrators group accounts, 134
advanced cable testers, 192, 315
AFP (AppleTalk Filing Protocol), 73, 315

amplifiers, 75, 315
analog signaling, *53*, 78, *78*, 315
analyzers, protocol, 152, 185, 202–204, *203*
AppleShare protocol, 73, 315
AppleTalk protocol suite, 72–73, *73*, 315
Application layer, 12–14, 315
application servers, 7–8, 316
architectures, data bus, 148. *See also* bus topologies
ARP (Address Resolution Protocol), 71, 186, 316
assigning IP addresses with DHCP, 7, 127, 323
asynchronous, 82, 316
ATM (Asynchronous Transfer Mode), 79, 82, *82*, 316
ATP (AppleTalk Transaction Protocol), 73, 316
attenuation, 54, 74, 316
AUI (Attachment Unit Interface) connectors, 59, 316
auto-sensing, 189

B

backbones, 64, 317
back ends, 128–129, 317
Backup Operators group accounts, 134
backup systems, 142
bandwidth, 53, 317
baseband transmission, 53, *53*, 317
baselines, 141
Basic Rate ISDN (BRI), 81, 317
bridges. *See also* connectivity devices
    defined, 15, 318
    overview of, 75, *75*
    source-routing bridges, 343
    transparent bridges, 347
broadband transmission, 52–53, *53*, 318
broadcast storms, **196–201**. *See also* troubleshooting
    causes of, 196, *196*
    defined, 196, 318
    recognizing, 198–201
    resolving, 197, *197*, 201
    study questions on, 213
brouters, 14, 77, 318
bus architectures, 148
bus topologies, 5, 64, *64*, 318

C

cable media, **55–59**. *See also* media; network planning
    advanced cable testers, 192, 315
    coaxial cable, 17, 57–58, *58*, 193, 320
    connectors
        AUI connectors, 59, 316
        DIX connectors, 316

NICs and, 148
RG-8 or 11 connectors, 193
RG-58 connectors, 59, 193, **340**
RG-62U connectors, 193
RJ-45 connectors, 59, **340**
in Ethernet networks, 16–17
fiber-optic cable, 55, 58–59, *59*, **326**
NICs and, 148
STP (shielded twisted-pair) cable, 18, 55, 57, *57*, **341**
Thicknet coaxial cable, 17, 55, 57–58, 193, **346**
Thinnet coaxial cable, 17, 55, 57–58, 193, **346**
in Token Ring networks, 18
troubleshooting, 191–193
twisted-pair cable, 17, 56–57, *56*, *57*, **347**
UTP (unshielded twisted-pair) cable, 18, 55–56, *56*, **319**, **348**
Carrier Sense (CS) protocol, 16, 321
categories of UTP cable, 56, 319
CD (Collision Detect) protocol, 16, 321
cell relay, 316
cells, 316, 319
channels, 61
chip creep, 319
chips, 61
choosing protocols, 127
chromatic dispersion, 54, 319
cladding, 58, 320
clients
client-server databases, **128–129**, **320**
client-server networks, 8–10, *8*, *9*, **320**, **341**
configuring Microsoft clients, 129, *130*
configuring NetWare clients, *129*, 131
defined, *8*, **8**, **320**
coaxial cable, 17, 57–58, *58*, 193, 320
Collision Detect (CD) protocol, 16, 321
collisions, 320
communication errors, 185–191. *See also* troubleshooting
in modems, 190
in protocols, 188–189
in RAS (Remote Access Service), 190–191
study questions on, 207–210
tools for finding, 185–187, *187*
viewing event logs with Event Viewer, 152, 185, 186–187, *187*, 191
communication technologies, 52–53, *53*, *54*
computers, stand-alone, 3, 343
configuring multiple NICs, 146. *See also* network configuration
connectionless communications, 11, 321
connection-oriented communications, 11, 321
connectivity devices, 74–77. *See also* network planning
bridges
defined, **15**, **318**
overview of, *75*, **75**
source-routing bridges, **343**
transparent bridges, **347**
brouters, **14**, 77, **318**
gateways
default gateways, 189, **323**
defined, **14**, **327**
expanding networks with, 126

overview of, 77
troubleshooting, 189
overview of, 14, 15, 74
repeaters
defined, **339**
multiport repeaters, **314**
overview of, 74–75, *74*
signal-regenerating repeaters, 75, **342**
routers, **14**, 76–77, *76*, **340**
study questions on, 99–101
troubleshooting, 193–194
connectivity problems, 191–195. *See also* troubleshooting
with cables, 191–193
with connectivity devices, 193–194
in Ethernet networks, 194
with NICs, 194
overview of, 191
study questions on, 210–213
in Token Ring networks, 195, *195*
connectors. *See also* media
AUI connectors, 59, **316**
DIX connectors, **316**
NICs and, 148
overview of, 59, 193
RG-8 or 11 connectors, 193
RG-58 connectors, 59, 193, **340**
RG-62U connectors, 193
RJ-45 connectors, 59, **340**
contention, 15, 321
counters in Windows NT, 153–154, *153*, *154*
crashes. *See* disaster recovery plans
crosstalk, 54, 321
CS (Carrier Sense) protocol, 16, 321
CSMA/CD (Carrier Sense Multiple Access/Collision Detect)
protocols, 15, 16, **321**

D

data bus architectures, 148. *See also* bus topologies
Data Link Control (DLC) protocol
defined, **68**, **324**
troubleshooting, 188, 193
Windows NT and, 68, *69*
Data Link layer
defined, **322**
LLC (Logical Link Control) sublayer, 15, **331**
MAC (Media Access Control) sublayer, 15, **331**
overview of, 12–13, 14–15
database applications, 128–129
database back-ends, 128–129, 317
Datagram Delivery Protocol (DDP), 73, 322
datagrams, 13, 14, 335. *See also* packets
dedicated lines, 322
dedicated servers, 8, 322, 341
default gateways, 189, 323
demultiplexing, 53, *54*, 333
DHCP (Dynamic Host Configuration Protocol), 7, 127, 323
Diagnostics, Windows NT, 152, 204–205, *205*

dial-up lines, 79, 323
differential backups, 142
digital signaling, 53, 78, 78, 323
digital voltmeters (DVMs), 192, 323
disaster recovery plans, 141–146. *See also* network implementation;
    troubleshooting
    backup systems, 142
    fault-tolerant disk schemes, 144, *144*, 325
    overview of, 141
    RAID, 144, 339
    redundant WAN links, 144–146, *145*
    study questions on, 161–164
    UPS systems, 143, *143*
dispersion, chromatic, 54, 319
distance-vector routing, 77, 323
DIX connectors, 316
DLC (Data Link Control) protocol
    defined, 68, 324
    troubleshooting, 188, 193
    Windows NT and, 68, 69
DNS (Domain Name Service), 7, 128, 189, 324
documenting networks, 126
domains, 324
duplicate IP addresses, troubleshooting, 188
DVMs (digital voltmeters), 192, 323
Dynamic Host Configuration Protocol (DHCP), 7, 127, 323
dynamic routing, 77, 324

E

802.*x* standards, 15–18. *See also* network standards
    802.3 Ethernet networks, 16–17
    802.5 Token Ring networks, 16, 17–18
    defined, 15, 328
    overview of, 15–16
EISA (Extended Industry Standard Architecture), 148, 324
EMI (electromagnetic interference), 54, 324
enabling printer sharing, 135, *135*
encoding signals, 78, 325
Error events in Event Viewer, 187
errors. *See* disaster recovery plans; network monitoring tools;
    troubleshooting
Ethernet networks. *See also* network standards
    cable media in, 16–17
    CSMA/CD protocol of, 15, 16, **321**
    defined, 325
    protocols in, 68
    troubleshooting, 194
event logs, 152, 185, 186–187, *187*, 191
expanding networks with routers and gateways, 126
Extended Industry Standard Architecture (EISA), 148, 324

F

Failure Audit events in Event Viewer, 187
fault-tolerant disk schemes, *144*, 144, 325
FDM (frequency-division multiplexing), 53, 326, 333
fiber-optic cable, 55, 58–59, *59*, 326

file and printer shares, 135–137, *135*, *136*
file servers, 7–8, 326
File Transfer Protocol (FTP), 71, 326
file-level security, 10
Frame Relay, 79, 80, *81*, 326
frame types, 189
frames, 15, 326
frequency-division multiplexing (FDM), 53, 326, 333
FTP (File Transfer Protocol), 71, 326
full backups, 142

G

gateways. *See also* connectivity devices
    default gateways, 189, 323
    defined, 14, 327
    expanding networks with, 126
    overview of, 77
    troubleshooting, 189
global groups, 134
ground, 57
group accounts, 125, 133–134, *135*
Guest user accounts, 131
Guests group accounts, 134

H

hardware addresses, 146, 327
hardware conflicts, IRQs and, 149–150
hardware crashes. *See* disaster recovery plans
high-power, single-frequency radio wave, 60–61, 327
hops, 61, 327
host name resolution with DNS, 7, 128, 189, 324
hosts, 327
HOSTS name files, 128
HTTP (Hypertext Transfer Protocol), 6, 327
hubs
    active hubs, 66, 314
    defined, 64, *65*, 327
    intelligent hubs, 66, 328
    passive hubs, 66, 336
hybrid networks, 10, 328
Hypertext Transfer Protocol (HTTP), 6, 327

I

icons in Event Viewer, 187
Identification tab of Network dialog box, 129, *130*
IEEE 802.*x* standards, 15–18. *See also* network standards
    802.3 Ethernet networks, 16–17
    802.5 Token Ring networks, 16, 17–18
    defined, 15, 328
    overview of, 15–16
IEEE (Institute of Electrical and Electronic Engineers), 15, 328
implementation. *See* network implementation
incremental backups, 142
Industry Standard Architecture (ISA), 148, 330

information sources on troubleshooting, 205–206, *206*
Informational events in Event Viewer, 187
infrared transmissions, 61, 62, 328
installing multiple NICs, 146
Integrated Services Digital Network (ISDN), 79, 80–81, *81*, 330
intelligent hubs, 66, 328
interconnectivity devices, 329. *See also* connectivity devices
Internet Protocol suite, 70–71, *70*, 329. *See also* IP; TCP/IP
Internetwork Packet eXchange (IPX) protocol, 68, 72, 330
internetworks, 74, 329
interrupt requests (IRQs), 149–150, 329
IP addresses
    assigning with DHCP, 7, 127, 323
    defined, 330
    resolving NetBios names to, 6, 127, 189, 349
    troubleshooting, 188
IP (Internet Protocol), 6, 71, 329. *See also* Internet Protocol suite
IPX (Internetwork Packet eXchange) protocol, 68, 72, 330
IPX/SPX (Internetwork Packet eXchange/Sequenced Packet eXchange) protocol suite
    defined, 6, 330
    overview of, 71–72, *72*
    SPX, 72, 343
IRQs (interrupt requests), 149–150, 329
ISA (Industry Standard Architecture), 148, 330
ISDN (Integrated Services Digital Network), 79, 80–81, *81*, 330

J

jabber packets, 196, 330

L

LANs (local area networks), 3, *4*, 330
LAPB (Link Access Procedures-Balanced) protocol, 80
leased lines, 79, 322, 330
links, redundant WAN, 144–146, *145*
link-state routing, 77, 330
LLC (Logical Link Control) sublayer, 15, 331
local area networks (LANs), 3, *4*, 330
local groups, 134
logical topologies, 63, 331
logs, event, 152, 185, 186–187, *187*, 191
low-power, single-frequency radio wave, 60–61, 331

M

MA (Multiple Access) protocol, 16, 321
MAC addresses, 146, 327
MAC (Media Access Control) sublayer, 15, 146, 331
MANs (metropolitan area networks), 4, *4*, 16, 331
MAUs (multistation access units), 17. *See also* MSAUs
MCSE Tests. *See also* study questions
    sample test answers
        Unit 1, 254–259
        Unit 2, 271–278

        Unit 3, 288–293
        Unit 4, 300–303
        Unit 5, 304–311
    sample tests
        Unit 1: standards and terminology, 35–47
        Unit 2: planning, 105–122
        Unit 3: implementation, 171–181
        Unit 4: troubleshooting, 216–223
        Unit 5: final review, 226–242
test objectives on
    implementation, 124
    planning, 50–51
    standards and terminology, 2
    troubleshooting, 184
media, 52–63. *See also* network planning
    bandwidth and, **53**, **317**
    baseband transmission and, 53, *53*, **317**
    broadband transmission and, 52–53, *53*, **318**
    cable connectors
        AUI connectors, 59, **316**
        DIX connectors, **316**
        NICs and, 148
        overview of, 59, **193**
        RG-8 or 11 connectors, 193
        RG-58 connectors, 59, 193, **340**
        RG-62U connectors, 193
        RJ-45 connectors, 59, **340**
    cable media, 55–59
        coaxial cable, 17, 57–58, *58*, 193, **320**
        in Ethernet networks, 16–17
        fiber-optic cable, 55, 58–59, *59*, **326**
        overview of, 55
        STP cable, 18, 55, 57, *57*
        Thicknet coaxial cable, 17, 55, 57–58, 193, **346**
        Thinnet coaxial cable, 17, 55, 57–58, 193, **346**
        in Token Ring networks, 17–18
        twisted-pair cable, 17, 56–57, *56*, *57*, **347**
        UTP cable, 18, 55–56, *56*, **319**
    communication technologies and, 52–53, *53*, *54*
    contention and, **15**, **321**
    CSMA/CD protocol and, 15, 16, **321**
    defined, **3**, **347**
    demultiplexing and, 53, *54*, **333**
    in IEEE 802.*x* network standards, 15–18
    media access protocols, **331**
    multiplexing and, 53, *54*, **333**, **349**
    overview of, 52, 55
    study questions on, 84–93
    token passing and, 15, 17–18, **346**
    transmission degradation and, 54
    wireless media, 60–63
        defined, **349**
        high-power, single-frequency radio wave, 60–61, **327**
        infrared, 61, 62, **328**
        low-power, single-frequency radio wave, 60–61, **331**
        microwaves defined, 60–61, **332**
        overview of, 60–61
        radio waves defined, **338**
        RF (radio frequency), 61, **338**

satellite microwave, 62, *63*, 341
spread-spectrum radio wave, 60–61, 343
terrestrial microwave, 62, *62*, 345
Media Access Control (MAC) sublayer, 15, 146, 331
mesh topologies, 66, *67*, 331
metropolitan area networks (MANs), *4*, 4, 16, 331
MicroChannel bus architecture, 148, 332
Microsoft clients, 129, *130*
Microsoft SMS (Systems Management Server), 141, 342
Microsoft Training & Certification Web site, 2
Microsoft Windows 95 security, 139–140, *140*
Microsoft Windows NT
  Books Online, 205–206, *206*
  counters in, 153–154, *153*, *154*
  Diagnostics (WinMSD), 152, 204–205, *205*
  DLC (Data Link Control) protocol and, 68, *69*
  enabling security logging in, 186
  Event Viewer, 152, 186–187, *187*
  multiple NICs in, 147, *147*
  NetBEUI protocol and, 68, *69*
  Network Monitor, 152, 202–204, *203*
  objects in, 153–154, *153*, *154*
  OSI reference model and, 69
  Performance Monitor, 153–154, *153*, *154*, 202
  protocols and, 68–69, *69*
  security, 137–139
  Servers as routers, 147, *147*
  TCP/IP and, 68–69, *69*
Microsoft WINS (Windows Internet Name Service), 6, 127, 189, 349
microwaves. *See also* wireless media
  defined, 60–61, 332
  satellite microwave, 62, *63*, 341
  terrestrial microwave, 62, *62*, 345
modems, 190, 332
modulating signals, 78, 332
monitoring. *See* network monitoring tools
monitors, active, 18, 314
MSAUs (Multiple Station Access Units), 17, *195*, *195*, 332
MSUs, 332. *See also* MSAUs
multihoming, 146, 147, *147*, 332
Multiple Access (MA) protocol, 16, 321
multiple NICs. *See* NICs
multiplexing, 53, *54*, 333, 349
multiport repeaters, 314
mux, 53

N

names
  DNS (Domain Name Service), 7, 128, 189, 324
  HOSTS name files, 128
  NetBIOS names
    NetBIOS defined, 333
    resolving with WINS, 6, 127, 189, 349
    study questions on, 167–169
  UNC (Universal Naming Convention), 151, 348
  user names, 132, 348
  WINS (Windows Internet Name Service), 6, 127, 189, 349
Nbtstat troubleshooting tool, 186

NCP (NetWare Core Protocol), 72, 333
NDIS (Network Driver Interface Standard), 19, 333
NetBEUI (NetBIOS Extended User Interface) protocol
  defined, 6, 68, 333
  overview of, 69–70, 151
  troubleshooting, 188, 193
  Windows NT and, 68, *69*
NetBIOS (Network Basic Input/Output System) names
  NetBIOS defined, 333
  overview of, 151
  resolving with WINS, 6, 127, 189, 349
  study questions on, 167–169
NetWare clients, *129*, 131
NetWare Core Protocol (NCP), 72, 333
network adapters. *See* NICs
network analyzers, 152, 185, 202–204, *203*
network configuration, 126–131. *See also* network implementation
  assigning IP addresses with DHCP, 7, 127, 323
  choosing protocols, 127
  database applications and, 128–129
  documenting networks, 126
  expanding with routers and gateways, 126
  HOSTS name files and, 128
  of Microsoft clients, 129, *130*
  of NetWare clients, *129*, 131
  overview of, 126
  planning for network growth, 126–128
  resolving host names with DNS, 7, 128, 189, 324
  resolving NetBIOS names with WINS, 6, 127, 189, 349
  security and, 126
Network dialog box, 129, *130*
Network Driver Interface Standard (NDIS), 19, 333
Network File System (NFS) protocol, 68, 71, 334
network implementation, 124–181. *See also* network monitoring tools
  administrative plans, 125–141. *See also* network configuration
    for account management, 131–134, *132*, *135*
    client operating systems and, 129–131, *129*, *130*
    database applications and, 128–129
    for file and printer shares, 135–137, *135*, *136*
    for group accounts, 125, 133–134, *135*
    network configuration and, 126–131, *129*, *130*
    for network growth, 126–128
    for performance management, 140–141
    for security management, 126, 137–140, *140*
    study questions on, 155–161
    for user accounts, 125, 131–133, *132*
  disaster recovery plans, 141–146
    backup systems, 142
    fault-tolerant disk schemes, 144, *144*, 325
    RAID, 144, 339
    redundant WAN links, 144–146, *145*
    study questions on, 161–164
    UPS systems, 143, *143*
  multiple NICs, 146–150
    accessing multiple networks with, 147, *147*
    cabling, connectors and, 148
    configuring and installing, 146
    data bus architectures and, 148
    hardware conflicts and, 149–150
    multi-homing techniques, 146, 147, *147*, 332

NIC defined, **146**, **334**
segmenting networks with, 147, *147*, **341**
study questions on, 164–167
troubleshooting, 194
NetBIOS names
NetBIOS defined, **333**
resolving with WINS, **6**, **127**, 189, **349**
study questions on, 167–169
sample test on, 171–181
test objectives for, 124
network interface cards. *See* NICs
Network layer, 12–13, 14, **334**
network monitoring tools, 152–154, 202–205. *See also* network
implementation
defined, **185**, **334**
event logs, **152**, **185**, 186–187, *187*, 191
Network Monitor, 152, 202–204, *203*
overview of, 140–141, 152
Performance Monitor, 153–154, *153*, *154*, 202
protocol analyzers, **152**, **185**, 202–204, *203*
SMS (Systems Management Server), 141, **342**
study questions on, 169–170
Windows NT Diagnostics, 152, 204–205, *205*
network planning, 50–122. *See also* connectivity devices; media;
protocols
connectivity devices, **74–77**
bridges, **15**, **75**, *75*, **318**
brouters, **14**, 77, **318**
gateways, **14**, 77, **327**
repeaters, 74–75, *74*, **339**
routers, **14**, 76–77, *76*, **340**
study questions on, 99–101
troubleshooting, 193–194
for growth, 126–128
media, **52–63**
bandwidth and, **53**, **317**
baseband transmission and, **53**, *53*, **317**
broadband transmission and, 52–53, *53*, **318**
cable connectors, 59, 193
cable media, 55–59, *55–59*
coaxial cable, 17, 57–58, *58*, 193, **320**
communication technologies and, 52–53, *53*, *54*
demultiplexing and, *53*, *54*, **333**
fiber-optic cable, 55, 58–59, *59*, **326**
multiplexing and, *53*, *54*, **333**, **349**
STP cable, 18, 55, 57, *57*
study questions on, 84–93
Thicknet coaxial cable, 17, 55, 57–58, 193, **346**
Thinnet coaxial cable, 17, 55, 57–58, 193, **346**
transmission degradation and, 54
twisted-pair cable, 17, 56–57, *56*, *57*, **347**
UTP cable, 18, 55–56, *56*, **319**
wireless media, 60–62, *62*, *63*
protocols, **66–73**
AppleTalk protocol suite, 72–73, *73*, **315**
Internet Protocol suite, 70–71, *70*, **329**
IPX/SPX protocol suite, **6**, 71–72, *72*, **330**
NetBEUI protocol, **6**, 68–70, *69*, 151, **333**
study questions on, 95–99
Windows NT and, 68–69, *69*

sample test on, 105–122
test objectives for, 50–51
topologies, **63–67**
bus topologies, **5**, 64, *64*, **318**
hierarchical topologies, 64
logical topologies, 63, **331**
mesh topologies, 66, 67, **331**
physical topologies, 63, **336**
ring topologies, **5**, 64, *65*, **340**
star topologies, **5**, 64–66, *65*, **343**
study questions on, 93–95
tree topologies, 64
WAN connection services, 78–83
analog signaling and, *53*, 78, *78*, **315**
ATM, 79, 82, *82*, **316**
dial-up lines and, 79, **323**
digital signaling and, *53*, 78, *78*, **323**
Frame Relay, 79, 80, *81*, **326**
ISDN, 79, 80–81, *81*, **330**
leased lines and, 79, **322**, **330**
redundant WAN links, 144–146, *145*
SONET, 83, **342**
study questions on, 101–104
Switched 56, 83, **344**
T1 lines, 83, 145–146, *145*, **345**
T3 lines, 83, **345**
WANs defined, **4**, *5*, **349**
X.25, 79–80, *80*, **350**
network shares, 125
network standards, 15–19
IEEE 802.*x* standards
802.3 Ethernet networks, 16–17
802.5 Token Ring networks, 16, 17–18
NDIS (Network Driver Interface Standard), 19, **333**
ODI (Open Data Link Interface) standard, 19, **335**
sample test on, 35–47
study questions on, 30–34
test objectives for, 2
network terminology, 2–15
access permissions security, **10**, **125**, **314**
application servers, **7–8**, **316**
brouters, **14**, 77, **318**
bus topologies, **5**, 64, *64*, **318**
clients, *8*, **8**, **320**
client-server networks, 8–10, *8*, *9*, **320**, **341**
connectionless communications, **11**, **321**
connection-oriented communications, **11**, **321**
connectivity devices, 14, 15, 74–77
dedicated servers, **8**, **322**, **341**
DHCP protocol, **7**, **127**, **323**
DNS (Domain Name Service), **7**, **128**, 189, **324**
file servers, **7–8**, **326**
gateways, **14**, 77, **327**
HTTP (Hypertext Transfer Protocol), **6**, **327**
hybrid networks, **10**, **328**
Internet Protocol suite, 70–71, *70*, **329**
IP (Internet Protocol), **6**, 71, **329**
IPX/SPX protocol suite, **6**, 71–72, *72*, **330**
LANs (local area networks), **3**, *4*
MANs (metropolitan area networks), *4*, **4**, 16, **331**

NetBEUI protocol, 6, 68–70, *69*, 151, 333
networks, 3, 333
OSI reference model, 12–15, 335
packets, **14**
peers, 8, 336
peer-to-peer networks, 8–10, *8*, *9*, 336
PPP protocol, 11–12, 337
print servers, 7–8, 337
protocol suites, 6, 338
protocols, 6, 338
ring topologies, 5, 64, *65*
routers, 14, 76–77, *76*, 340
sample test on, 35–47
security terms, 10
servers, 8, *9*, 341
share-level security, 10
SLIP protocol, 11–12, 342
stand-alone computers, 3, 343
star topologies, 5, 64–66, *65*, 343
study questions on, 20–30
TCP protocol, 6, 71, 345
TCP/IP networking services, 6–7
test objectives for, 2
topologies, 5, 347
transmission media, 3, 347
WANs (wide area networks), **4**, *5*, 349
WINS (Windows Internet Name Service), 6, 127, 189, 349
networks
accessing multiple networks, 147, *147*
client-server networks, 8–10, *8*, *9*, 320, 341
defined, 3, 333
documenting, 126
expanding with routers and gateways, 126
hybrid networks, **10**, 328
internetworks, 74, 329
LANs (local area networks), 3, *4*, 330
MANs (metropolitan area networks), **4**, *4*, 16, 331
network addresses, 334
peer-to-peer networks, 8–10, *8*, *9*, 336
planning for growth, 126–128
segmenting, 147, *147*, 341
subnetworks (subnets), 76, **76**, 188, 344
WANs (wide area networks), **4**, *5*, 349
New Local Group dialog box, 134, *135*
New User dialog box, 132–133, *132*
NFS (Network File System) protocol, 68, 71, 334
NICs (network interface cards), multiple, **146–150**. *See also* network
    implementation
    accessing multiple networks with, 147, *147*
    cabling, connectors and, 148
    configuring and installing, 149
    data bus architectures and, 148
    defined, **146**, 334
    hardware conflicts and, 149–150
    multi-homing techniques, **146**, 147, *147*, 332
    segmenting networks with, 147, *147*, 341
    study questions on, 164–167
    troubleshooting, 194

NSLookup troubleshooting tool, 186
NTFS (New Technology File System), 138–139, 334
NWLink protocol, 68–69, *69*, 189, 334

O

objects in Windows NT, 153–154, *153*, *154*
ODI (Open Data Link Interface) network standard, 19, 335
ohmage of coaxial cable, 58, 193
100BaseT Ethernet cable, 17, 314
100BaseVG-AnyLAN Ethernet cable, 16, 314
Open Shortest Path First (OSPF) protocol, 71, 77, 335
oscilloscopes, 192, 335
OSI reference model, 12–15
    AppleTalk protocol suite and, *73*
    Application layer, 12–14, 315
    Data Link layer
        LLC (Logical Link Control) sublayer, 15, 331
        MAC (Media Access Control) sublayer, 15, 331
    defined, **335**
    Internet Protocol suite and, *70*
    IPX/SPX protocol suite and, *72*
    Network layer, 12–13, 14, 334
    Physical layer, 12–13, 14–15, 336
    Presentation layer, 12–14, 337
    Session layer, 12–14, 341
    Transport layer, 12–13, 14, 347
    WAN connection services and, 79–82
        ATM, 79, *82*
        Frame Relay, 79, *81*
        ISDN, 79, *81*
        X.25, 79–80, *80*, 350
    Windows NT and, *69*
OSPF (Open Shortest Path First) protocol, 71, 77, 335

P

Packet Internet Groper (Ping) troubleshooting tool, 186, 337
packets
    defined, **14**, 335
    jabber packets, 196, 330
    packet switching, 335
    virtual circuit packet switching, 348
passive hubs, 66, 336
password properties, 133
password-protected security, 10, 336
PCI (Peripheral Component Interconnect) bus architecture, 148, 336
peers, 8, 336
peer-to-peer networks, 8–10, *8*, *9*, 336
performance management, 140–141. *See also* network monitoring
    tools
Performance Monitor, 153–154, *153*, *154*, 202
permissions. *See also* security
    access permissions, **10**, 125, 314
    defined, **10**, 125, 336
    NTFS permissions, 138–139, 334
    share permissions, 125, 138

physical addresses, 327
Physical layer, 12–13, 14–15, 336
physical topologies, 63, 336
Ping (Packet Internet Groper) troubleshooting tool, 186, 337
planning. *See* network planning
power outages, 202
Power Users group accounts, 134
PPP (Point-to-Point Protocol), 11–12, 337
Presentation layer, 12–14, 337
PRI (Primary Rate ISDN), 81, 337
print servers, 7–8, 337
printers, sharing
    enabling, 135, *135*
    scheduling print jobs, 136, *136*
    setting spooler options, 136–137, 343
private lines, 322, 330
problems. *See* disaster recovery plans; network monitoring tools;
        troubleshooting
PROM (Programmable Read-Only Memory), 146
properties of user accounts, 132–133, *132*
protocol analyzers, 152, 185, 202–204, *203*
protocols, 66–73. *See also* network planning
    AFP (AppleTalk Filing Protocol), 73, 315
    AppleShare, 73
    AppleTalk protocol suite, 72–73, *73*, 315
    ARP (Address Resolution Protocol), 71, 186, 316
    ATP (AppleTalk Transaction Protocol), 73, 316
    choosing, 127
    CSMA/CD, 15, 16, 321
    DDP (Datagram Delivery Protocol), 73, 322
    defined, 6, 338
    DHCP (Dynamic Host Configuration Protocol), 7, 127, 323
    DLC (Data Link Control)
        troubleshooting, 188, 193
        Windows NT and, 68, *69*
    in Ethernet networks, 68
    FTP (File Transfer Protocol), 71, 326
    HTTP (Hypertext Transfer Protocol), 6, 327
    Internet Protocol suite, 70–71, *70*, 329
    IP (Internet Protocol), 6, 71, 329
    IPX (Internetwork Packet eXchange), 68, 72, 330
    IPX/SPX protocol suite, 6, 71–72, *72*, 330
    LAPB (Link Access Procedures-Balanced), 80
    media access protocols, 331
    NCP (NetWare Core Protocol), 72, 333
    NetBEUI
        defined, 6, 68, 333
        overview of, 69–70, 151
        troubleshooting, 188, 193
        Windows NT and, 68, *69*
    NFS (Network File System), 68, 71, 334
    NWLink, 68–69, 69, 189, 334
    OSPF (Open Shortest Path First), 71, 77, 335
    overview of, 66, 68
    PPP (Point-to-Point Protocol), 11–12, 337
    protocol stacks, 335, 338
    protocol suites, 6, 338
    RIP (Routing Information Protocol), 71, 77, 340

SLIP (Serial Line Internet Protocol), 11–12, 189, 342
SMB (Server Message Blocks), 68, 342
SMTP (Simple Mail Transfer Protocol), 71, 342
SPX (Sequenced Packet eXchange), 72, 343
study questions on, 95–99
TCP (Transmission Control Protocol), 6, 71, 345
TCP/IP
    defined, 68, 345
    networking services, 6–7
    troubleshooting, 186, 188–189
    Windows NT and, 68–69, *69*
in Token Ring networks, 68
troubleshooting, 188–189
UDP (User Datagram Protocol), 71, 348
Windows NT and, 68–69, *69*
PSTN (public switched telephone network), 79, 338

Q

questions. *See* study questions

R

radio waves
    defined, 338
    high-power, single-frequency radio wave, 60–61, 327
    low-power, single-frequency radio wave, 60–61, 331
    RF (radio frequency), 61, 338
    spread-spectrum radio wave, 60–61, 343
RAID (Redundant Array of Independent Disks), 144, 339
RAS (Remote Access Service), 190–191, 339
redundant WAN links, 144–146, *145*
repeaters. *See also* connectivity devices
    defined, 339
    multiport repeaters, 314
    overview of, 74–75, *74*
    signal-regenerating repeaters, 75, 342
Replicator group accounts, 134
resolving
    host names with DNS, 7, 128, 189, 324
    NetBIOS names with WINS, 6, 127, 189, 349
resources, 125, 339
RF (radio frequency), 61, 338
RG-8 or 11 connectors, 193
RG-58 connectors, 59, 193, 340
RG-62U connectors, 193
rights, 125. *See also* permissions
ring topologies, 5, 64, *65*, 340
RIP (Routing Information Protocol), 71, 77, 340
RJ-45 connectors, 59, 340
Route troubleshooting tool, 186
routers
    defined, 14, 340
    expanding networks with, 126
    overview of, 76–77, *76*
    stopping broadcast storms with, 197, *197*
    Windows NT Servers as, 147, *147*

routing
  distance-vector routing, 77, 323
  dynamic routing, 77, 324
  link-state routing, 77, 330
  static routing, 77, 343

S

sample tests. *See* MCSE Tests
satellite microwave, 62, *63*, 341
scheduling print jobs, 136, *136*
security, 137–140
  access level security, **139**, *140*
  access permissions security, **10**, 125, 137
  enabling Windows NT security logging, 186
  file-level security, **138**
  network growth and, 126
  NTFS permissions, 138–139, 334
  overview of, 126, 137
  password-protected security, **10**, 336
  permissions, **10**, 125, 336
  setting user password properties, 133
  share permissions, 138
  share-level security, **10**, 139
  user-level security, **138**, 139–140
  on Windows 95, 139–140, *140*
  on Windows NT, 137 139
segmenting networks with multiple NICs, 147, *147*, 341
Sequenced Packet eXchange (SPX) protocol, **72**, 343. *See also* IPX/SPX
Serial Line Internet Protocol (SLIP), 11–12, 189, 342
Server Message Blocks (SMB) protocol, 68, 342
Server service in Windows NT, 190
servers
  application servers, 7–8, 316
  client-server databases, **128–129**, 320
  client-server networks, 8–10, *8*, *9*, 320, 341
  dedicated servers, 8, 322, 341
  defined, **8**, *9*, 341
  file servers, 7–8, 326
  print servers, 7–8, 337
  troubleshooting, 201, 202
  Windows NT Servers as routers, 147, *147*
services, networking, 6–7
Session layer, 12–14, 341
sessions, 13
share permissions, 125, 138
share-level security, 10
shares, 125
sharing files and printers, 135–137, *135*, *136*
shielded twisted-pair (STP) cable, 18, 55, 57, *57*, 341
signaling
  analog signaling, 53, 78, *78*, 315
  defined, **342**
  digital signaling, 53, 78, *78*, 323
signal-regenerating repeaters, 75, 342
sizes of coaxial cable, 58
SLIP (Serial Line Internet Protocol), 11–12, 189, 342
SMB (Server Message Blocks) protocol, 68, 342
SMS (Systems Management Server) software, **141**, 342

SMTP (Simple Mail Transfer Protocol), 71, 342
SONET (Synchronous Optical Network), 83, 342
spooler options for printers, 136–137, 343
spread-spectrum radio wave, 60–61, 343
SPX (Sequenced Packet eXchange) protocol, **72**, 343. *See also* IPX/SPX
stand-alone computers, 3, 343
standards. *See* network standards
star topologies, 5, 64–66, *65*, 343
static routing, 77, 343
STP (shielded twisted-pair) cable, 18, 55, 57, *57*, 341
study questions. *See also* MCSE Tests
  answers
    Unit 1, 244–253
    Unit 2, 259–271
    Unit 3, 278–288
    Unit 4, 294–300
  Unit 1, **20–34**
    standards, 30–34
    terminology, 20–30
  Unit 2, **84 104**
    connectivity devices, 99–101
    media, 84–93
    protocols, 95–99
    topologies, 93–95
    WAN connection services, 101–104
  Unit 3, **155–170**
    administrative plans, 155–161
    disaster recovery plans, 161–164
    multiple NICs, 164–167
    NetBIOS names, 167–169
    network monitoring tools, 169–170
  Unit 4, **207–215**
    broadcast storms, 213
    communication errors, 207–210
    connectivity problems, 210–213
    troubleshooting tools, 214–215
subnet masks, 188, 344
subnetworks (subnets), 76, *76*, 344
Success Audit events in Event Viewer, 187
Switched 56 connection service, 83, 344
switches, 64, *65*, 66, 344
switching
  defined, **344**
  packet switching, 335
  virtual circuit packet switching, 348
Synchronous Optical Network (SONET), 83, 342
system crashes. *See* disaster recovery plans
System Log in Event Viewer, 186–187, *187*
Systems Management Server (SMS) software, **141**, 342

T

T1 lines connection service, 83, 145–146, *145*, 345
T3 lines connection service, 83, 345
TCP (Transmission Control Protocol), 6, 71, 345
TCP/IP (Transmission Control Protocol/Internet Protocol)
  defined, **68**, 345
  Internet Protocol suite, 70–71, *70*, 329
  IP (Internet Protocol), 6, 71, 329

networking services, 6–7
troubleshooting, 186, 188–189
Windows NT and, 68–69, *69*
TDI (Transport Driver Interface), 68, *69*, 345
TDM (time-division multiplexing), 53, 333, 346
TDRs (time-domain reflectometers), 192, 346
10Base2 Ethernet cable, 17, 314
10Base5 Ethernet cable, 17, 314
10BaseT Ethernet cable, 17, 314
terminology. *See* network terminology
terrestrial microwave, *62, 62,* 345
testers, advanced cable, 192, 315
tests. *See* MCSE Tests
Thicknet coaxial cable, 17, 55, 57–58, 193, 346
Thinnet coaxial cable, 17, 55, 57–58, 193, 346
time-division multiplexing (TDM), 53, 333, 346
time-domain reflectometers (TDRs), 192, 346
token masters, 18
token passing, 15, 17–18, 346
Token Ring networks. *See also* network standards
    cable media in, 18
    defined, **17**, 347
    overview of, 16, 64
    protocols in, 68
    token passing in, **15**, 17–18, 346
    troubleshooting, 195, *195*
tokens, 17, 346
tools. *See* network monitoring tools; troubleshooting, tools
topologies, 63–67. *See also* network planning
    bus topologies, 5, 64, *64,* 318
    defined, **5**, 347
    hierarchical topologies, **64**
    logical topologies, 63, 331
    mesh topologies, 66, *67,* 331
    overview of, 63
    physical topologies, 63, 336
    ring topologies, 5, 64, *65,* 340
    star topologies, 5, 64–66, *65,* 343
    study questions on, 93–95
    tree topologies, 64
Tracert troubleshooting tool, 186
Transmission Control Protocol (TCP), 6, 71, 345. *See also* TCP/IP
transmission degradation, 54
transmission media, 3, 347. *See also* media
Transport Driver Interface (TDI), 68, *69,* 345
Transport layer, 12–13, 14, 347
tree topologies, 64
troubleshooting, 184–223. *See also* disaster recovery plans; network
        monitoring tools
    broadcast storms, 196–201
        causes of, 196, *196*
        defined, **196**, 318
        recognizing, 198–201
        resolving, 197, *197,* 201
        study questions on, 213
    communication errors, **185–191**
        in modems, 190
        in protocols, 188–189
        in RAS (Remote Access Service), 190–191

study questions on, 207–210
tools for finding, 185–187, *187*
viewing event logs with Event Viewer, **152**, 185, 186–187,
        187, 191
connectivity problems, **191–195**
    with cables, 191–193
    with connectivity devices, 193–194
    in Ethernet networks, 194
    with NICs, 194
    study questions on, 210–213
    in Token Ring networks, 195, *195*
DLC protocol, 188, 193
duplicate IP addresses, 188
incorrect DNS and WINS information, 189
incorrect or missing default gateways, 189
incorrect subnet masks, 188, **344**
information sources on, 205–206, *206*
NetBEUI protocol, 188, 193
NWLink protocol, 189
power outages, 202
sample test on, 216–223
server crashes, 201
server upgrade failures, 202
SLIP protocol, 189
study questions on, 207–215
TCP/IP networks, 186, 188–189
test objectives for, 184
tools for, **202–206**
    diagnosing cable problems, 192
    Event Viewer, **152**, 186–187, *187*
    finding communication errors, 185–187, *187*
    Nbtstat, 186
    Network Monitor, 152, 202–204, *203*
    NSLookup, 186
    Performance Monitor, 153–154, *153, 154,* 202
    Ping, **186**, 337
    resolving broadcast storms, 197, *197*
    Route, **186**
    study questions on, 214–215
    Tracert, **186**
    Windows NT Diagnostics (WinMSD), 152, 204–205, *205*
twisted-pair cable, 17, 56–57, *56, 57,* 347

U

UDP (User Datagram Protocol), 71, 348
UNC (Universal Naming Convention), 151, 348
upgrade failures, 202
UPS (uninterruptible power supply) systems, 143, *143*
users
    Guest user accounts, **131**
    user accounts, 125, 131–133, *132*
    user names, 132, 348
    user-level security, 10
    Users group accounts, 134
UTP (unshielded twisted-pair) cable, 18, 55–56, *56,* 319, 348

V

virtual circuit packet switching, 348
voltmeters, digital (DVMs), 192, 323

W

WAN (wide area network) connection services, 78–83. *See also*
    network planning
    analog signaling and, *53*, 78, *78*, 315
    ATM, 79, 82, *82*, 316
    dial-up lines and, 79, **323**
    digital signaling and, *53*, 78, *78*, 323
    Frame Relay, 79, 80, *81*, 326
    ISDN, 79, 80–81, *81*, 330
    leased lines and, 79, **322**, 330
    overview of, 78, 79
    redundant WAN links, 144–146, *145*
    SONET, 83, **342**
    study questions on, 101–104
    Switched 56, 83, **344**
    T1 lines, 83, 145–146, *145*, 345
    T3 lines, 83, 345
    WANs defined, 4, *5*, **349**
    X.25, 79–80, *80*, **350**
Warning events in Event Viewer, 187
warnings
    broadcast storms, 194
    NetWare servers, 131
    UPS devices, 143
Web sites, Microsoft Training & Certification, 2
wide area network. *See* WAN
Windows. *See* Microsoft Windows
WinMSD (Windows NT Diagnostics), 152, 204–205, *205*
WINS (Windows Internet Name Service), 6, 127, 189, 349
wireless media, 60–63. *See also* media; network planning
    defined, **349**
    infrared, 61, 62, **328**
    microwaves
        defined, **60–61**, 332
        satellite microwave, **62**, *63*, 341
        terrestrial microwave, *62*, **62**, 345
    overview of, 60–61
    radio waves
        defined, 338
        high-power, single-frequency radio wave, **60–61**, 327
        low-power, single-frequency radio wave, 60–61, 331
        RF (radio frequency), **61**, 338
        spread-spectrum radio wave, **60–61**, 343
Workstation service in Windows NT, 190
workstations, accessing two networks from, 147, *147*

X

X.25 connection service, 79–80, *80*, 350

MCSE CORE REQUIREMENT STUDY GUIDES FROM NETWORK PRESS

Sybex's Network Press expands the definitive study guide series for MCSE candidates.

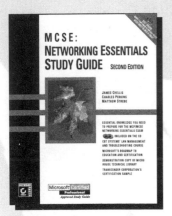

MCSE: NETWORKING ESSENTIALS STUDY GUIDE SECOND EDITION

JAMES CHELLIS
CHARLES PERKINS
MATTHEW STREBE

ESSENTIAL KNOWLEDGE YOU NEED TO PREPARE FOR THE MCP/MCSE NETWORKING ESSENTIALS EXAM
INCLUDED ON THE CD:
CBT SYSTEMS' LAN MANAGEMENT AND TROUBLESHOOTING COURSE
MICROSOFT'S ROADMAP TO EDUCATION AND CERTIFICATION
DEMONSTRATION COPY OF MICRO HOUSE TECHNICAL LIBRARY
TRANSCENDER CORPORATION'S CERTIFICATION SAMPLE

ISBN: 0-7821-2220-5
704pp; 7¹/₂" x 9"; Hardcover
$49.99

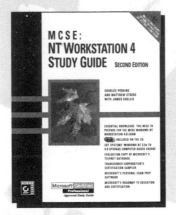

MCSE: NT WORKSTATION 4 STUDY GUIDE SECOND EDITION

CHARLES PERKINS
AND MATTHEW STREBE
WITH JAMES CHELLIS

ESSENTIAL KNOWLEDGE YOU NEED TO PREPARE FOR THE MCSE WINDOWS NT WORKSTATION 4.0 EXAM
INCLUDED ON THE CD:
CBT SYSTEMS' WINDOWS NT 3.5x TO 4.0 UPGRADE COMPUTER-BASED COURSE
EVALUATION COPY OF MICROSOFT'S TECHNET DATABASE
TRANSCENDER CORPORATION'S CERTIFICATION SAMPLER
MICROSOFT'S PERSONAL EXAM PREP SOFTWARE
MICROSOFT'S ROADMAP TO EDUCATION AND CERTIFICATION

ISBN: 0-7821-2223-X
784pp; 7¹/₂" x 9"; Hardcover
$49.99

MCSE: NT SERVER 4 STUDY GUIDE SECOND EDITION

MATTHEW STREBE
CHARLES PERKINS
WITH JAMES CHELLIS

ESSENTIAL KNOWLEDGE YOU NEED TO PREPARE FOR THE MCSE WINDOWS NT SERVER 4.0 EXAM
INCLUDED ON THE CD:
THE EDGE TEST FOR NT SERVER 4.0 DEMO
TRANSCENDER CORPORATION'S NT-ENTERPRISECERT 4.0 DEMO
EVALUATION COPY OF MICROSOFT'S TECHNET DATABASE
MICROSOFT'S TRAIN_CERT OFFLINE
MICROSOFT'S INTERNET EXPLORER 3.0

ISBN: 0-7821-2222-1
832pp; 7¹/₂" x 9"; Hardcover
$49.99

MCSE: NT SERVER 4 IN THE ENTERPRISE STUDY GUIDE SECOND EDITION

LISA DONALD
WITH JAMES CHELLIS

ESSENTIAL KNOWLEDGE YOU NEED TO PREPARE FOR THE MCSE WINDOWS NT SERVER 4 IN THE ENTERPRISE EXAM
INCLUDED ON THE CD:
THE EDGE TEST FOR NT SERVER 4.0 IN THE ENTERPRISE DEMO
TRANSCENDER CORPORATION'S NT-ENTERPRISECERT 4.0 DEMO
EVALUATION COPY OF MICROSOFT'S TECHNET DATABASE
MICROSOFT'S TRAIN_CERT OFFLINE
MICROSOFT'S INTERNET EXPLORER 3.0

ISBN: 0-7821-2221-3
704pp; 7¹/₂" x 9"; Hardcover
$49.99

MCSE: WINDOWS 95 STUDY GUIDE

LANCE MORTENSEN
RICH SAWTELL

ESSENTIAL INFORMATION YOU NEED TO PREPARE FOR THE WINDOWS 95 EXAM
INCLUDED ON THE CD:
EVALUATION COPY OF MICROSOFT'S TECHNET DATABASE
TRANSCENDER CORPORATION'S CERTIFICATION SAMPLER
MICROSOFT'S PERSONAL EXAM PREP SOFTWARE
MICROSOFT'S ROADMAP TO EDUCATION AND CERTIFICCATION

ISBN: 0-7821-2092-X
720pp; 7¹/₂" x 9"; Hardcover
$49.99

A $50.00! SAVINGS

MCSE Core Requirements
Box Set
ISBN: 0-7821-2245-0
4 hardcover books;
3,024pp total; $149.96

Microsoft Certified **Professional**
Approved Study Guide

NETWORK PRESS

STUDY GUIDES FOR THE MICROSOFT CERTIFIED SYSTEMS ENGINEER EXAMS

MCSE ELECTIVE STUDY GUIDES
FROM NETWORK PRESS

Sybex's Network Press expands the definitive study guide series for MCSE candidates.

ISBN: 0-7821-2173-X
640pp; 7¹/₂" x 9"; Hardcover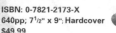
$49.99

ISBN: 0-7821-1967-0
656pp; 7¹/₂" x 9"; Hardcover
$49.99

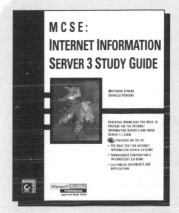

ISBN: 0-7821-2110-1
559pp; 7¹/₂" x 9"; Hardcover
$49.99

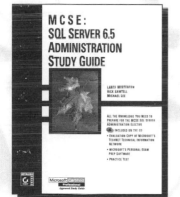

ISBN: 0-7821-2172-1
672pp; 7¹/₂" x 9"; Hardcover
$49.99

ISBN: 0-7821-2194-2
576pp; 7¹/₂" x 9"; Hardcover
$49.99

A **$25.00!** SAVINGS

MCSE Internet Systems
Specialist Box Set
ISBN: 0-7821-2176-4
3 hardcover books;
1,984pp total; $124.97

Microsoft Certified
Professional
Approved Study Guide

NETWORK PRESS
SYBEX®

STUDY GUIDES FOR THE MICROSOFT CERTIFIED SYSTEMS ENGINEER EXAMS

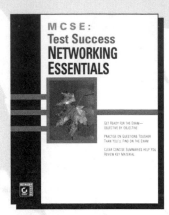